The Split Economy

SUNY series in Theology and Continental Thought

Douglas L. Donkel, editor

The Split Economy
Saint Paul Goes to Wall Street

NIMI WARIBOKO

Published by State University of New York Press, Albany

© 2020 State University of New York

All rights reserved

No part of this book may be used or reproduced in any manner whatsoever without written permission. No part of this book may be stored in a retrieval system or transmitted in any form or by any means including electronic, electrostatic, magnetic tape, mechanical, photocopying, recording, or otherwise without the prior permission in writing of the publisher.

For information, contact State University of New York Press, Albany, NY
www.sunypress.edu

Library of Congress Cataloging-in-Publication Data

Names: Wariboko, Nimi, author.
Title: The split economy : Saint Paul goes to Wall Street / Nimi Wariboko.
Description: Albany : State University of New York Press, [2020] | Series: SUNY series in Theology and Continental Thought | Includes bibliographical references and index.
Identifiers: ISBN 9781438480596 (hardcover : alk. paper) | ISBN 9781438480589 (pbk. : alk. paper) | 9781438480602 (ebook)
Further information is available at the Library of Congress.

10 9 8 7 6 5 4 3 2 1

For Max Lynn Stackhouse
(1935–2016)

Contents

Acknowledgments ix

Introduction 1

Part I
Ontology. Subject in General: A Theory of Cracks

Chapter 1   Sickness unto Excess 27

Chapter 2   Saint Paul's Notion of Split Subjectivity 49

Chapter 3   The Split Economy 67

Part II
Particular Subject: Logic of the World of Finance

Chapter 4   The Fantasy of Harmony 99

Chapter 5   The Ethical Form of Finance 117

Part III
Singular-Plural Subjects:
Deactivation of the Capitalist Future

Chapter 6   Abolish the Future 139

Chapter 7	Abundance, Scarcity, and Pluralism: A New Direction for Economic Theology	157
Epilogue		181
Notes		187
Works Cited		211
Index		219

Acknowledgments

Books hold, in their narrative layers, turns of phrase and flows of argument, the entanglements of knowledge, debts of insight and gratitude, and well-wishes accumulated by their authors. It is a supreme irony that such unpayable intellectual debts are clean slated simply through public acknowledgment of indebtedness. This is human grace at its best. I would be remiss to complete my writing without joyfully recognizing a Wall Street–defying level of debt to those who helped me along the way. These magnificent representatives supported and encouraged me as I carried the "fire" of this book from the Olympian heights of past cultural heroes of human creativity to a wide circle of readers.

Three present and former acquisitions editors at the State University of New York Press worked with me at various stages: Christopher Ahn, Andrew Kenyon, and Rafael Chaiken. Diane Ganeles, Anne Valentine, and others at SUNY also did wonderful work toward bringing this book to fruition. Thanks to Anwuli Ojogwu of Lagos who copy edited the manuscript with professionalism, care, and dedication. My gratitude also goes to Dr. Alexis Felder, who as a doctoral student at Boston University School of Theology worked as my research assistant on this project in the spring of 2016. Finally, let me thank Springer Nature for permission to re-use portions (pp. 21–23, 25–27) of chapter 1 of my book *Economics in Spirit and Truth: A Moral Philosophy of Finance* (2014), reproduced here with permission of Palgrave Macmillan.

Introduction

This book identifies the key character of the economy as provision for the future. This is the feature of the economy that is true both for premodern and modern economies, primitive and industrialized economies, and agriculture or service-based economies. The economy was born when humans first began to make provision for the future by restricting today's consumption and thereby creating savings or surplus as "seed" for tomorrow's survival, well-being, and flourishing. (Incidentally, by "flourishing," "human flourishing," a term you will encounter many times in this book, I mean a set of virtues, capabilities, and conditions that generates higher levels of well-being, the good life, prosperity, as well as generating new relations, practices, and realities that support the actualization of potentialities of a person, group, or community. The goal of the drive toward human flourishing is to create community that perpetually permits every human being to be the best that she can be given her gifts, talents, and communal-institutional support for her sake and that of her community, individual and community aiming for the highest human good, *eudaimonia*.)

With the creation of surplus or savings, we have assets and liabilities: the present supplying the wherewithal for tomorrow (creating assets), and the future holding the surplus (and its increments) as liability. The present is credited the value, and the future is debited the same amount, as rudimentary accounting teaches us. Thus we see here that the birth of provision for the future is in a sense the birth of credit and debt in their most elementary forms.

The emergence of credit and debt is also the emergence of money (as a pure accounting device), which is basically credit and debit, the accounting exchange of assets and liabilities, goods and its equivalents.

Accompanying is the birth of finance, where savings are set aside in the present to generate or augment production beyond the present.

The objective of this book is to trace and analyze the logic and dynamics of the split, the division of produced magnitude (which was initially meant for the immediate, that is, today's consumption) into consumption goods (today's allocation) and investible goods (for tomorrow's well-being). My task is to study the split between present and future, between no provision and provision for the future, and its logics from the primordial economy to the twenty-first century economy. I then investigate the ethical impact of the split not only on contemporary human flourishing, but also on how philosophers, theologians, and ethicists study the modern economy.

That the economy is about making provision for the future is discernible in many ancient and contemporary texts. Moses did not want the Israelites wandering in the wilderness to "build" an economy based on God's generous gift of manna, so he prohibited them from gathering beyond what they needed for daily survival (Exodus 16:4–26). It appears that the nature of the economic activities as provision for the future was clearly understood by Max Weber. In his book *The Protestant Ethic and the Spirit of Capitalism*, Weber states that the rational organization of economic life depends "on the provision for the future."[1] Milton Friedman makes a similar point with regard to consumption and saving in his book *The Theory of the Consumption Function*.[2] Friedman argues that saving is a provision for the future, and not necessarily what is left after consumption. Before him, economists explained savings as residual; but Friedman holds that consumer choices are ultimately based on a longtime horizon and that saving is a way of evening out consumption over a life span. One of the major contributions of Friedman's book to economic thought is that he posited that economic actors have some consumption program that informs their everyday budgeting decisions based on their expectation of income and accumulated savings (wealth). The most relevant point in Friedman's book to our thesis is that savings and consumption as integral parts of economic life are clearly laid out as dependent on the desire to make provision for the future. A key argument I will make in this book is that the fundamental split that marked the tendency of primordial producer-consumer to choose with regard to the future is the best place to start thinking about the emergence of the modern economy and how it informed the logic and dynamics of capitalism.

The knowledge of economy as the split that engendered the human process of making provision for the future, which Weber and Friedman took for granted in the analysis of the economy, has not been seriously considered as a possible organizing principle of philosophical or socio-ethical study of the contemporary economy. To address this shortcoming, I lift this principle as the organizing framework of my analysis of late capitalism and global finance. With this focus we come to understand that the tendency to make provision for the future is both the matrix and Moloch of the modern economy. Since an economy is fundamentally the process of making provision for the future, and the lean-in toward the future is its very source of strength and weakness, it means that economy is divided against itself. The economy is radically split. We have created an economy that is not in (or cannot come into) full identity with itself; we are forever interacting with an economic reality that is "ontologically" incomplete.

The overall result of this study is that we get a better theoretical understanding of how capitalism functions and thus garner insights on how to pragmatically resist it in the name of human flourishing and social justice. Now that I have given the *Reader's Digest* version of the book, let me begin again more properly. Every beginning is always already a part of another beginning. This time we begin with a focus on the ethical problem of the modern economy.

Karl Marx identified the primary ethical problem of capitalism as injustice and inequality, Sigmund Freud called it repression, and Todd McGowan attributed the core problem to capitalism's psychic hold over all of us as subjects. McGowan's work builds on the scholarship of Marx and Freud, as well as Jacques Lacan, even as he contests and expands on their thoughts. This book also builds on the works of these scholars: it contests, expands, and amplifies their brilliant insights. The argument of the book is that the ethical problems of capitalism are largely traceable to the split nature of the modern economy, an economy divided against itself: an economy that cannot coincide (or reconcile) with itself. A fundamental negativity at the core of the economy continually disturbs its stability and identity, thus generating its destructive drive.

According to McGowan, subjects are invested in the capitalist narrative of dissatisfaction, which it claims capitalism is uniquely situated to address under its promise of future enrichment or fulfillment. Relying on the psychoanalytic theory of Lacan, McGowan maintains that subjects are split as speaking beings: divided by language as signifier and signified. This fundamental split is linked to the libidinal (subjective) economy of the capitalist system, the structure of signification, and the gap it creates in the subject, which is connected to a sense of loss or lack, which induces desire. This sense of loss, which is not empirical but only retroactively posited by the subject, induces a desire for the lost object that no particular commodity can satisfy. The subject is thus always seeking the ultimate object of desire, and capitalism is always promising the subject the next (ultimate) commodity that will satisfy her, which will prove to be hollow, as demonstrated in her previous consumptions—because commodities are never able to give what they promise. "With the onset of capitalism, the speaking being enters a system that promises relief from the absence that inheres within the basic structure of signification."[3]

The overall thesis of McGowan's brilliant book *Capitalism and Desire* is that the split subject's desires are driven by the promise of full (future) satisfaction, yet the subject does not realize that her repeated failure to find full satisfaction is the very mechanism of capitalism's psychic hold over her. This epistemological obstacle points to her entrapment in capitalism's economic and ideological structuring, its powerful inducement into the logic of desire.

McGowan develops his thesis further by adding that the relentless dissatisfaction of the split subject, the logic of promise of a better future, and the orientation to desire (the desire to desire) are products of modernity and capitalism, and the death of God (*big Other*) that decentered subjectivity and delivered subjects to the abyss of freedom. All this is the logic and nature of capitalism that has not been effectively grasped by scholars and activists; hence, all talks or praxes about dismantling capitalism have been inoperative.

McGowan viewed the inability of many analysts and subjects to understand their psychic investment as epistemological. This is to say there is a cognitive failure on the part of us all in the thralldom of the fundamental capitalist fantasy—promise of future fulfillment or a better future—to grasp the *Thing* of capitalism that engenders its most intractable ethical problem. To better understand capitalism, we must transform the epistemological challenge into an "ontological" impossibility that characterizes every capitalist economy. The failure of the subject to grasp the *Thing*, the X that eludes her, is reconceived as a feature of capitalism, an obstacle, a split inscribed into the core of capitalism itself.

The capitalist economy functions around negativity at its core. It arose from this negativity, which birthed the promise of future enrichment and underlines the relentless dissatisfaction with the present.

The thesis of this book, however, is that it is not only subjectivity that is split: the capitalist economy itself is split. The split predates the modern capitalist economy, and we cannot adequately understand the ethical challenge of capitalism until we develop a theoretical framework that integrates split subjectivity, split economy, the libidinal investments of today's consumers and producers in the allure and promise of capitalism and its calculated "excess future," and the material conditions of the reproduction of all three. This will be a theoretical framework that connects the subjective libidinal economy with the objective functioning of the economy, their mutual imbrication that suggests that our subjective attitude and any conception of objective functioning are two sides of the same coin. Our subjective attitude toward commodities does not exist deeply in us independently of its relations to the economy, and we must not forget that value in, or the functioning of, the economy is a social relation. The subjective attitude and the operations of the economy are parts of the same field—a field increasingly marked by the separation of form and content (*kenosis*), dematerialization, spectralization, spectacularization, and dissatisfaction. This book attempts to develop such a theoretical framework at the intersection of philosophy, psychoanalytic theory, theology, and political economy as a meditation on split economy and split subjectivity. Here the notion of split subjectivity, unlike McGowan's approach, is not staged through Lacan's theory of language, but through the law as Saint Paul theorized it in Romans 7. According to Paul, the law constitutes the subject as split, traversed by negativity, and decentralized owing to the problematic relation of law and its transgression.

The passage of the primordial economy to modern economy—the proto-economy that split into what we now call "economy and finance," and became alienated from itself—is akin to the passage of a self (substance) into a split subject. Though the economy and self are both split, each divided from within, there is a certain formal homology between the split economy and split subjectivity, which are both dimensions of our incomplete (ontological, social) reality. Like the Pauline subject that wants to escape the symbolic castration of the law that divides subjectivity through grace, in the present global consumerist capitalism, the consumer wants unconstrained consumption, with no symbolic castration (prohibition, restriction) to interrupt her flow of enjoyment. Could we also think about the homology between Lacanian split subjectivity and surplus enjoyment, Pauline split subjectivity and surplus future, and Marxist split subjectivity (alienated worker) and surplus value in the same field of capitalism and subjectivity?

Finally, the transdisciplinary theoretical framework that we are attempting to develop in this book will have huge implications for how continental philosophers, theological theorists, and social ethicists approach the study of economic theology under late capitalism. The task of radical economic theology is to enact an authentic division within the citizenry: a split between those who want to continue with the future as defined and promised by capitalism, and those who want change. Economic theology (philosophy) must open a space for citizens to make a decision based on a *prepared future* (that is, the new economy that flows from the trajectory of capitalism's past and present, and late capitalism's project of a better future) or a *proper future* that could arise from the unforeseeable new economy that asks for, creates, and sustains alternative possibilities, the unexpected, and risky paths. The all-pervasiveness of resistance against capitalism, which has permeated all spheres of life, allows no neutral (universal) position. The correct insight to bring to the task of today's thought is not synthesis of the citizenry into a harmonious whole, but, rather, separation, split, and distinction, and to posit the difference *as such*. Once again, Paul might help us to clarify the importance of approaching the "healing" of our society by introducing (generating an awareness of) a cut.

> The radical gap that [Saint Paul] posits between "life" and "death," between life in Christ and life in sin, is no need of further "synthesis"; it is itself the resolution of the "absolute contradiction" of law and sin, of the vicious cycle of their mutual implication. In other words, once the distinction is drawn, once the human subject becomes aware of the very existence of this other dimension beyond the vicious cycle of law and its transgression, the battle is formally already won.[4]

Is this not also the position of Georg Lukács in *History and Class Consciousness*, that consciousness, the act of knowing, changes its object, transforms reality, and that both subject and object are changed in the process of knowing?[5] For instance, Lukács writes that when the proletariat becomes aware of its historic mission—that is, gains self-consciousness—it becomes a revolutionary subject; it acts differently. There is a subjective transformation of an objective social category: the working class becomes the proletariat.

Now that we have set out the base line of the argument of this book, let us turn to an issue that might be troubling readers at this junction. Readers may want to counter one of the basic pillars of this book's argument by saying that human beings have always set something aside for future consumption, so the split I have identified is not so fundamental after all. My response is that the proper way to conceive the split is to view it as a *gain of the future*. This is not the promise of the future based on a simple denial of immediate consumption or leaving what could be immediately consumed now for another time, but the additional future provided by the very formal process in early humans' effort in the primordial economy to attain the future. Let us call this surplus future or surplus promise.

I would call the stage of preparing for the future before the emergence of surplus future, pre-accumulative. After this stage, preparation for the future is what serves to make the future grow or to be always postponed. At some point in history, something changed in the human orientation to productive activities and consumption. We are not going to burn brain cells pondering what brought on this change—if it was the hunter-gatherers, or early agriculturalists, participants in early forms of the market, or some unknown step in the evolution of civilization; the important point is that at a certain historic and historical juncture, the future became surplus future, a stand-in for something sacrificed today in order to create more satisfaction later: surplus jouissance. The future became what could be grown and accumulated.

Of course, our ancestors never quite gained that extra future, as more (better) future is always the enemy of (present, attained) future. This surplus future, the pursuit of the gain-of-future, is caught up in the compulsion to repeat. The gain-of-future operates through repetition: "one misses the goal and repeats the movement, trying again and again, so that the true aim is no longer the intended goal but the repetitive movement of attempting to reach it."[6] Therefore, the gain-of-future is "attained" by the repeated performance to reach it, the surplus enjoyment in working toward it, but not reaching the intended goal.

Given this sociohistorical or psychoanalytic knowledge, the allure of commodities—which in capitalism rides on the promise of future enrichment—is not a corruption of human beings' authentic relation to the production and consumption of economic objects, but the symptomal point at which the split, surplus promise, or surplus future, operative from the beginning, breaks out into the open.[7] The gap that, in McGowan's theory, separates capitalism's commodity economy from the pre-capitalist, premodern, original economy is thus transposed back into the original (proto-) economy itself.

From the foregoing, we can surmise that the major ethical challenge, which has crucial implications for political organization and resistance, is how to *abolish the future*, formatted with the capitalist promise that incites consumers' desire for desire, inflames our dissatisfaction with the consumption of every commodity, and constricts our freedom. The abolition of the future is not simply a rejection of the future or an indifference to futurity; it is to go against the future of capital and the capital-parliamentary politics of preprogrammed ends. The aim of this stance is to exit the capitalist discourse and mechanisms of the future, the psychic investment in the governing fantasy of the future, and enact the liberation of our future from the commodity form.

As German philosopher Frank Ruda argues in his book *Abolishing Freedom*, we must act as if the end of time has come, as if there is no tomorrow, no future.[8] He says: "Act as if the apocalypse has already happened! Act as if you were dead! Act as if everything is already lost!" We must relearn how to live in the present without the perpetual pursuit of abundance in the name of a better future. To heal ourselves, we must enact another form of split, that is, to separate ourselves from the capitalist machine of jouissance, and learn to be "omnipotent" before the harsh face of late capitalism by reckoning with our *impotentiality* (a term further explained below). Human freedom is fast losing its impotentiality: we are becoming less and less able to abstain from doing what capitalism demands. The world of markets now constitutes a state of exception in which the distinction between human freedom and the freedom of capital are rendered inoperable. Human potentiality (disconnected from its impotentiality) is subservient to the actuality of capitalism. Human freedom is made to serve the predetermined ends of capital.

Generally, things move from potentiality to actuality, but potentiality does not exist only in act. When potentiality passes into actuality, does it exhaust itself? Giorgio Agamben, following Aristotle, says no.[9] Potentiality does not exhaust itself in actualization. A part of it will always remain as impotentiality (based on the theory of to "be able not to-do," potentiality to not-be, potentiality that "conserves itself and saves itself in actuality").

There are two types of potentiality: generic and existing. Generic potentiality is a person's capacity to act on something and become altered after exercising her potentiality. For instance, a child learns, and in the process of realizing her potential she is changed. On the other hand, a scribe has the potentiality to write, but faces the choice whether to bring this potentiality into actuality or not. This is the potentiality to "not do" or "not be." The scribe is able or not to exercise his own potentiality. Agamben sheds light on this form of potentiality, or, as earlier indicated, *impotentiality*:

> This is not to say that human beings are the living beings that, existing in the mode of potentiality, are capable just as much of one thing as its opposite, to do just as to not do. This exposes them, more than any other living being, to the risk of error; but, at the same time, it permits human beings to accumulate and freely master their own capacities, to transform them into "faculties." It is not the measure of what someone can do, but also and primarily the capacity of maintaining oneself in relation to one's own possibility to not do, that defines the status of one's action. While fire can only burn, and other living beings are only capable of their own specific potentialities—they are capable of only this or that behavior inscribed into their biological vocation—human beings are the animals capable of their impotentiality."[10]

Freedom is defined by ambivalence in human beings' potentiality. In their existing potentiality, they always have the power "to do" and "to not do," and are capable of their own impotentiality.[11] Human freedom is not merely the capacity to actualize, to be or to do, but also the potential to not-be or to not-do. Freedom, as Agamben sees it, is primarily in the domain of impotentiality, not in actualization. He maintains that it is possible to see how the root of freedom is in the abyss of potentiality. "To be free is not simply to have the power to do this or that thing, nor is it simply to have the power to refuse to do this or that thing. To be free is, in the sense we have seen, *to be capable of one's own impotentiality, to be in relation to one's privation.*"[12]

It is now clear what I mean by becoming omnipotent in the face of capitalism: citizens are not to enjoy the destruction of their impotentiality, not to be estranged from their impotentiality. Put differently, in the words of Guy Le Gaufey commenting on Jacques Lacan's insight on power: "Omnipotence is for Lacan not a kind of maximum, apex, or even infinitization of potency—to which one often reduces it in order to deny its actual existence—but a beyond of potency which appears only in the latter's failure. It does not appear on the slope of impotence but on the slope of what remains 'all-in-potentiality,' without ever passing over into the dimension of an act which belongs to the domain of some determinate potency/power."[13]

Something about the vastness of our topic—the split economy—forces me to think strategically about how best to elucidate it in a book that is not infinite. I have decided to focus on finance capital and on the United States, and thus other countries and sectors must appear on "the slope of what remains 'all-in-potentiality.'" Given this self-imposed restriction, we traced the emergence of the primordial split to—to mark its nature and logic through—*finance*. For indeed, the split began when the proto-economy divided itself into economy and finance. The split occurred when some consumption was sacrificed *today* to generate investible resources to fund production *tomorrow*, as our ancestors in the remote past hoped to improve on the present, to ameliorate common insecurity via future enrichment.

To be precise, the movement from harvest into consumption and saved consumption had an intermediary stage. Perhaps, the harvest (gathering, catch, output, intake) was split into (a) a portion for immediate consumption; (b) a portion set aside for next day (time) consumption, and (c) a portion saved to yield a future amount equal to itself and surplus. The split that cracked the primordial economy is the third one. Its emergence was driven by hope of meeting future needs, which, as Marx informed us, always has two parts: bodily needs and fantasmatic needs.[14] This generative split occurred, probably, because of human response to insecurity and anxiety. It might also be connected to what Lacan describes as "all needs are contaminated by being involved in an other satisfaction that they may never live up to."[15] Thus, biological needs are not merely physiological; they are often caught up in meeting psychological needs, supported by a fantasmatic screen. And once desire and drive come into play, every satisfaction fails; no object can fully stand in for the object of desire and no amount of surplus is enough. No object or surplus could be "it." Every object or surplus appears as a form of lack as no one object can yield satisfaction of desire. The consumer, the subject repeatedly circulates around the object of desire.

The process of saving for tomorrow and expecting better or fuller satisfaction has continued ever since, and yet insecurity, fragility, and dissatisfaction have not vanished from our collective existence. In fact, increasing wealth and higher levels of consumption of commodities have not only raised our sense of collective anxiety, but also elevated the fragilities of our social fabric. The United States, the bastion of capitalism and headquarters of global finance capital, is wracked by these kinds of ambiguities and incongruences.

America is a split society. Its single garment of destiny hangs over several gaps: racism, rising income inequalities, gender pay differential, sexism, and so on. America is flung over several clotheslines like a torn fabric in the sun.[16] This America, this frayed fabric was woven, purchased, or preserved by an economy that is the "sun," around which national households of our planet earth rotate. This economy is itself split, between Wall Street and Main Street, divided between finance and the rest of the economy, divided between mother and daughter, with the child devouring the mother. The devouring child—finance—is itself split.

This book tells the story of how finance became split from its mother-economy and turned to this "being" that is feeding on the entrails of its mother and nibbling on the lifeline of every citizen. Finance is itself always undergoing a split. Its products are increasingly emptied of real contents and have become voids—forms with no content sold as complex things that are less than nothing. Do *naked* credit default swaps—which do not promise a stream of cash flow to its buyers, but only sell them risk assessments based on the gamble that the original issuers of securities will or will not default in their payments to the holders of the securities—not remind us of the "voids" in Elizabethan England? In those days, the rich would feed sumptuously in large banqueting rooms, consuming substantial meals, and then retire to the small rooms to eat their desserts. The desserts over time became known as "voids," and they were often shaped as fake animals, birds, or fruits with an empty, insubstantial middle. Is Wall Street's securities culture not being used in the same way? The rapacious banking elites feed on the substance of the United States' economy, afterward retiring to their posh enclaves, their exclusive cultural spaces, which stand in actual and ornamental opposition to the flourishing and well-being of the rest of us.

The struggle between finance and economy or the struggle within finance is not caused by an external force or agency, but by a tearing-apart from the inside, like the body fighting against itself that occurs in some forms of cancer. Our modern economy fights against itself, chewing and tearing itself from within. This internal contestation, this self-devouring act, began at the very time the economy emerged—when output of production in the primitive household became split between part for consumption and part as input for future production. It continued when the primordial household (a combined single producing-and-consuming unit) was split with the advent of the market when consumption and production became separated between different households.

The primordial split evolved and in the twentieth century became the monstrous split between finance and industry, what the great British economist John Maynard Keynes called financial and industrial circulations of money. Today, the split is still running its course, and we discern it in the form of separation between content (cash flow stream) and form (risk) in credit default swaps: a mere trading of risk upon risk. (More on this later.) The various iterations of the primordial split have, somewhat, paralleled the major phases of the development of the capitalist economy: premodern economy to industrial economy to postindustrial (late capitalism as a paradise of financialization). The primordial split of economy and finance has also mimicked the process of modern dematerialization of money.

How do we think of or theorize this split, theologically or philosophically, in ways that can enable us to make sense of it in terms of human flourishing for all citizens? How do we trace the contours of the split as the red thread running through the delicate fabric of the American economy? Saint Paul (of Romans 7) is one of the earliest thinkers in the Western intellectual tradition to point to the grave issues that might arise from a body that fights against itself, when a self becomes split. I will use Paul's theory of split human subjectivity to investigate the global financial system, including the credit and debit processes. To paraphrase Karl Marx: Wall Street commodities are not simple; they are not obvious objects that investors buy and consume. They are full of theological niceties, and even metaphysical subtleties—philosophically strange things, indeed. Pauline thought (appropriated through a Lacanian psychoanalytic reading) provides us with a good lens to closely examine the strange world, the queerness of Wall Street. In so doing, I lean toward the recent turn of continental philosophers to Paul's theology to flesh out the framework for my analysis of Wall Street. Thus, this work is located more in the scholarship of continental philosophy (as inflected by critique of political economy, and critical-theoretical psychoanalysis) than in constructive theology or theological ethics. No wonder: recall that the opening lines of our ethical critique in this introductory chapter began with Marx and Freud.

Beginnings always have their own beginnings. So, let us re-begin, again, by carefully explicating the title of this book, *The Split Economy: Saint Paul Goes to Wall Street*. The unfamiliar term in the title is "split economy," so let us start with that. What is a split economy? I am using the term in four senses. First, by split economy I mean every modern economy is troubled by multiple splits and antagonisms. Precisely, the term refers to the difference of the economy from itself, its noncoincidence with itself. There is a fracture within the economy that cannot be reduced to the usual polarities or negations within an economy. The split refers to an economy that is divided by and in itself. The economy is an internally inconsistent and incomplete whole. This is a notion of economy that says an economy is not in (or cannot come into) full identity with itself, and it is forever interacting with a reality that is ontologically incomplete. This understanding of how an economy functions has serious implications for how we think about economic ethics or how we go about addressing social injustice.

Second, any modern economy (capitalist or not) is split in itself, and split against itself. We will later demonstrate that finance is nothing but an economy split against itself. Finance emerged when the primordial economy divided against itself from itself. Every economy is fundamentally divided between two agonist sides: economy (Main Street) and finance (Wall Street). This split is primordial in the sense that it engenders the birth of the modern economy and is older than capitalism and thus fundamental to how every economy functions.

Third, there is a split in financial commodities; that is, content is split from form. Before now, financial products, arguably, had this structure: (a) an instrument that encodes the contents of a future stream of payments, materiality, and assets, and (b) the risk that attends the stream of payment or assets. We may liken the projected stream of cash flow as the "matter" of the financial commodity and the risk as the "form." But with the development of collateralized debt obligations (CDOs) such as credit default swaps, risk has become its own content; risk has come to occupy the position formerly occupied by content or asset. Form (risk) functions both as matter and form, as a drive, and as a kind of material surplus of empty-form.[17] The market has become so sophisticated that those who have no stake in the original investments or loans will buy CDOs. These types of CDOs are known as "naked credit default swaps" and serve to give speculators a chance to take positions on the credit-worthiness of the original issuers of bonds. (The value of naked CDS derives from mathematical estimations of the value of a third person's ability to keep its promise to pay.) This class of speculative traders is betting on the risk that supervenes the original risk of those who hold the bonds of the reference entities. Risk has curved in on itself. Risk on Wall Street is now reflexive. Form (risk, self-referentiality of risk) appropriates itself as asset, as content, in order to be the *drive* for investment (ethical) action. Financial products such as naked CDS stand as the commodity of the lack of the commodity, the content as the lack of content.

Finally, these three types, which represent progressively deepening levels of splitting (primordial economy ➡ economy: finance ➡ finance: financial commodities), reinforce one another. I consider their collective form as an index of any one of them and of the falsity of any notion of inherent or automatic harmony and wholeness of any modern economy.

Now that I have explained the technical dimensions and deep structure of my notion of split economy, let me now broadly describe the nature of a split economy. I open the discussion with a poem by Bertolt Brecht, in one of his "Hollywood Elegies":

> The village of Hollywood was planned according to the
>   notion
> People in these parts have of heaven. In these parts
> They have come to the conclusion that God
> Requiring a heaven and a hell, didn't need to
> Plan two establishments but
> Just the one: heaven. It
> Serves the unprosperous, unsuccessful
> As hell.[18]

Is this notion of heaven not operative in the United States, and nearly every other country in the world? In the same space that the rich enjoy their obscene lifestyle, the rest of their fellow citizens live in servitude. Abundance and poverty, freedom and slavery are in one place; heaven is also hell. Our economy is split. The increase in wealth owing to the continuous self-revolutionizing movement of capitalism has fueled rising social antagonisms (between the haves and the have-nots). Progress, success, or development is birthing instabilities, inequalities, and antagonisms. The success of capitalist accumulation and expansion, the very rise of productivity, renders every condition of employment precarious, and produces more unemployment. Exclusion, not embrace, is at the core of today's economy. Arguably, most people are excluded from the benefits of capitalist development, yet the capitalist market includes them. There is now a huge gap between creditors and debtors in the economy, yet the hapless debtors are part of the comprehensive creditor-debtor nexus that marks and defines today's economy. There is also a split between the economy and the environment. Giving life to capital, that is, creating vast amounts of wealth, means delivering death to the ecosystem, which in all seriousness owns the economy or capitalism. Rising income inequality offers us another picture of a deeply split economy; the widening gap between the rich and the poor reflects the deepening of the split, a crack or division in the economy.

Workers' freedom is split between potentiality to-do and impotentiality to-not-do. What is happening in late capitalism is that the impotentiality that human beings have is being treated as already lost. What is lost is something beyond the mere, easygoing obedience to the demands of the market. What is lost is resistance, the exercise of spirited, responsible freedom that imaginatively and effectively opposes obedience to subjugation to capital. This is not a mere reframing of freedom or action, but the destruction of frame of freedom, the disappearance of the potentiality to not-do or not-be as the support of every potentiality to-do. The so-called freedom of choice that persons exercise limits them to existing frame of possibilities. The person as consumer has the free choice and permissiveness to consume all he or she wants. This notion of freedom that limits it to only the potentiality to-do is a particular way of exercising freedom that subverts a holistic understanding of freedom. The freedom to only do, to only act, is the opposite itself of authentic (full ply of) freedom, because through the severance of impotentiality from potentiality citizens lose their freedom. The effective content of this amputated freedom to-do is subjugation to capital or market. The overall result of this one-armed freedom is that the Western citizen's celebrated freedom—freedom of choice—is the vey form of unfreedoms.

It is on these kinds of unity of opposites that today's economy thrives. The economy of any modern country is a multiplicity of splits.

The economy is split from itself. There is a split/antagonism in the very core of what we call the economy. How do we search the multiplicity of splits to reach the real, the principal, the ultimate one? Which of these splits are not just temporary disturbances or disequilibria but structurally necessary?

These splits are not only opposed to human flourishing of the majority of the world's populations, they define their predicament today and structure what the poor and the rich, or financial industry and the whole economy, experience as reality. My point in this argument or explanation of split economy is not just the claim that the split is the bane of our current socioeconomic fabric, but that Wall Street, the financial industry, or the economy's own identity and self-revolutionizing force, is also simultaneously grounded in the split. Wall Street is caught in its own split. All this calls attention to the fundamental splits that sustain the functioning of an economy, and no less fundamental splits must sustain every attempt to either undermine or transform the functioning of an economic system. We must learn to split from the familiar narrativity of capitalist futurism and divide the citizenry into camps for or against commodified futurism.

The foregoing takes care of the first part of the title of this book. Now, you may ask: what has Saint Paul got to do with split economy? Let me begin my response with a biblical passage.

> What shall we say, then? Is the law sinful? Certainly not! Nevertheless, I would not have known what sin was had it not been for the law. For I would not have known what coveting really was if the law had not said, "You shall not covet." But sin, seizing the opportunity afforded by the commandment, produced in me every kind of coveting. For apart from the law, sin was dead. Once I was alive apart from the law; but when the commandment came, sin sprang to life and I died. I found that the very commandment that was intended to bring life actually brought death. For sin, seizing the opportunity afforded by the commandment, deceived me, and through the commandment put me to death. So then, the law is holy, and the commandment is holy, righteous and good.
>
> Did that which is good, then, become death to me? By no means! Nevertheless, in order that sin might be recognized as sin, it used what is good to bring about my death, so that

through the commandment sin might become utterly sinful. We know that the law is spiritual; but I am unspiritual, sold as a slave to sin. I do not understand what I do. For what I want to do I do not do, but what I hate I do. And if I do what I do not want to do, I agree that the law is good. As it is, it is no longer I myself who do it, but it is sin living in me. For I know that good itself does not dwell in me, that is, in my sinful nature. For I have the desire to do what is good, but I cannot carry it out. For I do not do the good I want to do, but the evil I do not want to do—this I keep on doing. Now if I do what I do not want to do, it is no longer I who do it, but it is sin living in me that does it.

So I find this law at work: Although I want to do good, evil is right there with me. For in my inner being I delight in God's law; but I see another law at work in me, waging war against the law of my mind and making me a prisoner of the law of sin at work within me. What a wretched man I am! (Rom. 7:7–24, NIV).

Paul is saying that the human being is caught in a vicious cycle between law and sin, one engendering the other; hence, she is a divided subject. Law is what brings sin to life, birthing transgressive desires. Caught in this destructive cycle, she wants to obey the law but ends up in sin, and yet without the law there would be no sin. Law and sin mutually implicate and strengthen each other; prohibition and desire are intertwined. This antagonism or predicament is constitutive of human subjectivity. The split subject is caught between law and desire/flesh. Thus, Slavoj Žižek sums up the Pauline notion of subjectivity as fashioned by a pulsating mass of law and desire in this manner:

> The direct result of the intervention of the Law is thus that it *divides* the subject and introduces a morbid confusion between life and death: the subject is divided between (conscious) obedience to the Law and (unconscious) desire for its transgression generated by the legal prohibition itself. It is not I, the subject, who transgress the Law, it is non-subjectivized "Sin" itself, the sinful impulses in which I do not recognize myself, and which I even hate. Because of this split, my (conscious) Self is ultimately experienced as "dead," as deprived of living

impetus; while "life," ecstatic affirmation of living energy, can appear only in the guise of "Sin," of a transgression that gives rise to a morbid sense of guilt. My actual life impulse, my desire, appears to me as a foreign automatism that persists in following its path independently of my conscious Will and intentions. St. Paul's problem is thus not the standard morbid moralistic one (how to crush transgressive impulses, how finally to purify myself of sinful urges), but its exact opposite: how can I break out of this vicious cycle of the Law and desire, of the Prohibition and its transgression, within which I can assert my living passions only in the guise of their opposite, as a morbid death drive?[19]

According to Paul in the Romans passage, sin is not some invasion of the self by an external agency, but a split within the self, the subject torn between desire and its prohibition. The subject is split, de-completed by the other within, the law. The other says, "Thou shall not covet," "do not desire," but it stimulates the life of desire, and the subject is animated by it. Do not desire . . . what? Without knowing exactly what is proscribed or prohibited with just the formal, empty form of obligation, the law takes the form of "a trial in the Kafkaesque sense of the term, perpetual self-accusation without a precept."[20] The "do not covet," is like the abstract *Sollen* ("ought to be") of the Kantian categorical imperative in its formal indeterminacy. Paul, in radically abbreviating the commandment to this form instead of the way Moses had, portrays the law as giving life to death, and the knowledge of it becomes "only a knowledge of guilt."[21] As Giorgio Agamben put it:

> Paul's drastic abbreviation of Moses' commandment—which did not simply say, "Do not desire," but "Do not desire the woman, the house, the slave, the mule, and so on . . . of thy neighbor"—renders the commandment unobservable and equally impossible to formulate. . . . The law here is no longer *entole*, a norm that clearly prescribes or prohibits something.[22]

For Paul, this split (law and desire) in the subject is only the first form of division within the subject. There is a second division: between law and spirit, representing two ways of living one's life. The way of the flesh that leads to death versus the way of the Spirit that leads to life.

The new life of the Spirit that a person acquires through Christ scatters the joint operation of the law and desire and delivers her from the way of death (flesh and law) to the way of life, grace (spirit and love).

Paul's conception of human subjectivity is indicative of social systems; they are always incomplete and unfinished. A system cannot come to identity with itself. Social systems have no master-signifier guaranteeing the harmonious order of reality or their wholeness. There are always splits and cracks in them. Phenomenal reality is also incomplete, inconsistent, and *non-all*. Social systems can follow either one of the two subjective stances to life: one that leads to human flourishing for all or the other that leads to social death, that is, systems detached from others and not sharing the goods of life with others.

The issue here is: How does Paul's understanding of the immanent logic of law and sin enable us to comprehend the immanent logic of the global financial system? Paul demonstrates in Romans 7 that the human subject is divided because the split between law and sin decenters her. Law invites and generates sin, transgression against its prohibition. The immanent logic of finance capital (which is not different from the logic of capitalism itself) pushes toward split identity. The condition of possibility for the unleashing of the productive forces of capitalism, precisely the innovativeness of Wall Street, the full deployment of the creativity of the financial industry is simultaneously the condition of impossibility of achieving a non-split economy. Just as human subjectivity has an inherent obstacle/antagonism that prevents it from fully coinciding with itself, Wall Street harbors an inherent transgression/antagonism that prevents it from coinciding with itself or with its general economy. It is also increasingly being detached from the general economy and from the ethical substance of its society. One of the major interests of this study is to demonstrate how the gap in human subjectivity (or more precisely, the gap or wound of the *Real* internal to any symbolic order) repeats itself in the processes of debt and credit, in the agnostic tension of finance and economy, or in the activities that constitute economic reality.

Finance represents the tension between the "ground" and existence of an economy. In its primordial past, human beings were forced to choose between production that accrues beyond immediate satisfaction, stored value and nonexistence of stored value. The split, the passage from nothing (an economy without accumulation) to something (the beginning of an economy with surplus) as the "ground" that threatens every "economic existence," is indicative of the death drive of the economy. This gap is the evil or the source of evil that many liberal scholars see in/as evil, the sin of Wall Street. Their hope is to overcome this evil in the name of some substantial good. I am afraid the evil that is the split, the death drive of finance, cannot be overcome but only "accounted for and accommodated. Evil is not finally and fully subject to the good but the good arises from and is ultimately subject to the evil which precedes it."[23] The "fall" (finance) is at the origin of the economy so that it precedes the very possibility of the "good" arising from the modern economy and makes possible the creative force of human economic reality. The point to note is that the gap that separates global finance, Wall Street, speculative finance from the rest of the economy, is transposed into the economy itself, and the proper insight to garner here is that the very feature that appears to separate finance and economy turns out to unite them.[24]

The ethical analysis in this book is geared toward uncovering why Wall Street, the financial system, has to act the way it does; that is to say, what are the imperatives of a split economy, the inner logic of financial products, that compel individuals as a group to accept them and act in a certain way? What is it about the nature of a split economy—precisely the global financial industry—that it is geared to neither serve ordinary customers nor attend to the common good? Karl Marx noted that the preference of the individual entrepreneur in the capitalist system is for "the production of surplus value, or the making of profits, [which] is the absolute law of this mode of production."[25] But in this book, we go beyond this obvious and common truth or the general wrongdoing of capitalism to investigate the particular work of finance capital as the radical negativity at the heart of the capitalist economy. Finance "embodies" or is the metonym of the "nothing" that is the "creative force" at the very center of the economic order of being. Finance is the death drive of capitalism. Finance is the *Real*, the gap, and the crack through which the death drive borne by the vibrancy and revolutionizing life of capitalism makes its appearance. It is the productive/destructive gap of the modern economy, which is "unassimilable" into the fabric of the economy.

It is important at this juncture to distinguish this project from books such as Thomas R. Blanton and Raymond Pickett (eds.), *Paul and Economics* (2017), and Blanton's *A Spiritual Economy: Gift in the Letters of Paul Tarsus*.[26] Given their titles, some readers may wonder what differentiates them from this book. These books offer brilliant profiles of economic conditions of Paul's congregation, including a detailed look at the Roman economy. The books give us excellent accounts of the economic conditions of the communities that Paul established and the economic aspects of his letters and communities in order to set Paul in the socioeconomic context and cultural practices of the Greco-Roman world. The concerns of *The Split Economy* are very different from those of *Paul and Economics* and *A Spiritual Economy*. Taking provocation from continental philosophy and Lacanian-Žižekian studies, this book mines Paul's notion of sin as it relates specifically and narrowly to split subjectivity to approach the split character of economy and finance.[27]

While *Paul and Economics* and *A Spiritual Economy* could be put under the rubric of Pauline studies, offering theological and biblical interventions into recent advances in scholarship, *The Split Economy* is not in the same category. It is based on recent political philosophical readings of Paul, not on exegetical tradition. It is a philosophical-theological analysis of the contemporary global capitalism that draws fundamental theoretical instigations from a particular interpretation of the notion of split subjectivity, arguably, embedded in Romans 7. Thus, this project does not seek to illuminate Pauline theology through the readings of philosophers; rather, its goal is to illuminate economic theology (or the logic and dynamics of the modern economy) through crucial passages in Paul's letters. This endeavor, though circumscribed, is necessarily transdisciplinary as I mobilize resources from fields such as economics, social ethics, theology, psychoanalysis, and philosophy. Like Blanton I plead that "readers are invited to exercise clemency in their judgements regarding the book's success in this endeavor: these fields are broad—each one too broad to be fully mastered by a single individual, and collectively far too large for such mastery even to be conceived."[28]

This book integrates economics and continental philosophy with Pauline theology, Marxist critique of political economy, and psychoanalytic theory to investigate the global financial system, including the credit and debt processes. It demonstrates the similarity between the theory of split subjectivity worked out by Paul and Lacan and the split character of economy and finance. Our meditation on the similarity is partly filtered through the lens of Kantian, Hegelian, and Marxist philosophies. The book goes further to show how the insights from this transdisciplinary assemblage of knowledges might improve the study of economy and theology.

In this effort to bring together constructive theology and economics, I have relied on radical continental political philosophers. I need to quickly add that in this engagement with critical theories that illuminate Paul's thinking, no attempt is made to offer a comprehensive interpretation of the political (or economic) readings of Paul; rather, I have limited my focus to the Lacanian-Žižekian tradition of split subjectivity, cracks, ontological incompleteness. This entails philosophers' psychoanalytic approach to reading Pauline thought. Though I locate this book in this tradition, its analyses push their ideas to new terrains and offer fresh insights to the working of the modern economy. This book demonstrates that the construct or critique of the modern economy developed by the Lacanian-Žižekian tradition (or for that matter, Giorgio Agamben) cannot be taken as the definitive account of what constitutes the philosophical exploration of economic theology. It is by combining philosophers' psychoanalytic readings of Paul's notions of sin, law, and love with economic research that I offer my interpretation of the split character of the modern economy.

I have taken the ideas of the Lacanian-Žižekian notion of split or crack in all phenomenological reality into three new directions in my analyses of contemporary capitalism. First, I demonstrate how the notion of split helps us to understand or explain the "origin" of the primordial economy and how the logic of this primitive economy continues to condition the operations of modern economy or late capitalism. The cut or the moment of the emergence of the gap, crack, is outside of the symbolic of modern economic life. The split may be considered as a form of an "encounter with the Real," an encounter that returns to haunt economic life. The cut in time that created the future, that is, the insatiable provision for the uncertain future (*objet a* of indeterminate provision), is like a traumatic encounter with the Real, which haunts every economy. The demand of the *provision-for-the-future* is terrifyingly indeterminate. This book traces the sources of the traumatic return of the piece of the Real, *objet petit a*, in different guises in the modern economy.

Second, this book identifies humanity's struggle with the uncertainty of the future and the need to make provisions for the future as *the* fundamental drive of economic activities, showing that an ethical analysis of today's capitalism must pay attention to temporality, uncertainty, and the logics of capitalist investments. Third, the book demonstrates how the notion of split offers crucial insights into the emergence and development of the finance sector in the modern economy, giving us a better understanding of the everyday working of global finance capitalism. The split between finance and "economy" is not merely the effect of greed or logic of finance capital but is also the ground. Overall, neither Lacan nor Žižek reached this level of depth in their radical critiques of capitalism or modern society. Of course I would not have been able to go as far as I did in my own study of late capitalism if I did not stand on their shoulders.

The book is divided into three parts. Part I (ontology) includes chapters 1, 2, and 3. This part, building on the insights of this introduction, sets out the basic critical ontology of the modern economy. The key point is that our economic reality is split, incomplete, and shot through with fundamental antagonism. This conception of reality is also taken as a basic premise of our analysis of human subjectivity: it is also traversed by split or impossibility. Chapters 4 and 5, constituting part II, move from the universal, ontological dimension of our theory to its particular dimension by focusing on the inner workings of finance capital as exemplified on Wall Street. Part III, comprised of chapters 6 and 7, is the singular dimension of the critique of economic theology. In the light of the theorization and findings of the book, I cast an ethical vision. This vision has two dimensions: first, I attempt to offer suggestions to address the social problems raised in parts I and II; and, second, I cast a vision for the discipline of economic theology.[29] I close with an epilogue that serves as a theorization of split as a possible fundament and fountain of social ethical reasoning and praxis.

What does this study contribute to knowledge? *The Split Economy: Saint Paul Goes to Wall Street* brings a new approach to the study of political and social theory of finance capital by weaving Kantian-Hegelian-Marxist-Lacanian philosophical-psychoanalytic insights into the woof and warp of economics. The wisdoms from the interplay of disciplines enable us to see deeply into the inner workings of the modern economy. The rift between Wall Street and Main Street, which is commonly regarded as a contingent feature of our twenty-first century American economy, standing in need of some special explanation, is presented in this book as a necessary feature of all economies across time and place. This insight invites us to traverse our fantasy of building or returning to a harmonious, non-split economy.

More importantly, the book opens our understanding of the social world, demonstrating how the social embodiments of the relationships of the major players in the financial sectors are connected to the logic and dynamic of split. The primordial split is embodied in practices and commodities of the financial sector. Put differently, this book attempts to show how the moral agency of a philosophy, worldview, or social imaginary rooted in the logics and dynamics of a splitting economy could be socially embodied—at least, embodied in the commodity form.

All these have implications for how we implement strategies of struggles for social justice. This study of split economy provides us with lessons for the present political and social praxis of resisting capitalism in the name of human flourishing. More importantly, it opens up a space to make a decision on whether we want to continue with the capitalist project of a better future society or take a risky path.

PART I

Ontology. Subject in General
A Theory of Cracks

Chapter 1

Sickness unto Excess

Introduction

In the book's Introduction we stated multiple times that to properly understand the modern economy we must translate the epistemological obstacle that prevents us from properly understanding an economy as an obstacle within the economy itself, a split inscribed into the core of capitalism. This is to say that our inability to grasp the Thing of capitalism that engenders its most intractable ethical problem is not due to epistemological failure but is an inherent negativity of capitalism. This means that the economy is cracked. Taking this as my point of departure for our analysis is to hold onto a philosophical perspective and a methodological approach that are rooted both in premodern and modern philosophies.

Plato conceptualized being as cracked, split between ideal forms (ideal world) and the external appearance to the world, indicating a division within being. Kant categorized our existence into two distinctions: the phenomenal and noumenal realms: the thing and the thing-in-itself. He proceeded to argue that we can only know a thing as it appears to us (our experiences), which is at the phenomenal level, and not as it is in itself (the reality), at the noumenal level. Here Kant is theorizing an epistemological division of being that explains that our way of knowing or conceiving reality is shot through with an epistemological barrier that we can never overcome. Hegel shifted the focus by saying we have this divided approach to the world because reality itself is ontologically divided. The split between appearance and thing-in-itself is not in the knowing subject, but in things themselves. What creates the stumbling block for the knowing subject is a split, crack, rupture within being. For Hegel, reality is appearance qua appearance. All these insights are also important for understanding how the Hegelian dialectics work. The so-called synthesis of thesis and antithesis is not really a third item from outside of the two opposing positions, not a fusion of the thesis and antithesis; it is only a parallax shift, which reveals that the antithesis is already in the thesis. Take, for instance, law and crime, a thesis and its antithesis; the synthesis is the subject's realization that law itself is big crime, founded on a criminal, constituting violence. Law is only a universalized crime. In the synthesis, law encounters itself in the form of its opposite, and we realize that the antagonism between thesis and the antithesis is internal to the thesis itself.

Let us return to the crack, the rupture in being. Lacan also conceives being as cracked, with a gap that forever disturbs it. He postulates this gap through his theory of language. Whereas Ferdinand de Saussure analyzes language as a structure of difference put in play by signifiers, Lacan is more interested in understanding the emergence of signifiers from a rupture or gap in being and how the whole signification process circulates or functions around this gap. The signifier that emerged from the division within being repeats the division within being. Furthermore, the signifier separates the knowing subject from the natural world. For Lacan, human beings are subjects of the signifier, which has also introduced a gap between need and desire. The emergence of speaking beings transformed their needs in contrast to animals. For the human subject, according to Lacan, "There is no . . . state of pure need. From the origin, need is motivated on the plane of desire, that is to say, of something that is destined in man to have a certain relationship with the signifier."[1] In the words of Paul Eisenstein and Todd McGowan, "Lacan identifies the radical kernel of the linguistic turn as the cut in being that the signifier illuminates . . . The cut gives birth to the subject and the unconscious. The unconscious is the register of the signifier's rupture. It is what remains of the revolutionary cut that occurs with the emergence of the signifier."[2]

Paul theorizes human subjectivity as a crack in the human being; the law divides the self from within through the destructive cycle of law and its transgression (Romans 7). The focus on grace in Pauline theology represses the scandal of the law, covers the scandal of the creation (emergence) of sin through law. So the rescued Christian, the one saved by Christ, is at once the result of the scandal of the law and its repression. Paul here in the fashion of Plato, Kant, Hegel, and Lacan gives us another insight into the cut in being. Paul moves very quickly to heal the gap, the wound through his Christological notion of grace and thus refuses to testify to the perpetual being's constitutive incompleteness.

Yet it seems Paul could not avoid the language of division in being. His theology of grace or the relationship between Jews and the law under the regime of grace accents endless radical divisions within being, as if he could not stop circulating around the possibility that the rupture of the law inaugurated. Paul in his writing acknowledges several partitions in the law, from the fundamental division of the law as Jews and non-Jews, the law that divides the self from within, the law that divides itself, to the division between circumcision and foreskin. "How does Paul tackle these divisions? . . . Paul puts another division to work, one that does not coincide with the preceding ones but is not exterior to them either. The messianic aphorism works on the divisions of the law themselves, imposing upon them a further cut. This cut is that of *sarx/pneuma*, the cut of 'flesh/breath.'"[3] Giorgio Agamben goes on to state in another place about Paul's proclivity toward finding divisions in the law:

> Under the effect of the cut of Apelles, the partition of the law (Jew/non-Jew), is no longer clear or exhaustive, for there will be some Jews who are not Jews, and some non-Jews who are not non-Jews. Paul states it clearly: "Not all those of Israel are Israel" (Rom. 9:6); and, further on, citing Hosea, "I will call my own people a non-people" (Rom. 9:25). This means that messianic division introduces a remnant [*resto*] into the law's overall division of the people, and Jews and non-Jews are constitutively "not all."[4]

Even without going to this length to uncover the imbrication of Paul's thought in fractured being, we can also see that Paul's investment in a monotheistic God and his grace signals that humans are not confined to a completed world. God and grace, in the thought-world Paul signifies, marks a break or gap within the signifying chain of existence. God and grace mark a rupture between subjects and their environment (or *situation*, to use Alain Badiou's term).

In this chapter, and in the book as a whole, I want to explore how the primordial economy repeated the gesture of rupture in being, how it is carried forward in capitalism, especially finance capital, and how such a gap in the economy is generating an excess that destabilizes and decentralizes social existence. This excess manifests itself in concrete and abstract values, in harvest that is deemed a surplus for investment, as excess orientation to the future, and as excess investment in the psychic appeal of the promise of better and fuller future satisfaction.

Thus, in this text I am not only interested in the emergence of the primordial crack in the economy and the structures it inaugurates, but also how this excess (sometimes concrete, other times as abstract, exuberant content-less forms of financial commodities swaps, and yet at another time as the unmasterable excess of finite content of naked swaps) seeps into our social bodies or into our ethical substance. My interest is to use various philosophical apparatuses to foreground the centrality of the crack (in being and in the economy) in economic ethics and its methodology. All economic experience is preceded by the crack, led by the crack, and made by the crack. Economic acts, like political ones and historical ruptures, "are possible[,] and transformative change can occur because being is always at odds with itself, and this self-division is both destabilizing and productive."[5]

The Birth of the Split Economy

The modern economy was born when finance began as a "crack" of the primordial general economy. The beginning is traceable to the generation of the first set of surplus, seed for the future production in the evolutionary process of the primitive economy. This is to say the modern economy emerged when the basic harvest, gathering, or kill was divided between immediate consumption and a surplus to prepare or plan for tomorrow's kill or production. In neoclassical economic language, we are referring to the beginning of saving geared toward having claims on future resources or output. In psychological terms, it may well refer to the dawn of an insatiable drive for economic security.

When we say that finance split off from the economy it is not meant to convey the sense of fantasy or that the prehistoric economy in the splitting discovered a version of the structure of fantasy as we have it in today's economy. The pre-split economy was not a period or stage of abundance, which was lost or turned into a time of scarcity with the splitting, only for the subjects to head toward an Eden of over-abundance—the recovery of lost original abundance. The setting aside of a portion of today's consumption for tomorrow's consumption and the hope of future abundance emerged as a struggle with scarcity. The logic of the split or the whole economy has ever since not approached the access to future abundance apart from scarcity.

The primordial split is also an indication of the division of labor in a double sense. Here we have the product of labor divided along temporal lines: use in the here and now, and use later. We also have the impulse toward the division of labor: somewhere and "elsewhen" society's members will be divided between those who manage the social product for today's consumption and those who would convert what is not consumed into capital for future generation and increment of social production.

In the beginning was the split, and the split was with the economy, and the split was the economy. My basic starting point for analyzing or examining today's economy and the complex relationship between finance capital and the rest of the economy is that in the beginning the split already existed, and what we know as the economy today is the work and working out of the "big bang" of the split. This split is an ambiguous power, a mixture of good and evil. This good that is mixed up with evil cannot simply be extracted or the evil expunged so that we can heal the divisions. The fundamental arguments of this book express the claim that the economy is split, and can never be harmonious; finance is split, not whole, financial commodities are split, not whole, and splitting is the engine, the self-revolutionizing power of the economy, particularly the financial sector. What Wall Street does is to coordinate these split parts into profitable ways of doing business in the face of competition without making them holistically coherent or harmonious, only alive and profitable. This ongoing coordination for profit is subject to ethical evaluation at two distinguishable but related levels.

It is often said that the financial market, like all markets, has no inherent moral character. The advocates of this viewpoint hold that the moral problems of the financial sector arise from greed and failure of governments to properly regulate the players in the markets. This book, however, argues that the financial market, Wall Street, and finance capital have an inherent moral character that precedes, transcends, and interacts with greed and government regulations. Its inherent logic is that of split, division, separation of content from form, timeless drifting from and taking advantage of the general economy. This tendency is profoundly moral. The fundamental character of finance is splitting, to divide and tear apart and celebrate fragments as spectacles. The fundamental character and its engendered practices *speak* certain values that may or may not resonate with the majority of us. This is the basic primordial (or overarching) context in which actors' greed is played out and governments' policies operate for the benefits of special interests. The logic or character of finance capital, the financial market, is not neutral, and it serves a purpose or an interest, so we cannot in all honesty argue that it has no inherent morality. Social processes or institutions, before they are manipulated by or corrupted for special interests, have an inherent logic, purpose, bias, interest, rationality, or directionality, all subject to ethical evaluation.

The work of this book is to enable us to *think* of the split, understand its logic and dynamics, figure its impact on human lives, and develop the ethical framework to properly address it. The control of Wall Street or finance capital must bet on social justice, democracy, and pluralism without risking killing the self-revolutionizing dynamics (motor of accumulation) of capitalism.[6] I must admit that I am not optimistic about how as a society we can efficiently or effectively do this. Though there are enough reasons for despair, I want to believe that if we explore the critical nexus between economics and politics we can discern a way out. Ultimately, controlling Wall Street will boil down to politics—that is, sustained activists' actions to push the *polis* toward more democracy, pluralism, social justice, and equalitarian economic opportunities.

The ravenous nature of Wall Street is a predictable consequence of the dynamic of the split in free modern economy. This is so because the event of the primordial split is "demonic." "To call capitalism [or Wall Street] demonic means that it is a structure of evil characterized by the ambiguous unity of creative and destructive powers. Tillich stresses that the demonic is no individual act of evil based on the free decision of personality. Rather, it is 'a structure of evil beyond the moral power of good will, which produces social and individual tragedy precisely through the inseparable mixture of good and evil in every human act.'"[7] All this points to the tragic quality of the primordial split triggered by desire and economic insecurity. "A situation is tragic in which the very elements which are most valuable by their very value drive it to self-destruction."[8] The split as manifested on Wall Street is driving the economy as a whole toward self-destruction. The economy is a "life" in which separation is continuously posited but cannot be overcome by reunion.

I hope to think and theorize all these within the disciplinary location of economic ethics, and not within theology or neoclassical economics. Economic ethics studies rationally, systematically, and methodically the political, normative, and moral purposes of economic institutions, socioeconomic dynamics, and public policies for the ideal organization of society for human flourishing.[9] Unlike neoclassical economic analysts, I do not deem the ethical purposes of economic institutions and public policies to be defined, driven, or circumscribed by self-interest (or self-interest properly defined), but by community, stories of living well with others, and what it means to allow all human beings to be the best they can be. Again, unlike neoclassical economists or the run-of-the-mill liberal (conservative) scholars of political theory, I do not think that the quest for the ideal organization of society for human flourishing should be limited to the distribution of power in any given society, but should be expanded to include transformation of the coordinates that organize our existence, eliciting an interruption of the flow of social life. This is to say, in the fashion of Paul Eisenstein and Todd McGowan, economic ethics must become (include) a political theory that is not restricted to the creation and maintenance of "a reasonable, just, and stable social order."[10] It must become a theory of rapture. "Rapture is the occurrence of the impossible, when the very ground under our feet shifts in order to transform the point from which we see" our socioeconomic reality.[11]

At this point, the reader may well ask, why then do you deploy Paul's theology? Has Paul not been too domesticated and coopted into Christendom to aid any revolutionary thinking? I turn to Paul's theory of human subjectivity not to undergird the study of economic ethics with (dogmatic) theology *per se*, but to extract the universalizable philosophical dimensions of his thought and deploy them for my limited task in this work. Is his theory of human subjectivity not about the destructive cycle of law and its transgression, and the consequent division of the subject? The split caused by the law becomes an obstacle that prevents the human subject from attaining its full identity with herself. I hope to make the insights of Pauline theology to speak to both Christians and non-Christians in their quest to address the universal predicament imposed on all humanity by finance capital.

The split economy is born from excess (surplus) that needs to be stored to generate future excess. Excess, as soon as it emerges, can never be fully integrated into the economic life process; instead, it pushes the economy into continuing renovation and causes instabilities and human suffering. Finance is a metonym of this excess. Is the story of finance not about how the "animal economy," proto-human economy contracted this excess of economic life, which makes it a "human economy"?[12] Can't we say that finance gives body to the primordial split, occupying the space of the gap, the space between economic life and its excess, current production, and fixation on an imaginary absent point of reference? All these do not mean a modern economy is equal to financial economy; it is an economy equal to one in which the excess or finance intervenes as something that prevents the economy from attaining its full identity.[13]

The split economy is never just an *economy*, "it is always sustained by an excess of life which, phenomenally, appears as the paradoxical wound that makes [it] 'undead,' which prevents [it] from dying [standing still]."[14] The primordial economy generates an excess, a surplus on account of which the economy "can no longer be contained in itself," which marks its constitutive exception, announcing a rupture that signifies the "possibility of new possibilities," to expand.[15] The possibility of new possibility should remind us of the unstable limit of an economy known as the production possibilities frontier, the void the economy must constantly stumble upon.[16] The economy retains its *economicity* only insofar as it is "incomplete," constitutively divided, and harbors a foreign kernel that resists its grasp or full incorporation. The economy is therefore always a process, which works by including its failures, struggling to include this kernel—the constant circulation around the "object" that mediates its innovations.

The thought of a Wall Street–less economy, an economy in harmony with itself, a financial industry fully integrated to support Main Street's productive activities is the thought of Paradise—the "name of [economic] life delivered of the burden of this disturbing excess."[17] The unfortunate burden of all liberal paradiasical thought is then the paradoxical task of prohibiting the excess, which the economy generates and disturbs it from within, without ever stifling the economy.

The fundamental argument of this chapter is that the economy is sick with an excess of the future; the focus on finance is only a slice, an authenticating sample of this concern. I trace the origin of the split back to the moment when the *animal economy* (i.e., an economy where production is for spontaneous biological life) was contaminated by something that caused it to leave production for immediate satisfaction and for the *here and now* to become truly economic, truly human, a truly *human economy* (i.e., an economy grasping for a better future and the not-yet or what is to come).

What makes an animal economy truly a human economy is *excess*—an excess of enjoyment of life, a strange drive to enjoy satisfaction, contentment that abolishes uncertainty—a dimension far beyond ordinary animal economy. What makes an animal economy truly human is *excess of production*: an excess of daily production for daily consumption, an attachment to the stored value that enables human beings to exceed the mere production and consumption for the temporal now. This stored value is the financial. The stored value is the metonym of human unconstrained propensity to insist on taking care of our needs and desires ahead of time.

This excess that turns animal economy into human economy is what most threatens the modern economy. Regulations, symbolic laws, and morality aimed at restricting, controlling, or damming this excess, this "too-muchness" manifested on Wall Street, never quite succeed in realizing their aim. The "sin" of Wall Street is the sin of the primordial split, the excess with which animal economy is contaminated. This "sin" of the split manifests as the separation between the financial and industrial circulations of money, the split in financial commodities, and the split between content and form that is behind the marketing of "voids" such as credit default swaps.

This excess, this malignant cancer, reminds me of the Kierkegaardian notion of "sickness unto death." Most liberal scholars and citizens, tired of the severe shortcomings of Wall Street, desperately want to rid the economy of this excess, want the dangerous finance sector to disappear, to relieve themselves of the hell of the excess, but they cannot do it, for the economy is condemned to the perpetual life of the excess. It appears that even the usual concepts of grace and love that conservative scholars (and even some of their liberal counterparts) throw around cannot save us from this excess. The logic of the split has divided grace, and grace cannot coincide with itself.

The notion of grace is not a strange beast to neoclassical economists. The grace implied here is grounded in Adam Smith's understanding of the market, the invisible hand as a particular operation, the work of providential grace. Knowing that grace is at the bedrock of the functioning of the modern economy, we are compelled to ask why love (as returned, reciprocated grace) cannot accompany it, allowing us to strengthen human flourishing. By *love* here, I am not thinking of love as a return to pre-split, smooth functioning animal economy. A return is impossible; a life of harmony is blocked. The invisible hand of the market is the outcome of the impact (theoretical appropriation) of the Christian message (orientation, doctrine) of grace, but it is also its unfinished impact, a split, divided, practical appropriation.[18]

A quick look at the Smithian appropriation of grace immediately reveals that grace is split on Wall Street: grace received is estranged from grace returned, and we are naming grace returned (reciprocated) as love.[19] Here love is not sentimentality, but an extension of received grace from one to another. We are conceptualizing love as grace, returned grace, or the circulation of grace. Theologian Leonardo Boff agrees with us on this point when he writes: "the gratuitousness of love is the gratuitousness of grace itself. . . . To love as the grace of God can never be interpreted in purely individualistic terms. Its structure is eminently social. The more a society creates real forms of human relationship, brotherhood, justice, and love among human beings and nations, the more it manifests grace as love in the world."[20]

Recently, other scholars have noted and questioned the separation of "the gratuitousness of love from the gratuitousness of grace" among the capitalist or business class. Gar Alperovitz and Lew Daly argue that: "If much of what we have comes to us as the free gift of many generations of historical contribution, there is a profound question as to how much can reasonably be said to be 'earned' by any one person, now or in the future."[21] Joseph Stiglitz, the Nobel Memorial Prize–winning economist, adds his voice to this debate when he writes:

> For one thing, the government sets the basic rules of the game [economic growth]. It enforces the laws. More generally, it provides the soft and hard infrastructure that enables a society and an economy to function. If the government doesn't provide roads, ports, education, or basic research—or see to it that someone else does, or at least provides the conditions under which someone else could—then ordinary business cannot flourish. Economists call such investments "public goods," a technical term referring to the fact that everyone can enjoy the benefits of, say, basic knowledge.

A modern society requires collective action, the country acting together to make these investments. The broad societal benefits that flow from them cannot be captured by any private investor, which is why leaving it to the market will result in underinvestment.[22]

In the conceptualization I have just sketched out, love is grace writ large. Paul wrote this about love in I Corinthians 13: 1–13:

If I speak in the tongues of men or of angels, but do not have love, I am only a resounding gong or a clanging cymbal. If I have the gift of prophecy and can fathom all mysteries and all knowledge, and if I have a faith that can move mountains, but do not have love, I am nothing. If I give all I possess to the poor and give over my body to hardship that I may boast, but do not have love, I gain nothing. Love is patient, love is kind. It does not envy, it does not boast, it is not proud. It does not dishonor others, it is not self-seeking, it is not easily angered, it keeps no record of wrongs. Love does not delight in evil but rejoices with the truth. It always protects, always trusts, always hopes, always perseveres. Love never fails. But where there are prophecies, they will cease; where there are tongues, they will be stilled; where there is knowledge, it will pass away. For we know in part and we prophesy in part, but when completeness comes, what is in part disappears. When I was a child, I talked like a child, I thought like a child, I reasoned like a child. When I became a man, I put the ways of childhood behind me. For now we see only a reflection as in a mirror; then we shall see face to face. Now I know in part; then I shall know fully, even as I am fully known. And now these three remain: faith, hope and love. But the greatest of these is love.

Love as thus described appears as grace phenomenalized as concrete action and disposition from one person to his or her beloved. Love is the result of grace—grace becoming a product of itself. Love is grace in the process of its own actualization. Here, love is seen not as something that engenders itself, but as grace existing in and through labor, and the disposition of persons who are grateful for having received it and are thus faithful to it, engaged with it, motivated by it, and committed to extending it to others. Love is the articulation and extension of the grace one has received to others.

The relationship between grace and love reminds us of that between value and surplus, value as Karl Marx conceived it. Capitalists pay workers for the value of the commodity (labor power) that they are selling, and the source of surplus value lies (not necessarily in underpayment) in the fact that "the use-value of this commodity [labor power] is unique, it produces a new value greater than its own value."[23] The point to note here is that the difference in the values is not because capitalists (like merchants) buy low and sell high, but the capacity of labor power to produce new value. Grace does its work of salvation in an individual, but it has this unique potential to produce new value, to keep adding something to itself and hence producing new value greater than itself (at least, as it started with or initially released or received). This new value, the production of new value, value greater than its starting power, is love. As Paul said, without love all gain is nothing (I Corinthians 13:3), a capitalist production process is nothing without surplus value.

Paul also argues that even with love we are nothing, that love always renders us incomplete even when we have every knowledge. Though the one that gives love by extending grace is very aware of her lack, grace is not something she can possess or become one with. However, it is this awareness that paradoxically makes her rich in love, propels her, and enables her to enjoy her work of love. "Only a lacking vulnerable being is capable of love; the ultimate mystery of love is therefore that incompleteness is in a way higher than completion."[24] The accumulation of surplus value does not give the capitalist rest to enjoy unlimited jouissance. It does not free him from the self-revolutionizing movement of capital. The capitalist in principle is always lacking and vulnerable. It appears that Wall Street—with its legendary ability to make super-profits and bend the regulatory rules of the country to its advantage—no longer feels vulnerable.

We started this long discussion about excess as sickness in the economy that needs healing and discovered that we cannot move too quickly toward the so-called healing with the typical religious (or liberal) platitudes about grace and love. This is a methodological move of this book. In trying to work out the relevant ethical approach to addressing the split in the economy, I do not quickly move to fill the gaps. But I accentuate the divisions and widen the splits, until we discover an intuition or brilliant idea that emerges and transforms the way we think about the split. In their deepest and widest separation, we begin to discern that such a chasm is already inherent to any of the sides. The evolution of separation having attained a wide berth acts retroactively upon each side, disclosing dimensions and logic hitherto uncomprehended. The separation appears in different light and hence the economy reveals itself differently.

The widening separation eventually brings the sides together. Take this game we used to play as children. Two children start by standing and facing each other. They are then asked by others to move apart, taking backward steps and in this way increasing the space between them. Eventually their backs meet, and the gulf has disappeared. Their very movements of separation have traversed their difference, and they meet with no preordained force harmoniously bringing them together. Inherent in their own separate movements is the dynamic logic that enables them to traverse the gap.

Take for instance the split between abundance and scarcity. Theologians claim that one of the problems of neoliberal economics is its focus on scarcity, while a kingdom-of-God economics will be focused on abundance. There are liberal theologians who have driven the gap between these two approaches to economic conceptualization as wide as they can. The more they drive these two positions apart, the more I see them as joined, or the more I see theologians as partaking in the logic that they are contesting. Theologians believe that capitalist production can overcome the barriers of scarcity, and capitalists also want to overcome the barriers of scarcity for the fantasy of producing enough to meet unrestricted desires of consumers. Both theologians and capitalists are focused on producing abundance. The typical theological stance on abundance misses a crucial point. The crises that have rocked capitalism are not crises of scarcity, but that of too much goods, as consumers at some point do not have enough money to buy all the goods produced and put on the market. Capitalism always wants to produce an infinite amount of goods to satisfy every desire and demand. Capitalists always want to increase productivity, production, to flood the earth with every conceivable object to realize more and more profits. But this drive to increase the productivity of labor, to realize greater profits eventually works to lower the rate of profits. In the words of Marx, "the profit rate does not fall because labour becomes less productive but rather because it becomes more productive. The rise in the rate of surplus value and the fall in the rate of profit are similarly particular forms that express the growing productivity of labour in capitalist terms."[25]

The constant complaint of theological critics of capitalism is that as an economic system its fascination with a logic of scarcity rather than abundance actually plays into the vortex of the capitalist game. The promise of abundance for perpetual enrichment of entrepreneurs and consumers is the foundation of the capitalist system. The theologians who abandon the notion of scarcity for the so-called divine gift of abundance on earth feeds into the capitalist promise and logic of better future. The logics of scarcity and abundance, among their advocates, might have started as a gap of difference doomed to widen forever, but in reality, the very logic or orientation that separates the two sides brings them together and we are able to see the capitalist economy in a different light—an attack is either incorporated into the system or made to speak its truth. Both capitalists and liberal theologians are invested in the capitalism's psychic appeal of abundance as the basis and promise of better future—what Todd McGowan calls "the fundamental capitalist fantasy."[26] Later (in chapter 7) we will return to the theological-philosophical concerns of scarcity and abundance as we seek solutions to the problems of finance capital in pluralistic societies. In this chapter, we conceive pluralism is an acknowledgment of our mutual lack and vulnerability, our *ex-position* to one another.

As mentioned, it certainly appears that Wall Street, with its rejection of love (reciprocal grace) and its legendary ability to generate gains at the expense of the rest of society, no longer feels vulnerable. Our primordial (ancestors) producers did not recognize that economy as such is in principle split. With the engendering of the finance sector, they gained the perspective of split. But the players in the financial sector came to see finance as the split—not the economy as such. Because they did not know this (the economy as split), they see themselves as the only sector free to split, free to move to the extreme of differentiation, particularization, and be void of content. These players, seeing their sector of the economy as the only one free to split at will, collectively became a despot, and not part of the overall economy.

But today we as citizens of the United States, under the hammer of late capitalism, have attained the consciousness that economy *qua* economy is split, that it is the logic of split that constitutes its peculiar nature. Political praxis under this consciousness is how to maintain the economy as a self-differentiated whole (split into sectors) while preserving individual and collective human flourishing.

The economy as split is never complete and self-identical. It is constituted by fragmentary and sometimes incoherent sets of sectors. To resort to the language of Jean-Luc Nancy, the "community" of sectors is nothing but exposition, each is exposed to the economy and to itself. The truth of the economy resides in the split sectors being-together (not being of togetherness). The split economy entails the exposition, the presence of each sector to all. The presence of sector to sector precludes thinking of the economy as an essence or effectuating its own essence as something beyond the exposition of sector to sector. An economy is this exposition: the co-appearing of finite sectors, and ensembles of transactions, exposed to an outside (another ensemble of transactions). The "being" of the economy is the exposition of sectors, which "are themselves constituted by sharing, they are distributed and placed, or rather *spaced*, by the sharing that makes them *others*: other for one another," and "whose relationship—the sharing itself—is not a communion."[27] Thus, without this exposure and sharing the economy would not exist.

The whole economy turns on this gap, the co-appearing without harmonization as none of its sectors can stabilize its relations with another sector or the whole economy. The split parts of the split economy are not searching for their missing parts—as in Aristophanes's tale of love as the search for one's soul mate—to achieve perfect complementarity. Each of the split parts turns on the cut that generated the split and this puts each sector in a "permanent condition of disruption and yet this disruption is the source" of vitality that the whole economy provides.[28] It is the self-division, noncoincidence of each sector or the whole economy with itself that triggers its movement. Each sector can never stabilize itself because each wants from the other what it does not have. To harmonize fully with the others—to subdue and master their otherness will effectively destroy them and eliminate them as objects of satisfaction. Thus, a perfectly harmonized economy will destroy itself exactly at the moment it achieved total harmony. The split economy must leave each sector or itself with gaps and incompletion, and this incompletion must be seen as indication of its liveliness rather than its failure or problem. Its inability to achieve self-identity rather than its specific features is the focus of our philosophical analysis.

From Split Economy to Split Commodity

Let us begin by denoting the process of harvest ➡ saved consumption ➡ harvest in the primordial economy as H-SC-H. Later, with the emergence of a ruling or dominant class, which could extract the SC from the oppressed men and women, and which is also bent on producing more surplus, H-SC-H becomes SC-H-SC (or SC-H-SC^1, where SC^1 = SC +ΔSC, increase of value), and so SC assumes the drive or tendency for self-valorization.

The primordial split between the economy and finance somewhat anticipates the internal split of the commodity between use value and exchange value that Marx talked about. The use value of a commodity, the bundle of qualities that is a sign of need and the consuming subject, became separated from its quantitative aspect. This split-off part now relates to other commodities similarly heaved off, that is, commodities now relate among themselves independent of the psychological subject, the subject of need. Similarly, the harvest (output, gathering) was split between the part that is used to meet needs and function as a sign of subject of need, and the part that would be exchanged for the future—exchange of today's consumption for consumption tomorrow. These exchange-parts (portions set aside for investments, "saved consumption") now relate to themselves on the basis of the social rate of time preference, that is, basically their time content. Time preference is the rate (which later came to be approximated by interest rate or social discount rate) at which society is willing to exchange present consumption for future consumption.[29] Therefore, the more time value or content a "saved consumption" contains, the better it is. A society with a low time preference rate usually has the bulk of its investments in the short time. The point to note is that with the split, saved consumption is now evaluated on the basis of lower preference for future consumption or strong preference for today's consumption. The higher the relative worth (desirability) of a saved consumption to meet satisfaction in the future, in the mechanics of the intertemporal and interspatial flows of goods and services within and between societies, the higher is its value. The values of saved consumptions are based on difference to one another. Later, money evolved not only to be the embodiment of a society's valuation of the time and space contents of its savings and consumptions, but also a drive of the focus and orientation toward future satisfaction.[30]

What is traded in the transactions of "saved consumption" (either between households or intertemporally between the same household) is not the process of time (flow of time), but time as a specific object (time-power, content of time). Time-power is the quantity of time it takes for saved consumption to produce itself and a surplus $(1 + r)$, where r is the rate of change in value of the saved consumption, for instance, between time zero (t_0) and time $1(t_1)$.

Time-power is actually an exception to the whole process of exchange between the saved-consumption parts, between the parts of the initial harvest (output, gathering, kill) that will be exchanged for the future. It is one split-off part (between time, immanent flow of time and time-power) undergirding both the initial harvests and their future values. Time-power is an element in this whole splitting and investment for the future that subverts it, undermining the universal concept of trading of rate of time preference. In the exchanges of saved consumptions (hereafter, SC) each SC receives equivalent exchange. But time-power is paradoxically a value that produces more than its value. It must produce a surplus in relation to the mere flow of time (its other part). If time has no power to "produce" (transform) value, to generate the surplus value needed to replace (reproduce) the SC, then the whole process is wasteful or at best will break even. So for the whole system of harvest and savings-to-produce-more to work, we must have a fair, equivalent exchange between saved consumptions, and a paradoxical exchange of time-power that must have value beyond itself for the universal system to hold. In this pre-capitalist scenario, time serves as the internal negation of the exchange process, but with capitalism and its pervasive commodification, the split between use value and exchange value of commodity is inscribed into labor that is measurable, according to Marx, by the labor time necessary for production. Labor power becomes the paradoxical exception or internal negation of the exchange process—or, more precisely, layers over this proto-exception.

The condensation of different kinds of harvests and the kinds of labors behind them into abstract time, which can be compared and exchanged on the basis of time-power, transformed subjectivity and time itself. The subject is now traversed by two forces: the motives of enjoyment and enrichment. First, saved consumption (SC) signifies the future, the site of surplus value and surplus enjoyment. The future becomes object of desire and cause of desire. In a certain sense, the future has also become an insatiable god that demands sacrifice and more sacrifice. Second, time became split (into process and power) and also a form of social relation. In the system of differences in which saved consumptions now dwell, the value of time became an exchange value, which is nothing but social relations between human *prosumers* (producers and consumers).[31] Time could be bought and sold by the same individual by imaginatively projecting himself into two time segments, or by different persons, to satisfy postponed desires anticipated to be richer in the future. Later, with the development of market and commodification and the splitting of producers and consumers, labor, precisely labor-time/labor-power became what the capitalist buys to produce surplus value. Quantifiable time became quantifiable subject in the form of labor power.

Split Economy and Split Time

The rupture in the productive activity or horizon that created saved consumption and the ensuing consequences of transformation of subjectivity and time itself (time becoming a social relation) imposes on us a thought about time. Under the hammer of thought grasping fractured being and excesses, we conceive time as also fractured.

The present is the past returning to itself, to self-identity. It points to an ontological desire to return to rest; an unconditional gift to itself.[32] The present contains a surplus, an excess. The future implies a surplus in the present in terms of what the past reckons with and beckons to return, to come to the dialectical rest. The rotary movement of the present generates more energy than it uses. It is like a centrifugal movement that generates a vortex in a bucket of water, creating enough energy and tension to keep the void while throwing off energy around the edges of the bucket. The future is the excess, so to speak, as the present seeks self-identity.

An *other* (an excess) interrupts this identity—an obstacle that splits the whole and dwells in it as a foreign body. This other is created by the past present in its very movement toward self-identity. This other prevents the present, the present-past identitarian movement from coinciding with itself. This obstacle is the future.

The movement of past and present is akin to the rotary drives of the Schelling's Godhead—the phase contraction.[33] F.W.J. Schelling theorized pre-creation Godhead as a tension between ground and existence, expansion and contraction; the rotary movement between natality and necessity within God. Schelling's audacious speculation of the existence of God begins with primordial "Freedom," a neutral "Will" that wants nothing.[34] This is only a potentiality, and in the process of conversion into actuality, in actualizing itself, the pure will (the primordial freedom) changes into a pure contraction, which translates to the annihilation of all determinate content. It actively wants nothing outside itself. In Schelling's reasoning, the perfect freedom, that is, self-contented will (the mode of potentiality), is no different from a destructive fury (mode of actuality) that threatens to swallow everything. A parallax shift of perspective is needed to see that this conversion is purely a formal one; the indifferent will and the will that actively wants "nothing" are of the same being: "the same principle carries and holds us in its ineffectiveness, which would consume and destroy us in its effectiveness."[35]

Note that the moment the primordial freedom attempts to actualize itself, the will is split into two: the will-to-contraction and the will-to-expansion. At the inception of this contraction (the fury of destruction), the will negates itself to become one that wants something, wants to expand. How is this tension within freedom going to be overcome? This positive will (expansion) cannot overcome the antagonism of the negative (contraction), and in this primordial tension the two wills frustratingly move in rotary form, with the positive will not able to break out. The Godhead cannot withdraw completely into itself or open itself up, to admit Otherness. God did eventually create, so expansion won. The future—thus in our paradigm of temporality—is the expansion and as such represents creativity, disruption, and irruption.

The future as we have stated is not something that comes from outside the past and present of time; rather the future is the internal drive of the past and the present to break through the limit of their forms to actualize the inexhaustible potency of their abyss. The present is the ecstatic element of the past and the future is the ecstatic element of the past and the present.

The future is the split, the cut into the ongoing automatism of social processes rooted in and driven by the present-past tango.[36] This future (the proper future of an economy) does not preexist the past or the present-past, but it is created as the present-past moves, in other words, as the production possibilities frontier (hereafter PPF) of an economy or the universe expands. What economists call PPF is a graph (with a bow-out curvature) that shows the most optimal allocation of resources in an economy given the effects of diminishing returns on production.[37] The graph shows how the total value of output will change as different allocations of land, labor, and capital are made. It plots out the output combinations at different allocation regimes of an economy's resources or factors of production. All points on and under the curve are attainable levels of production; those above it are not reachable given the limited supply of resources (capital, labor, technical know-how, management expertise, and so on).

Production levels that correspond to points on the PPF are theoretically considered efficient.[38] At those levels an economy is considered to be producing at levels where there is no waste of resources. At such levels, producers can increase the output of a product only at the expense of another—that is, by decreasing its production. Any attempt to increase the output of a product involves tradeoffs. But when the PPF of an economy shifts outward it can increase not only the production of all items, but might produce even new ones. The PPF shifts outward when there are technical improvements in the economy.

If the PPF defines the boundary of set of possibilities available for an economy to produce and manage its total output, then what is beyond this limit? Beyond the frontier (PPF) is a *void*. It is not a space; it is not conducive for "economic habitation" (for production and exchange). It is a nonplace, a nonexistent economic space. But as an economy expands and its constraints are loosened, it creates its own space. A cutting-edge economy creates the space into which it expands. With what "forces" does an expanding galaxy of economic activities unfurl the subsequent space it will inhabit? Technological breakthroughs and human capital improvements are some of the factors that usually shift the line (curve) outward.

I want to accent or reiterate one of the features of PPF's expansions: an economy creates the space into which it expands. Take, for instance, that decades ago there was no computer industry in the United States. There was no "there" of the computer industry into which the United States could move and occupy in order to expand its economy, to increase its gross domestic product. It had to create this new space into which it would then go. The creation and movement into the new space is simultaneous, in the same way the universe expands by creating its own space and expanding into it.

In this vein, we can now say that finance appears when the economy generates enough force to create its own future. Put differently, finance appears when the economy is able to grasp or invite the future, which is the splitting force of time, into its own rotary movement. This internal splitting of time gives birth to two elements, spheres, or flows: (a) self-sufficient finitude of the present-past, and (b) dependent infinitude of the future. The present-past collective or fabric is always trying to shut out the future as it endlessly pursues its immediate interest, but as we have seen the very endless rotary movement toward self-identity and contentment generates the future that shakes its resolve.[39]

Looking Forward

Let me recap the argument of this chapter by recalling a statement I made early in the chapter. In the beginning was the split, and the split was with the economy, and the split was the economy. In the beginning, *forward-looking claim* was the creative power that alighted on the "earth," that is the darkness of the productive ground of human activities, and separated light from darkness. The light in our exposition is called finance and the earthy darkness the general economy. Thus, the first day began with tremendous promise. But the light has not only done its work of separativeness too well, it has also become radioactive, shattering the "vessel," the earth/ground of economic production from whence it came, and sending shards of the vessel all over the space of human existence.

When it arose in the primitive human's will to have a forward-looking claim, the first step was to somewhat "withdraw" from immediate consumption, and conceal the infinite immediate desire to consume the limited output. This first constriction, restriction, self-limitation created the incipient world of finance. The withdrawal is a constriction that shed light on the potential of the future, and over time the intensity and influx of this released light, which is linked to the infinite desire of the human will, began to overwhelm the human capacity to control.

This chapter and the next two constitute part I of this text, the ontological examination of the split economy. In chapter 2 we will examine the issue of split subjectivity from the perspective of Saint Paul (Romans 7) as we explore how the fracture of being is implicated in both human subjectivity and the economy. Chapter 3 grapples with the notion of split economy. Therein, I do not focus on the technological or macroeconomic dynamics, but rather on the agonistic foundations of the economy of the United States. My analysis concerns, therefore, the "constants" of capitalism, understood not as its macroeconomic statistical regularities, but as its underpinning agonistic foundations. In chapters 4 and 5 (part II) I probe the logic of finance capital, which is today the representative face of capitalism. I provide here a detailed economic-philosophic explanation of the separative logic of finance capital. In chapters 6 and 7, I ask questions regarding how to heal the split: What slips into the split between finance and the economy to heal the crack? Would it be citizens' activism? Can the wound of the gap be healed (ameliorated) without hoping to make the economy whole? The responses to these questions are organized around how to conceive the future or *futureness* that emerged from the primordial economy and is now a full-blown capitalist gimmick or has acquired the commodity form. One of the conclusions of these chapters (chapter 6) is that when we focus only on the future that is envisaged by capitalist trajectory, we remain only within the realm of the possible, never questioning the coordinates of our social existence and thus never leaning toward the rupture that can install the impossible, which interrupts the familiar flow of social life.

In the final chapter, my epilogue, I offer a theory of split (a theory of rupture in being as reflected through split economy/finance capital) that identifies with the present and accents a subject that emerges as "a break within time and because of this break, the subject has the capacity to form values that make life worth living."[40] This break within time can only be gestured to and cannot be offered as a capitalist promise of the future. Hannah Arendt writes: "This small non-time-space in the very heart of time [i.e., the break within time], unlike the world and the culture into which we are born, can only be indicated, but cannot be inherited and handed down from the past; each new generation, indeed every new human being as he inserts himself between an infinite past and infinite future, must discover and ploddingly pave it anew."[41]

Chapter 2
Saint Paul's Notion of Split Subjectivity

Introduction

In the previous chapter we learned that Paul both construed and denied incompleteness of being. He contested the completeness of our world insofar as he conceived God as the missing signifier (which must remain transcendent) of its completeness. For Paul, the necessity of a missing God and belief in God in the world must be conceived together. Paul is balancing fidelity to belief in rupture in being with rapture (solace and bliss in God's authority). We see this deft interplay of rupture (radicality) and rapture (conservatism) in his analysis of human subjectivity. He acknowledges the rupture in the self as occasioned by the divine law in Romans 7, but his question: "Who will rescue me from this body that is subject to death?" serves as a rapturous knock on an open door to a site of bliss, ultimacy, and access to empowering meaningful knowledge. The question is only a short prelude to the messianic closure of the hole in signification, the split in being. His cry "who can rescue me?" assumes there is a *big Other* to perform the rescue.[1] The law that splits Paul's subject is from the big Other. The cry signifies a belief in the existence of a big Other who can close the split in being.

The economy or the market refuses such closure, as the players in it have no such fantasy framing their actions and thoughts—at least, as we are conceptualizing it here. The operators play the market believing that rupture (and its attendant missing signifier) ultimately subtends every structure that they interact with or, possibly, every transaction that they enter into. The recognition of this fact—acceding to the irrevocable split in being—does not represent anti-Paulism, but instead a Paulism estranged from itself. The issue with the Pauline conception of the rupture in human beings is that it is too occupied with what stands on either side of the divide—God and the estranged human subject. Paul is not really invested in the divide within the self—the rupture in itself. Quick to seek salvific (social) harmony between the sides—as indeed one expects him to do given his location—he does not see the divide within the self as a source of value.

Contrary to Paul, our analysis of the split economy or split subjectivity locates values in the cut, seeing it as ontological. We avow the fecundity of the cut. In this chapter, following Paul's discourse in Roman 7, we analyze the split in human subjectivity, and in chapters 3, 4, and 5 we pursue—without resorting to the utopian dream of social harmony—the role of the cut in the subject and the economy, and how the cut foundationlessly grounds and haunts values. I refuse the fantasy of social harmony or ideal form of society because I have no prior knowledge of the perfect community; that is, I have no understanding of society before the fundamental antagonism traverses it. Put slightly differently, I reject giving epistemological privilege to, or positing the ontological priority of, the ideal form. Do we, today, still believe like Plato that there are ideal forms of worldly appearances? Or do we now believe that appearance *qua* appearance is self-divided? It is the self-division of appearance rather than external, eternal form that gives the illusion of an ideal form, something outside the limits of appearing. We see an object (especially if it has flaws), and we think that there must be a better one, a flawless one somewhere else outside history. The mere encounter with an object, according to Alain Badiou, produces the idea that it is out of place, that is, there is an ideal form of it. Why? He holds that: "All that is relates to itself at a distance from itself owing to its place where it is."[2] This simply means every particular object is split "between its place and its being, which always exceeds the particular's position in the world. Every particular appearance suffers from this self-division in which universality manifests itself."[3]

Basically, we will be examining the disruptiveness of the crack in being as an ethic of Wall Street, which has been deployed in ways that deform or challenge our received wisdom of social ethics and economic theology. Current forms of economic theology even when they acknowledge the split in being—the fundamental antagonism of society—posit that the split can be translated into a positive form or into an ideal form.

This kind of scholarship does not identify with the rupture and hence does not think it—at least, does not think it as the fundamental impossibility, negativity around which the economy functions. The received wisdom is not a conscious philosophizing or theologizing of split in being or ruptures in economic ethics; thus, our text might in itself represent a rupture in the discipline. Social ethics in the academy is usually seen as the study of social cohesion and solidarity as strengthened, undermined, or transformed by morality, order, and events as they are interpreted in the light of human flourishing. This book deliberately accents the events, or ruptures, in the study of social ethics. All this said, let us now turn to Paul's theory of human subjectivity as we begin in earnest to *think with* and *think against* Paul as he goes to Wall Street.

Paul and Split Subjectivity

What shall we say, then? Is the law sinful? Certainly not! Nevertheless, I would not have known what sin was had it not been for the law. For I would not have known what coveting really was if the law had not said, "You shall not covet." But sin, seizing the opportunity afforded by the commandment, produced in me every kind of coveting. For apart from the law, sin was dead. Once I was alive apart from the law; but when the commandment came, sin sprang to life and I died. I found that the very commandment that was intended to bring life actually brought death. For sin, seizing the opportunity afforded by the commandment, deceived me, and through the commandment put me to death. So then, the law is holy, and the commandment is holy, righteous and good. Did that which is good, then, become death to me? By no means! Nevertheless, in order that sin might be recognized as sin, it used what is good to bring about my death, so that through the commandment sin might become utterly sinful. We know that the law is spiritual; but I am unspiritual, sold as a slave to sin. I do not understand what I do. For what I want to do I do not do, but what I hate I do. And if I do what I do not want to do, I agree that the law is good. As it is, it is no longer I myself who do it, but it is sin living in me. For I know that good itself does not dwell in me, that is, in my sinful nature. For I have the desire to do what is good, but I cannot carry it out. For I do not do the good I want to do, but the evil I do not want to do—this I keep on doing. Now if I do what I do not want to do, it is no longer I who do it, but it is sin living in me that does it. So I find this law at work: Although I want to do good, evil is right there with me. For in my inner being I delight in God's law; but I see another law at work in me, waging war against the law of my mind and making me a prisoner of the law of sin at work within me. What a wretched man I am! Who will rescue me from this body that is subject to death? Thanks be to God, who delivers me through Jesus Christ our Lord! (Rom. 7:7–25 NIV)

To begin my philosophical-psychoanalytic meditation of this enigmatic passage, let me first offer Jacques Lacan's gloss on it:

> Is the Law the Thing? Certainly not. Yet I can only know of the Thing by means of the Law. In effect, I would not have had the idea to covet it if the Law hadn't said: "Thou shall not covet it." But the Thing finds a way by producing in me all kinds of covetousness thanks to the commandment, for without the Law the Thing is dead. But even without the Law, I was once alive. But when the commandment appeared, the Thing flared up, returned once again, I met my death. And for me, the commandment that was supposed to lead to life turned out to lead to death, for the Thing found a way and thanks to the commandment seduced me; through it I came to desire death.
>
> I believe that for a little while now some of you at least have begun to suspect that it is no longer I who have been speaking. In fact, with one small change, namely, "Thing" for "sin," this is the speech of Saint Paul on the subject of the relations between the law and the sin in the Epistle to the Romans, Chapter 7. [. . .]
>
> The relationship between the Thing and the Law could not be better defined than in these terms. . . . The dialectical relationship between desire and the Law causes our desire to flare up only in relation to the Law, through which it becomes the

desire for death. It is only because of the Law that sin . . . takes on an excessive, hyperbolic character. Freud's discovery—the ethics of psychoanalysis—does it leave us clinging to that dialectic?[4]

What do you think Paul is saying in Romans 7? Let me put it plainly so it is easy to grasp. Is law the sin? Has it become death to me? Certainly not! Yet I only know of insatiable longing, desire by means of the law. Really, I would not have the idea to long after sinful desires if the law had not prohibited me from taking certain actions. But the longing was producing in me all manner of evil desire, covetousness thanks to the law's prohibition, for without the prohibition the longing was dead. I was once alive without the prohibition. But when prohibition appeared, the longing revived, and I met my death. Now it is no longer I who is coveting, but the longing that dwells in me. And for me, the law that was supposed to lead me to a crucified, sanctified life, to swerve me away from hell, is bringing me into captivity of longing. The world found a way with me, thanks to insatiable longing that seduced me; through it I came to be dominated by the law of sin and death. I now desire death. Who will deliver me from this body of death?

We have noted several divisions of the self that are precipitated by law, but let us not forget to mention that the self is split in more than one way. Beyond being split by law into two conflicting sides, Paul's implicit assumption about it in his discourse of law/self/sin is that the "I" itself is split—even before the law hammers and cleaves it. There is the "I" as object of phenomenal experience, and the "I" as a thing-in-itself.[5] The former as an object of experiences and representations is what the law attacks (or attaches itself to) and separates from the latter. The struggle initiated by the coming (entrance) of the law acts against this background, and the struggle is between the "I" as an object of experience and the "I" that supposedly grounds it. The self cannot be a totalized simple entity; otherwise there would be no conflictual relation (set in motion by the law) between the simple totality and that which must be its internal other. Paul must have assumed that before the coming of the law, the two "I"s worked harmoniously. Or did he presuppose that one side dialectically integrated or swallowed up the other? Or did Paul in his interest to theorize the law and subject, or to find the antagonism of the law, disavow the knowledge that the human being from the beginning is an embodiment of antagonism?

The self-division, according to Paul, is caused by the law (Rom. 7:19). But here he acknowledges the law, which divides the self and decompletes the subject from within, is itself divided. The one who is divided sees "another law at work in me, waging war against the law of my mind [law of breath of life] and making me a prisoner of the law of the sin at work within me (7: 23, NIV)." The principle of the law for Paul, as Agamben argues, is division—always splitting groups.

> The principle of the law is thus division. The basic partition of Jewish law is the one between Jews and non-Jews, or in Paul's word, between *Ioudaioi* and *ethne*.[6]
>
> Let us take the fundamental division of the law to be that of the Jew/non-Jew. The criteria for how this division works is both clear (circumcised/foreskin) and exhaustive, for it divides all "men" into two subsets, without leaving a remainder [*resto*] or remnant.[7]

For Paul, then, subjectivity emerges from this division; indeed, subjectivity *is* the division, the split itself. Let me point out that there is a triple movement (sort of "objective-subjective-absolute") in the emergence of subjectivity.[8] It needs to make a journey through the law and desires to form itself as divided something. Law is objective reality that makes an impossible demand, such as "thou shall not desire," but does not tell me what not to desire. The self stands for the certainty of subjective self-awareness of foreign body within me; the "absolute" gestures to the inclusion of the subjective into the objective itself. The divided subjectivity emerges when the law is inscribed into the self and the subjective self-awareness is included into the law. The law is the otherness within the self that prevents it from achieving its full identity; and this otherness that creates inconsistency and incompleteness in the self coincides with the very inconsistency and splitting of the law. The law does not simply add to the self: it divides the self, therefore, creating a gap between the self and its desires.[9] The self embodies the prohibitions (demands) of the law into itself: "For I would not have known what coveting really was if the law had not said, 'You shall not covet.' But sin, seizing the opportunity afforded by the commandment, produced in me every kind of coveting." The subjective self-awareness is included in the law in the sense that law generates its own transgression. Paul makes us see how the objective law includes enticement in itself even as it stands as an obstacle to the satisfaction of desires. There is a splitting or duplication within the law itself, which can (re)produce itself and seize opportunity or chance.[10]

The divisions, demands, and "acts" are constitutive parts of the subject, and this is what makes subjectivity a crack in the substance of the subject. This crack, subjectivity-as-crack, is neither an essential entity that emerges from the interaction of the self and the other (law), nor a substance that shines through the interaction or pre-law self, nor a positive counter force to the person (personhood); "it is a result of the process (event) of its own becoming."[11] The self is always already a struggle between its real being and the demands coming from the Other. The split is the subject as such.

There is a fundamental internal split in the subject; parts of the same self (the "I") are locked in an agonizing and agonistic struggle, and it appears the "I" is given over to sin, and to death (Rom. 7:17). The subject is living under the influence of the "law of sin and death," or the "body of death." The subject split against itself is oriented toward death, living under the control of the death drive. This cannot be fully grasped outside sin's transgressive relationship to the law. As Lacan and Slavoj Žižek argue, the law through the obscene superego supplement generates its own transgressions. On a more philosophical note, Paul here shows that the subject is split between his conscious ego, "I," that wants to obey the law, and the unconscious self, decentered and dispersed by desire. The subject is thus compelled to transgress the law, to do what he does not want to do or hates. His transgression of the law and indulgence in jouissance is imbricated in the dynamics of law and desire—the prohibitions enforced by the law generate desires in the subject to transgress the law. The subject is split; the difference, that is, the gap between the two energetics, prevents the subject from reaching full self-identity. And subjectivity is constituted around this kernel, the obstacle within the subject.

Paul's position is that the person should be conscious of this mechanism and should not fall for it. He wants the person to break out of this trap, this perversion. Thus, Žižek writes:

> St. Paul's problem is thus not the standard morbid moralistic one (how to crush transgressive impulses; how finally to purify myself of sinful urges), but its exact opposite: how can I break out of the vicious cycle of the Law and desire,

of the Prohibition and its transgression, within which I can assert my living passions only in the guise of their opposite, as a morbid death drive? How would it be possible for me to experience my life-impulse not as a foreign automatism, as a blind "compulsion to repeat" making me transgress the Law, with the unacknowledged complicity of the Law itself, but as fully subjectivized, positive "Yes!" to my life.[12]

Žižek's point about breaking the vicious cycle of law is appropriately located in Paul's understanding of the two divisions that plague the subject. There is the division (law and desire), as we have noted, within the subject, and there is also the division between law/desire and Christian love, which enables the believer to break the deadlock of the dialectics of prohibitory law and its transgressive desire, escaping the particular perverse relationship to the law and not the law as such. Žižek holds that the Christian, who embraces the law of love, is able to escape; hence, he writes in *The Ticklish Subject*:

> It is as if St. Paul himself has answered Dostoyevsky's famous "If there is no God, everything is permitted!" In advance—for St Paul, *precisely since there is the God of Love everything is permitted to the Christian believer*—that is to say, the Law, which regulates and prohibits certain acts is suspended. For a Christian believer, the fact that he does not do certain things is based not on prohibition (which then generate the transgressive desire to indulge precisely in these things) but in the positive attitude of Love.[13]

Žižek considers the positing of relation between the law (the symbolic order) and the transgressive desire as the formal condition of subjectivity.[14] The subject is split between her own desires and what the Other (law, Big Other, symbolic order, social relations) demands from her. The gap separating the human being (her desires) from herself is the formative ground of her subjectivity. Subjectivity is always characterized in the Lacan-Žižekian register by an internal scission. "Subject designates the 'imperfection' of substance, the inherent gap, self-deferral, distance-from-itself, which forever prevents substance from fully realizing itself, from becoming 'fully itself.'"[15]

Pauline Subjectivity and Future Orientation of Capitalism

The cry (*who will rescue me? . . .*) is the groan of someone face to face with the image of dissatisfaction. Paul's cry is oriented to the future. There is a distance that separates this "tortured" subject from a possible harmony in the way he formulates the moral burden. The moral law addresses or encounters the subject with a duty that he ought to accomplish, but he is torn, split by this ought. The subject experiences the law as internalized and immanent, but depicts its ought (its harmonization) as "a future act to be accomplished rather than an act already done."[16] As long as the moral law and its harmonization as an accomplished act (that is, without the ought, *Sollen*, without its tormenting partial organ of a voice inside me) remains a possibility I need to reach, there is a distance between the self and the law. Never mind that Paul says the law has been internalized. The distance arises because implicit in the Paul's conception of the relationship between the subject and the law is the split between morality and its reality. On one hand, the moral law is immanent, within the subject, but on the other hand, it is also above the subject, as the starry heavens above. This is because, for Paul, morality is not conceived "as something already attained and accomplished," always with "a moral imperative to act in the future."[17] But following Hegel, if we privilege the moral deed rather than the ought or the partial-organ voice of the moral imperative, the emphasis on the failure or distance is cut off. Hegel in *Phenomenology of the Spirit* writes: "Consciousness starts from the idea that, *for it*, morality and reality do not harmonize; but it is not in earnest about this, for in the deed the presence of this harmony becomes *explicit for it.*"[18] For conceptualizing the deed as the site where morality and reality meet, Hegel disables or subtracts the ought of the "moral imperative to act in the future." But Paul's vision of morality does not subtract the future from it. The moral law lifts us out of our everyday struggle with the flesh when we experience its force, its demanding imperative and not when we accomplish the moral deed, for we cannot accomplish the moral deed, the good by ourselves. So, unlike Hegel, Paul insists morality and reality will ever remain split because morality is not a duty that has been accomplished and continues to be accomplished; rather, it is a moral duty that we ought to accomplish.[19]

The important point for excavating the accent on the future in Paul's theory of subjectivity is to show that subjectivity relies on distance: it is futural. We not only experience the law as embodied in the here and now, but also in the promise that it embodies, in the distant jouissance, which are desires of less traumatic encounter that it holds in front of us. Though the law is inside of us and constitutive of our subjectivity, we are perpetually at the edge of desire to be in harmony with it, but can never attain satisfaction, as we need God, the big Other to tide us over. So the Pauline subject is always at a constant state of desire and is bound to experience every satisfaction as dissatisfaction. Is this not what Paul is saying in Philippians 3:12–14? He is always pressing forward, expecting more satisfaction, working to penetrate just another sublime mystery. He is simultaneously enjoying himself in his knowledge of and confidence in Christ, and sincerely believing that there is something more just around the corner if only he can press on. Does all this not remind us of the fundamental fantasy of capitalism? Is this promise of better future, the enjoyment that we experience now, but could get more of it in the future not also what capitalism promises its subjects? Or is this not how capitalism molds us to relate to our various satisfaction?

Todd McGowan, relying on psychoanalysis, probes capitalism on the basis of its futural dimension of the satisfaction it provides and also promises:

> The fundamental gesture of capitalism is the promise, and the promise functions as the basis for capitalist ideology. One invests money with the promise of future returns; one starts a job with the promise of a higher salary; one takes a cruise with the promise of untold pleasure in the tropics; one buys the newest piece of electronics with the promise of easier access of what one wants. In every case the future embodies a type of satisfaction foreclosed to the present and dependent on one's investment in the capitalist system. The promise ensures a sense of dissatisfaction with the present in relation to the future.
>
> The promise of the better future is the foundation of the capitalist structure, the basis for all three economic areas—production, distribution, and consumption . . . Any sense of satisfaction with one's present condition would have a paralyzing effect on each of these regions of the capitalist economy.[20]

Pauline Subjectivity and Two Types of Militant Figures

Paul's way of theorizing subjectivity in Romans 7 raises the specter of two types of militant figures. There is the fundamentalist one who refuses to accept that the sublime mystery Paul is gesturing to has already been attained. Believers are accepted by Christ and are in Christ, and thus there is no mystery to unveil, and human subjectivity does not have a secret waiting to be revealed. The first kind of fundamentalist does not accept this and wants to keep looking, plugging more into the treadmill of satisfaction/dissatisfaction. The other type of militant figure (the revolutionary) believes that she has "touched the face" of Christ, and found genuine freedom and wants to divest from the treadmill. She already has what is promised. She wants to be fully immersed in her satisfaction of Christ. This is the figure that easily translates into Alain Badiou's revolutionary militant figure. She is not interested in any mystery or miracle. She is only interested in Christ resurrected, or only faithful to her being accepted in Christ and not to the future realization of sublime experience. Her investment in the sublime only translates to a belief in the transcendental capacity of human beings to initiate something new, the *novum* amid ongoing social automatism. This figure that decides to unplug from the too-muchness of religious enjoyment is potentially dangerous to capitalism. Marx states in the second volume of *Capital*: "For capitalism is already essentially abolished once we assume that it is enjoyment that is the driving motive and not enrichment itself."[21] McGowan, following Marx, argues in his *Capitalism and Desire* that capitalism (and we add here religion) "depends on a psychic investment in the promise of the future," buttressed by a sense that one's satisfaction is always incomplete. To learn this lesson and come to terms with one's satisfaction is the beginning of wisdom in revolutionary emancipation.[22]

The two figures point to a problem in the Pauline theory of subjectivity. By bringing the law from the transcendental distance and situating it within the self the sublimity of the law can actually be attained (embodied), paving the way for disappointment. The appeal of the fundamentalist is the broken promise of ultimate satisfaction in his encounter with the law, and he looks for the sublime future. He would prefer the sublimity of the law to be put at a distance, at a transcendental level as in the pre-Pauline conception of the Torah. Fundamentalism is in a certain sense a revolt against the form of closeness to the law the Pauline subjectivity provides. "The fundamentalist is not someone who fails to experience the satisfaction that [the proximity of the law] offers but someone, instead, who experiences it fully. This satisfaction is dissatisfying for the fledging fundamentalist because it doesn't live up to the promise that [the proximity] makes . . . This gap is the source of the fundamentalist disappointment."[23]

The two figures of fundamentalist and revolutionary can stand for two ways of relating to capitalism. There are those who are invested in the sublime mystery of the commodity and refuses to accept that satisfaction could actually be experienced. They do not want freedom from the stronghold of capitalist commodities or the Other's desire. The second figure—which McGowan portrays as the right way to resist capitalism—grasps that she derives satisfaction from acquiring the commodity and thus "can divest from the capitalist project of accumulation. The satisfaction that derives from the commodity can exhaust the desire for the accumulation of commodities."[24] The person has found her genuine freedom, no longer in the thralldom of pursuing ultimate enjoyment out there. McGowan further writes:

> True freedom is freedom in the face of the Other's desire—or, more properly freedom from the Other's desire. Freedom is an indifference toward the desire of the Other that the subject has when it finds itself fully immersed in its own satisfaction. The free subject ceases to concern itself with the question of the desire of the Other and pursues its own satisfaction regardless of its relationship to the other. It neither tries to follow the desire of the Other nor deviate from this desire. But capitalism has a profound allergy to this type of freedom and does all it can to ensure a preoccupation with the desire of the Other.[25]

Indeed, the Pauline theory of split subjectivity focuses our attention on subjects' dissatisfaction with their relation to the law and to a promise of a better future. It thus opens up a lens to understand capitalism, which is forever bombarding us with visions of our dissatisfaction in consuming this or that commodity and then promising to rescue us from our predicament with an enriched or better future, only to induce us to desire for more. One key difference between the Pauline and the capitalist split subjectivity is that eventually the Pauline subject (beyond

Romans 7) does not see herself (not the fundamentalist) as dissatisfied forever pursuing future satisfaction. She eventually comes to recognize the satisfaction she has found in Christ and in God's grace.

From Split in Subjectivity to Split Economy

The economy is a body. It has "power of being," weight, and "flesh." It lives by moving, interacting with other bodies, expanding and adding weight, renewing itself, and living as a super-natural entity to the human bodies that birthed it. It is traversed by the tension between what Hegel calls the "animality" and the "spiritual," the materiality of mechanical interactions of private interests and the collective work, self-interested actions and universal spiritual substance—the flesh and spirit. More importantly, the economy is split by language—the accounting language of debit and credit. Accounting is the fundamental scene where the constitutive difference of finance is made accessible to thought. Everything in finance begins with the relation of credit and debit. Finance (as an abstract thought of the primordial split) did not preexist the encounter (discovery) of credit and debit, particularly not before the duality of money. Inasmuch as finance is thinkable, it is so only from the point of the first and fundamental scene of the split in money. The split, by the way, did condition the emergence of debit and credit. Debit and credit is the originary power of the split, of money. (More on this later.)

In this transactional language, debit and credit are the signifiers, chains of zeros and ones, bearing only arbitrary relations to transactions as wealth (income) creation or destruction (depletion) that they signify. The link between the 0/1 or debit and credit and the signifieds is a matter of (arbitrary) convention. "With nothing to guarantee the link between the two component parts of any sign, all signs are inherently unstable. There is always a gap between the signifier and the signified."[26] The whole accounting language, like the language that we speak, depends on a system of differences. One knows the value of a transaction through its relation to other transactions in the system. The worth of a transaction is dependent on its place in the chain of signification that is perpetually in flux, and any attempt to know its value-in-itself is endlessly postponed or deferred; a journey to an unreachable destination or origin, always open to difference/deferrals. To add to this quandary, the signifier of the transaction lives on long after the transaction is "dead." The signifier (debit or credit, asset and liability), which was already referring to the transaction in its absence, standing in when the transaction is not present, goes on to live, exist long after the signified is dead.[27] Thus nothingness, absence, or death dwells at the center of the gap between the signifier and signified; rather, death is inscribed into the heart of life, an otherness at its intimate core.

The problem with the accounting system as the site of the language of the economy is that it is a bold, bald attempt to cover the foundational gap, to bring the signifying chain to a close, a closed harmony for any set of transactions.[28] Despite this attempt, the gap fractures the economy, making it susceptible to instability. Just as the self—as we have demonstrated earlier—is neither coherent nor constant, the economy (or the economy as a body) is inconsistent and unstable. It is split by a fundamental antagonism, signifier and signified—the language of debit and credit. The accounting system (language), like the spoken language, defines meaning (value) retroactively. The simple act of projecting future value (via the basic technique of valuation such as the discounted cash-flow model)[29] to determine value today (at time zero), which is repeated when the projected future date arrives, suggests three things: (a) the inexhaustibility of the process of valuation (meaning); (b) that there is always another future (signifier, S_2) to determine the value of what came before (today, S_1); and (c) the presupposition (convention) that there is a total milieu, a complete chain necessary to ascertain the value of any one transaction.[30] "The completeness of the system of signifiers [debit and credit] is both demanded and precluded by the same rule of language. Without the totality of the system of signifiers there can be no determination of meaning [value], and yet this very totality would prevent the *successive* consideration of signifiers that the rule requires."[31] There is a gap, split in the heart of the accounting system, the economy or finance capital.

Overall, the reading of Paul's Romans 7 in this chapter situates split subjectivity, the constitutive incompleteness of the subject, at the heart of our understanding of social reality. The point to note is that the specific reading of Romans 7 that we have accented in this chapter—and admittedly this is but one of many possible readings—holds that human subjectivity bears, harbors a gap within itself. And in this book, as we have already noted, we want to examine the theoretical consequences of split subjectivity on economic existence, more precisely as a lens to examine the nature and logic of the global financial system. One of the issues we will be treating in this book, based on the insight of the Pauline theory of subjectivity, is this: What can the split in subjectivity tell us about the split in the economy? How is the radical imbalance/tension of the Pauline subject related to that of the economy? Finance begins from the fact that there is a gap/split in the economy. Or do we say that it is because finance begins that the gap is produced?[32] Finance here coincides with the split, with the inconsistency, the radical disturbance/impossibility in the "being" of the economy. It is because of this inconsistency or incompleteness inherent to the economy that the new interruption, or event like finance can emerge. The development/separation of sectors or the periodic disturbance of finance is a *symptom* of the basic antagonism, the split that cuts across the economic whole. The sectoral developments, disturbances, and imbalances are not only the symptoms that keep repeating the primordial cut, but are also embodiments of the cut, which makes the economy *non-all*.

All this is indicative of an economic system that is always incomplete, unfinished. The economy is "non-all," non-whole, *pas-tout*. The economy is not only split, but also the principle of law of its development is division. Split as modality of the "real" is expressed in the various forms of sectoral developments, internal struggles, and distortions, and it is "the very structuring principle of these distortions."[33] The split not only represents symbolic failure of the economy to be self-identical, but also its point of excess. It structures the very terrain in (background against) which sectors of economy relate to one another and maintain their being-in-common.

The modern capitalist economy is a *universalism minus one*: minus the working class, the part of no-part, whose submission to the demands of capitalism and survival invites their exploitation and private concern about the protection and reproduction of biological life; hence, their excision from *politics proper* as an act of emancipation. The modern economy is constructed with a master signifier, which is an exception: money. Money is itself self-divided, always as credit and debit, asset and liabilities.

As stated earlier, our task in this book is to relentlessly examine the forms of split in the economy, or how the originary primordial split repeats itself today to the disastrous consequences, the radical tearing-apart of human lives and socalities. While we situate the split as the organizing principle for economic-ethical thought, we do not offer solutions to cover or foreshorten the crack. While in chapters 6 and 7 we advocate for extended dialogue and Jean-Luc Nancy's theory of exposition of beings as a way of identifying with ruptures as a disposition of being, we acknowledge the necessity of active citizens' resistance to the ethics and politics of Wall Street that appropriates the logic of rupture for filthy lucre. By not searching for closure—messianic or not—we part ways with a dominant thread in Pauline thought. Paul's struggle in Romans 7 reflects a belief in original wholeness, which has been split, warranting an expectation of return to oneness. But, unlike Paul, we view the self (economy) as primordially split, fragmented and composite originally. Paul is looking for a language, a code that will translate the communication between the two halves. Is this not the fundamentalist fantasy of all phallogocentrism? The French philosopher Jacques Rancière offers us an uncodified language to translate the basic insights of Paul's theory of subjectivity into a perspective of fundamental antagonism in the political economy of modern societies without the problematic fantasy that ultimately frames Paul's thought.

Rancière's notion of democracy provides another approach to applying Pauline insights about sin and the split self to the analysis of modern socioeconomy. Paul's analysis of the flesh suggests parallels with Rancière's notion of the *demos* as both part of, and the whole community.[34] For Paul, the flesh is simultaneously both part of the self (flesh plus spirit) and the whole of the self. Rancière believes that a society is internally split between the part that counts and the part that does not count, the *part of no-part*, which is identified with the whole community. A fundamental difference, antagonism exists between the parts of the community: while the part that does not count wants to undermine the order of distribution of bodies and places, the part that dominates aspires to maintain the harmony of specific human-being together, the way of being, the consensual practices that reject the political logic of the egalitarian act. The drive or the insistence on this harmony is the "sin" of what he calls the police logic of the distribution of places. For Paul, sin is not just the internal conflict, a split to be overcome by homostasis of the parts by rebasing the self on a principle of inner harmony. Sin is the very impossibility of the harmony, the noncoincidence of the self with itself. The split is fundamental; it makes the self itself non-whole, non-all. Sin is not a struggle between the self and its outside; but the self is cut from within the self. Herein, we see the similarity in the thoughts of Paul and Rancière.

Saint Paul's Notion of Split Subjectivity 65

For Paul, the self is divided against itself, and this is the basis of religion, at least the turn to God's Spirit (an agent outside the self-division of the body) to make the believer whole and achieve some "ethical" harmony. In Rancière's case, community is split between the rich (those who rule) and the *part of no-part*; thus, this is the basis of politics. In his terminology, "politics" is about how a society counts the parts of its community and allocates places. Human societies are counted in wholes, which are divisible into parts and functions. There is always a part of no-part. There is a conflict between the parts that count in the social body and the part that does not, and this latter part unsettles the whole because of the universal principle of equality, the equality of all speaking beings. The counting is based on two logics:

> Political conflict does not involve an opposition between groups with different interests. It forms an opposition between logics that count the parties and parts of the community in different ways. The combat between the "rich" and the "poor" is one over the very possibility of splitting these words into two, of instituting them as categories that inscribe another (ac)count of the community. Two ways of counting the parts of the community exist. The first counts real parts only—actual groups defined by differences in birth, and by different functions, places and interests that make up the social body to the exclusion of every supplement. The second, 'in addition' to this, counts a part of those without part. I call the first the *police* and the second *politics*.[35]

According to Rancière, politics starts when those not counted try to establish equality of all speaking beings, when they subjectivize the wrong. It starts when they realize the sheer contingency of any social order, the absence of any foundation for the counting parts in any community. The police order works precisely to cancel politics, maintain the order and mechanisms of dominance, and keep the "ethical" harmony of the way of being that refuses the logic of equality.

The conflict within the self in Romans 7 is not ultimately an opposition between parts of the self with different dispositions. The conflict is a manifestation of a gap in the self itself. It reveals the self in its difference to itself. It is an opposition between logics of distribution of parts into what counts and what does not count. Does the work (desires) of the flesh count? The confrontation is about making visible and recognizable that which has no reason to be seen or heard. Is the flesh articulating a spiritual, heaven-bound movement through its desires, or merely expressing its state of being as transformed dense clay? How is the relation in the shared "common" (the self) and the distribution between the flesh and spirit determined?

Paul is brilliant in recognizing this essential dissensus in the self (and by extension, society), but insofar as he accents *archi-spirituality*, which effaces the inherent litigiousness by unifying it and policing it under the law of the spirit, he expulses the flesh as part of no-part. The law of the spirit in Paul's summation is the law that unifies the various parts of the self, gives them a single foundation, and reveals itself as a way of life.

The split we have identified indicates how the economic world and its people are divided, who is excluded and who is allowed to participate in the full opportunities for human flourishing. The "essence" of the split lies in capturing the norms, the general rules, the modes of perception that define the partition, distributions of parts and benefits. The split is the *nemein* upon which the *nomoi* of the economy is founded. "The partition should be understood in the double sense of the word: on one hand, as that which separates and excludes, and on the other, as that which allows participation. A partition of the sensible refers to the manner in which a relation between a shared common (*un commun partagé*) and the distribution of exclusive parts is determined in sensory experience."[36]

In chapter 3 we will examine the manner of the relation in which the shared common of the United States' economy and the distribution of exclusive parts are determined in concrete life. This is to say, we will explore how the primordial split operates under various guises in the economy of the United States: the *nemein* upon which the *nomoi* of the split economy functions in the bastion of late capitalism.

Chapter 3

The Split Economy

Introduction

The observant reader will have noticed that I have used the introductory portions of the previous two chapters to explore specific dimensions of the theory of split being. The introductions serve as a guide to orient the reader to the more demanding theoretical moves and shifts in arguments that I will be making in each chapter. I will follow the same strategy in this final chapter of part I.

I want to tell the story of the split economy in the United States, and doing so requires a methodological approach of historicity that emphasizes ruptures and breaks in contexts, revealing self-division in context. This approach to narrative evades the operation of knowledge that claims mastery of context and causality in comprehending and explaining objects and events. In this way, I elevate the roles of ruptures, singularities, and breaks that fidelity to the logic of split demands. The method focuses on local stories, discontinuities, dislocations, or displacements that show not only where histories might be produced, but also the inherent incompleteness of the world (or so-called context and signifying structure) without transcending the universality of the fundamental antagonism that traverses the economy (society)—the split being. By naming the particular divisions and struggles, I hope to point the reader to the "antagonism that divides such struggles from themselves, and thus to the universality that connects them to other struggles."[1] The key interest of this philosophical approach to the narrative is to catch a glimpse of the disavowed kernel, the violent cut of the economy, that is far from the celebrated image of a smoothly functioning democratic economy. In this kind of narrative, the split in the economy is described through diversity of perspectives, often powerfully confronting us as the reality that emerges through the differences (parallax) in the various angles of analytical lens.

This philosophical method of analysis and narration (history) comes close to that of Michel Foucault, without completely identifying with it. We will locate ourselves between Foucault and Max Weber. Foucault explains his method in this way:

> Compared to the attempt to inscribe knowledge in the power-hierarchy typical of science, genealogy is, then, a sort of attempt to desubjugate historical knowledges, to set them free, or in other words to enable them to oppose and struggle against the coercion of a unitary, formal, and scientific theoretical discourse. The project of these disorderly and tattered genealogies is to reactivate local knowledges . . . against the scientific hierarchicalization of knowledge and its intrinsic power-effects.[2]

What I will be doing in this book is not genealogy, but an attempt to capture the spirit or horizon of genealogy in the sense of producing a multiplicity of discourses, to show the diversifying effects of the split of being that rejects the totalizing or unifying single lens to understanding its functioning in the system. The diversity of lens with which we will look at the struggles in the economy is not intended to show the U.S. economy as divided in a single all-encompassing manner, but to demonstrate the fundamental antagonism at work in various guises, or different *figures*. All this is why Weber's historicist method of narrating or analyzing the history of capitalism does not appeal much to my sensibility.

In his *The Protestant Ethic and the Spirit of Capitalism*, Weber tends to find the determining causes of the emergence of capitalism solely within the historical context of Protestantism, as if it were a single unified whole not pervaded by antagonisms.[3] He neglects to pay serious attention to the contradictions and negations through which the new capitalist universal emerges. The history or worldview of Protestantism cannot fully provide the causes that generated the capitalist universal, if one ignores the role of ruptures in being. "For example, Weber claims that the self-renunciation and sacrifice that capitalist production requires from its laborers has its origins in 'the spirit of Christian asceticism.' From Hegel's perspective, the 'protestant ethic' could not function as a coherent cause because it is not a unified ethic. The asceticism of the Protestant ethic depends on an ideal of future profligacy that both subtends and contradicts it. The new universal is not reducible to historical determinants that do not exist themselves."[4] Weber's analysis is too smooth, locating all determining causes in a certain historical context and neglecting the contextual antagonism. For the capitalist universal to emerge, there must be ruptures in the immediate being, a disjunction between the emergent capitalist universal and the Protestant context or worldview from which it came.

Here the views of Roland Barthes are very helpful in going beyond smoothen historical context to the wounds, cuts, ruptures that exist in it. Let us begin by considering history as a portrait, a painting of a people's past. When we look at a portrait as Barthes taught us to do, we can immediately see the obvious, the recognizable political, economic, religious, or cultural information or context about the people. This is not all; something else might jump out and grab us, so to speak. And it does—at least something in it reaches out to me, inviting me to think about it as what breaks, wounds, or pricks the fabric of being that is captured in the portrait. Barthes expressed some profound thought about this intriguing quality of photography as that "which arises from the scene shoots out of it like an arrow, and pierces me."[5] What arises from the photograph, painting, or historical portrait enables us to link the flat immobilized life of the portrait to the disruptiveness of ruptures in being. There are in a portrait or photograph two elements akin to an order of being and its excess (*event*), which can pop up and reconfigure the order of being or, at least, our understanding of it.

Following Barthes, we will call the two discontinuous elements of the historical portrait *studium* and *punctum*. His description of the nineteenth-century photograph of the Queen of England is illustrative of these two elements:

> Here is Queen Victoria photographed in 1863 by George W. Wilson; she is on horseback, her skirt suitably draping the entire animal (this is the historical interest, the *studium*); but beside her, attracting my eyes, a kilted groom holds the horse's bridle: this is the *punctum*; for even if I do not know just what the social status of this Scotsman may be (servant?

equerry?), I can see his function clearly: to supervise the horse's behavior: what if the horse suddenly began to rear? What would happen to the queen's skirt, i.e., to *her majesty?* The *punctum* fantastically "brings out" the Victorian nature (what else can one call it?) of the photograph, it endows this photograph with a blind field.[6]

I believe that economic ethicists should always approach a nation's history or political economy to find and distinguish these two elements and then latch onto the *punctum* as their point of departure in order to contextualize their work and also to find alternatives to hegemonic bourgeois (neoclassical economic) thought that is failing the world through the rise of inequality, racism, poverty, and virulent nationalism in Europe and America. In this chapter, I have described America's contemporary economic story in order to point beyond the *studium* of history and catch a glimpse of the *punctum* waiting to leap out or be triggered.

Given this stance, what we seek to grasp in this chapter is not an explanation of the U.S. economy via historical origin of its capitalist contradictions (sublated or repressed), but contradictions insofar as they are organized by the fundamental antagonism of the split. We are interested only in tracing the arché of the fundamental antagonism as a form whose traces or guises appear as political tensions and social disagreements. We take the pain to point out the traces (contradictions) not because we believe that they, through their anarchic impetus, are what will destroy the economy (and society) of the United States or capitalism for that matter. The traces of the primordial split now function in a manner similar to the well-known periodic crises of capitalism itself. Crises, like the traces of the split, are both the sickness and the solution to the capitalist economy's inherent inconsistencies. The eminent Japanese philosopher Kojin Karatani is right when he states the following:

> Crisis is *a chronic disease* inherent in the capitalist economy, yet also a *solution* to its internal defects. In other words, capitalism makes temporary repairs to its innate problem by crises, thus it will never collapse because of it. It can be compared with hysteria, the springboard of Freudian psychoanalysis. For an ill patient, hysteria is itself a solution, thanks to which the patient's stability is secured for the time being. But, for Freud, what was more crucial than hysteria was the mechanism of

unconscious that would cause it—which exists in a person whether or not he or she is ill. In the same way, for Marx, crisis was no longer the terminator of capitalist economy. It became important only because it would reveal the truth of the capitalist economy that is invisible in the everyday economy.[7]

Dimensions of Split Capitalist Economy

When we say that the economy is split, this is not to suggest a binary opposition between an economy and its other or other economies. Rather, "split" refers to the difference of the economy from itself, its non-coincidence with itself. This is the difference: the inherent gap between the economy and its structural place—the place of its inscription in our lives. The split is the inherent gap between the economy and the void, the mode of the drive. Here we are talking about the "hole" in which consumption becomes an end in itself, and expansion of values (self-valorization of capital) becomes an endless circular movement.[8] The economy in the symbolic order is our interpellation as individual subjects of desire and our collective participation as bearers and enforcers of the capitalist drive. The capitalist class displays the compulsion to increase profit, while consumers, haunted by anxiety, insecurity, and fragilities, are struggling to enact the direct loss (destruction) of their impotentiality.

The response of the consumer to her anxiety and fragility of social existence is to do more and more, plunging into activities as a way of protecting the self and its flourishing against the massive forces of fragility unleashed on society by late capitalism, when the appropriate response should be to do less. As capitalism limits the ability of the citizen to control her life, or exacerbates its entanglements in her world, or constrains her actions, she strives to be less and less defined by her human limitations. She works more, buys more smart technology, and seeks out miracle medicines so she will be less bound by limitations. She wants to be seen as capable, more capable than ever, the perfect American, with an impeccable "I can do it" attitude. A profound similarity exists between today's American consumer's permanent self-revolutionizing (that is, the endless struggle of the consumer to be flexible and amenable to the inexorable demands of the market) and the inherent self-propelling power of capitalism to exceed its limits. The echo of "I can do it" from the *objectified speaking mouth* of the consumer (American Citizen) is the form in which this capitalist *something* survives, sustains itself, and haunts her. This something is like a *superego* agency generating unbearable guilt within her for not doing enough or not being nimbly adaptive amid the changes around her and the demands upon her.

So there is always a pseudo-urgency to *act now*. She does not step back to perceive the violence inherent in this state of affairs. The urgency to act is often coming from a body and its desires that have been invaded and disciplined by capitalism and its forces. "At the immediate level of addressing individuals, capitalism, of course, interpellates them as consumers, as subjects of desire, soliciting in them ever new perverse and excessive desires (for which it offers products to satisfy them); furthermore, it obviously also manipulates the 'desire to desire,' celebrating the very desire to desire ever new objects and modes of pleasure."[9]

With this interpellation there is always an urgent injunction to act out her freedom of choice, which ultimately amounts to playing by the rules of the system, or self-destruction of her "impotentiality."[10] As Slavoj Žižek puts it: "At its most elementary, freedom is not the freedom to do as you like (that is, to follow your inclinations without any externally imposed constraints), but to do what you do not want to do, to thwart the 'spontaneous' realization of an impetus."[11]

The overall result of this inclination to do more and more is that American consumers seem to have severed themselves from the ability to not-be or to not-do in the market. American consumers appear to enjoy the destruction of their impotentiality as "an aesthetic pleasure of the first order." Giorgio Agamben laments this outcome of modern democracies and market systems:

> Separated from his impotentiality, deprived of the experience of what he cannot do, today's man believes himself capable of everything, and so he repeats his jovial "no problem," and his irresponsible "I can do it," precisely when he should instead realize that he has been consigned in unheard of measure to forces and processes over which he has lost all control. He has become blind not to his capacities but to his incapacities, not to what he can do but to what he cannot, or can not, do. . . . Nothing makes us more impoverished and less free than this estrangement from impotentiality.[12]

In the United States—in the competitive ambience of the new economy—there is a strong attachment to abilities and potential, which is taken as a positive and powerful character trait. The majority of American consumers are interested in the potential to-do, but there is also the potential to not-do, what is called impotentiality. There comes a time in life when in order to resist an unjust system or to keep our soul we need to focus on this potential to not-do. Modern democracies or late capitalism not only separate citizens from what they can do, but also from what they cannot do (the power to not-do). Everyone is seduced, cajoled, and driven to accept the flexibility that the market demands. Most of them have lost the capacity *not* to be flexible, forgotten how not to participate in the system to reproduce itself. The eager readiness of today's American woman to repeat "I can do it" indicates that she has actually been commandeered by the fierce free market system, which does not allow her to preserve any freedom that can undo the prevailing order in her incessant acts of selling her labor power, buying stuff with the proceeds, and guarding her ever-slipping economic security. Today, man's boastful "I can do it," that is, his potential to-do in late capitalism, has become an echo chamber of the freedom to do what he pleases with his property in the marketplace, and it resonates with the freedom to recklessly use the earth's resources for profit. This hubris is the pathetic arrogance of a man whose soul has been captured and reformatted by late capitalism for its profit.

We identify this as hubris because the response is pseudo-activity; the response to take actions, to intervene, is mistakenly considered as courage, as the character of a person who is the captain of his soul or fate, as a conquering spirit charging at his world with the powerful technology of the twenty-first century, *when it is actually none of these*. The effort is all empty theater, the impotence of man trapped under an unbearable weight of frustration and marked by a deep indifference to the Real and reality of late capitalism. While the all-powerful American consumer is boldly declaring, "I can do it," capital is saying back to him in a guttural voice, "I can do whatever I want with you!"

Let us also examine the place of the inscription of the economy in our lives from another perspective. The place the economy occupies in our lives is also the Void, the gap of the future. Its promise of full enjoyment is always postponed. We are libidinally invested in the *excess of life* it holds before us, and this is revealed by our fixation on a partial object—our consumerism is nothing but our self-destructive triumphing in our failure to create an economy in which there is "life and life more abundantly." We are "stuck" in the failure to reach our goal, and we now derive satisfaction from endlessly circulating around the goal in form of consumerism and the boastful "I can do it."

By this combined conceptualization of economy and void here, I am gesturing to a structural place, the empty formal place and the element that occupies it in our lives. In this place, there is only a minimal difference between lack and surplus, and the empty place and what fills it. Thus, the economy and the void point to the empty signifier of human flourishing (or essence) and the various elements that attempt to fill it. Human essence, for instance, is an empty indefinable property, an empty signifier;[13] an empty signifier "while deprived of all meaning, stands for the pure potentiality of meaning."[14] The "goods" of the economy attempt to fill this empty signifier of human essence with particular content and meaning. Human essence is a stand in for the "undead excess" of life, the too-muchness of life, non-castrated life-substance, the *inhuman* excess in the human that escaped symbolic colonization, the errant surplus, an excessive object of human life, lacking its place. So when we say an economy lacks its place in our lives (meaning the goods filling the empty place, contents without a permanent place), it means the same thing as saying human essence is an empty place, an elided signifier. Žižek writes:

> The point is not that there is simply the surplus of an element over the places available in the structure or the surplus of a place that has no element to fill it out. An empty place in the structure would still sustain the fantasy of an element that will emerge and fill out this place; an excessive element lacking its place would still sustain the fantasy of some as yet unknown place waiting for it. The point is, rather, that the empty place in the structure is strictly correlative to the errant element lacking its place: they are not two different entities, but the front and the back of one and the same entity, that is, one and the same entity inscribed into the two surfaces of a Moebius strip.[15]

When we say that the economy is split we have in mind the primordial splitting of finance from the general economy and its compulsive repetition. The financial sector is not only a fruit of the split economy, but it also enacts the economy of the split. The economy of split is the economy infinitely subtracting itself from itself. The economy is a site of continuous separation and articulation of human transactions. The economy is powerful only to the extent it is divided and continuously divides.[16]

Though the economy and finance sector are now two, it is important to understand that they are of one "substance," the network of transactions directed toward meeting human desires. It is this common substance (always divided because of the plurality of human desire, and because of debit and credit) that articulates itself in various economic sectors, each with its own specific determination, each an articulation of this collective network, multiplicity, reality, or disposition, and each an articulation and administration of human life, and running of mutual dependency. Each sector is a *signature* of how transactions (the self-production of man/woman) are differently *measured* (sets a particular temporary limit, bounds), *numbered* (the giving of specific form to the transaction), and *weighed* (draws them to motion or rest). Measure, number, and weight define the *ordo* of a portion of human transactions, and they imply a fracture within the praxis of every sector, which names a configuration (properties) of the incessant activity of humanity. The economy (collective transactions, the self-production of man/woman) is the genus, and the sectors are the species, so to speak.

The Gap between Finance and Industry

Hegel once said that every genus in the final analysis has only two species: the genus and its species, and this gap between them constitutes the specific, underlying difference in the genus. The difference here is between genus (economy) and its species "as such" (finance). Our term, the "economy" represents the genus as such, and "finance" stands for the difference within the genus as such, within the economy as such. The difference between them is the radical antagonistic gap that affects the entire universe of human productive activity.[17] Finance does not have a "relation" with the other sectors of the economy; there is a certain "impossibility" of economic relationship between finance and the whole economy. They are inscribed into two different sets.

All firms in the "economy" are subject to the limitations of the finance sector; that is, finance *cannot* totally meet all their needs—they can have only partial and limited enjoyment of the financial resources they need. But there is this fantasy that there are exceptions to this rule, of a firm or firms with unlimited access to financial resources for unlimited growth and expansion, or there exists a future time when a firm will have unmediated, unlimited access to all the financial resources it needs. This illusion of "having all the finance that one needs," the possibility of unmediated jouissance, the "impossible" enjoyment of finance enables them to bear their own present restriction.

Finance, on the other hand, is not subject to the restrictions of funding. With fractional banking—that is, banks creating money—a total of over 90 percent of the money supply in this country is created by banks. This does not mean that all firms, all financial institutions, escape the restriction of funding and can always preserve their full enjoyment of access to funds. Nor does it mean some part or project of a financial institution remains free of the limitation of access to funding (finance). Unlike the firms in the economy, which we can identify as members of a unified category subject to the limitation, firms in "finance" "are *radically singular*, not examples of a class or members of closed set, *but each one an exception*. They are an exception; however, not to a 'rule,' but to an open set, an infinite series of particular [financial houses], into which each [financial firm] enters 'one by one.'"[18] By definition, there is no common denominator of restriction to financial resources for the part of the economy that locates itself as finance, the custodian of the collective savings of the nation. By this logic, there is no way of characterizing "finance in general," whose price of access to a collective pot of gold is partial and limited jouissance.

An industrial firm's demand for finance is a thing apart from its productive life. But for the financial firm, it is its whole existence. The financial firm is entirely immersed in finance without restraint or reserve. There is no dimension of its economic life that is not permeated by it; for that very reason, the demand for finance is "not-all" for the financial firm, "it is forever accompanied by an uncanny fundamental indifference."[19] The financial firm knows that its symbolic title as a house of funding, a partner directing money to industry, is only a mask and there is nothing "beneath the mask," because there is no "real partner" of industry or human flourishing beneath its symbolic title. So as a group it does not make firm commitment to real economic development. While the industry may have some constitutive exceptions because it is constrained to produce something tangible, or because it still embraces the capitalist premise of brutal exploitation with its ideological communitarian sugar-coating (there are things one should not turn into a mere mask), for the financial group there is no exception—one should turn everything into a mask, into an empty form (see chapter 5 for further discussion).

The Gap between Economic Statistics and Concrete Human Lives

There is a split between "the reality" and "the Real" of the late capitalist economy, to resort to Lacanian terms. Increasingly in this era of spectral capitalism, what controls and often devastates the life of actual people are virtual forms of exchange (transaction) and futures trades and options that are transacted on the basis of economico-mathematical models. An economy is believed to be doing well among economists if the various models and their induced economic reports are showing good results. And these abstract models are considered to be directly reporting what is actually going on with real people and their issues. The economists who espouse this view are caught up in the ideology of capital. As Slavoj Žižek explains: "'Reality' is the social reality of the actual people involved in interactions and in the productive process; while the Real is the inexorable 'abstract' spectral logic of Capital, which determines what goes on in social reality."[20]

What it means to be caught in the ideology of capital today is not to disbelieve that capitalism or its agents ignore the reality of people and are caught up with the abstract or financial circulation of money. What it means to be caught up in ideology of late capitalism is not to disbelieve that there is a disconnect between virtual capitalism and concrete productive activities. It is precisely to ignore the "Real of spectrality, and pretend to address directly 'real people with real worries.' Visitors to the London Stock Exchange are given a free leaflet that explains to them that the stock exchange is not about some mysterious fluctuations, but about real people and their products—*this* is ideology at its purest"[21] Any theological-ethical critique that ignores the imbrication of economic models in the Real of spectrality of late capitalism ignores their role in defining the nomos of economic life or turns a blind eye to their normativity. Often social ethicists ignore the normativity of economic models with the presupposition that they are not normative. The presupposition that economic models are not normative is ideology at its finest.

Economic modeling implicitly or explicitly presupposes norms; among such presuppositions is the idea that profit maximization and competition provide a sound basis for ordering societies.[22] In the language of Bernard Lonergan, there are always moral imperatives in the immanent intelligibility of economic processes and models. To the extent that economic models are regulative of public policies, orient behaviors and thoughts, partly constitute the contextualized environment of economic actions, and are part of the teleoaffective structure of social practices in modern market economies, it is not correct to say that economic models are not normative in nature.[23]

Gap between Work and Reward

The economy is often taken as an integrated whole, master of its own rewards, where rewards are correlative to efforts, risk to return. Work (effort) is understood to lead smoothly to reward (profit) according to well-known "economic laws." This perspective takes work into account as determined by an ever-expanding exhaustive set of laws or as determined by the symbolic order of rewards. Certainly, this extant view does not take into account the split for which "I work where I am not profiting" and "I profit where I do not work." This is not to talk of the events that disrupt the supposed smoothing of the correlation between effort and reward. Indeed, many citizens cannot precisely correlate work and reward at the same time. If they know or ascertain work, the issue of reward necessarily remains unknown. If, for a moment, we consider the economy as a whole, a set of knowledges, then what we are saying is that "the set is incomplete, the whole is not whole, for there's an unfillable hole in the set," as Heisenberg's uncertainty principle teaches us.[24]

The bourgeois, neoclassical economic thought that relates work and reward is somewhat akin to the modernist philosophical thought that correlates being and thought. Descartes famously stated "I think therefore I am," thus conceptualizing that thinking and being coincides, overlaps. For Lacan, this supposition of identity of being and thought is mistaken because unconscious thought (the unconscious) often intrudes (surges forth) between conscious thought and being. The subject is forced to choose between being and thought/thinking and not both at the same time. (Thinking for him refers to unconscious thought.) Lacan states in Seminar XIV: "Either I am not thinking or I am not." The ego is not the master or author of its thought, and its thoughts do not correspond with external reality.[25] Bruce Fink writes:

> While beginning with the punctual (or pointlike) Cartesian subject, that is, the fleeting coincidence of thinking and being, Lacan turns Descartes on his head: ego thinking is mere conscious rationalizations (the ego's attempt to legitimate blunders and unintentional utterances by fabricating after-the-fact explanations which agree with the ideal self-image), and the being thus engendered can only be categorized as false or fake . . . The Lacanian subject remains separated from being.[26]

The Lacanian subject is a divided one (between ego, the false self, and the unconscious), and in fact the split is constitutive of the subject. The division is a product of language assimilation, according to Lacan. It is not necessary for us at this juncture to go into the details of how language causes the splitting of the "I," as we want only to register the limitations of the Cartesian mindset when it comes to understanding the relationship between work and reward. Just as *being* does not coincide with *thought*, *work* does not coincide with *reward*. If neoclassical economics is said to deal with the subject, it does this from the standpoint of the masterly Cartesian subjectivity wherein "being" coincides with "thought" and does not "take into account the split subject for whom "I am where I am not thinking" and "I think where I am not."[27] To deal with the subject in terms of the Lacanian or Pauline split subjectivity situated in some corner of the split economy where the lauded progress of the U.S. economy does not coincide with her own flourishing is to hear the "economic laws" declare these words: "I work where I am not profiting," and "I profit where I do not work." The working class, the 99 percent, hears the first declaration, and the 1 percent hears the second. For the 99 percent, Descartes's "I think therefore I am" is correlative to "I profit therefore I work." Profits from exploitation are retroactively claimed, fabricated as after-the-fact explanations of hard work and ingenuity.

The rich and powerful in most economies of the world have commandeered the powers of their nations' institutions and policy-making bodies for their own selfish gain. Often economies fail to develop or increasingly exclude the masses from flourishing lives not because their citizens are not entrepreneurially driven or innovative. They fail or perform poorly economically not because of their culture or geography. It is because their political systems have installed extractive institutions, which make the capture of state power the main (viable) means of production (wealth creation) in such societies. According to economists Daron Acemoglu and James Robinson, economies like Mexico, Colombia, and Nigeria are struggling to develop because of the legacy of extractive institutions. In their book *Why Nations Fail*, they state that these are pernicious institutions "which concentrate power and wealth in the hands of those controlling the state, opening the way for unrest, strife, and civil war. Extractive institutions also directly contribute to the gradual failing of the state by neglecting investment in the most basic public services."[28] The use of institutions, even democratic ones, to exclusively extract resources for the benefit of the upper class is not limited to countries in Asia, Africa, and Latin America. In the United States, it is not just the case that the upper class appropriates a giant share of the income and wealth of the country; a large group of its citizens is basically excluded from the possibility of prosperity.

The Color Gap: Poverty and Racialization

The American society is a divided one. There is a sharp division between the 1 percent and the rest of society. There is division between blacks and whites—between whites and *all* minorities. The American economy is split by racism and poverty. Joseph Stiglitz, the Nobel prize–winning economist, declares: "We do have a divided society . . . America has been growing apart, at an increasingly rapid rate."[29] Stiglitz laments that the impact of an increasingly divided society reaches beyond what the stark income inequality data portray. It shows up "in health, education, and crime—indeed in every metric of performance. While inequalities in parental income and education translate directly into inequalities of educational opportunity, inequalities of opportunity begin even before school—in the conditions that poor people face immediately before and after birth, differences in nutrition and the exposure to environmental pollutants that can have lifelong effects. So difficult is it for those born into poverty to escape that economists refer to the situation as a 'poverty trap.'"[30]

The American poverty trap has a color line. Minorities of color in general live below the standard of well-being of the white majority. Poverty is defined or marked by racism as much as anything else. Indeed, many scholars see poverty as related to the racialization of U.S. society—hence, the increasing attention drawn to the theme of "poverty and racialization of the economy" in the examination of economic inequality.

What is racialization and how does it cause poverty in the United States? Racialization is a difficult term to operationalize for deciphering the connection between economics and inequality in a society profoundly marked by racism. I will suggest multiple ways of conceptualizing racialization that make sense for political economic discourse. I do not want us to be too quick to reduce or constrict its meaning, so as not to hinder a robust discussion of its relation to the split economy. I offer five different ways of conceptualizing racialization of economy.

First, in a certain sense, racialization of the economy refers to the structural inequalities that exist in the United States and are keyed to, marked by, and driven by race or skin color discriminations. Second, racialization of the economy points to the increasing vulnerability of the citizens of color to early death and low life expectancy. Third, racialization is the near monopoly of benefits, positions, and opportunities of the economy of the United States by whites or racially privileged groups. Fourth, racialization of the economy is a form of exclusion of minorities from the necessary economic, social, and public resources in ways that destroy their capacities to actualize their God-given potentials. Finally, racialization of the economy is a form of police logic of the American empire, which renders certain racial groups permanent *part of no-part*, part of the demographic, economy, and polity that does not count.

The combined result of the logics and dynamics of these five forms of racialization is absolute and relative poverty of minority groups. This twin result of poverty and racialization is not accidental to the overall logic and social imaginary of the society, polity, and economy of the United States. Poverty and racism define America as much as wealth and military power. Poverty and racialization mark America as much as the stars and stripes mark the national flag.

Racialization of the U.S. economy is like a five-point star of the star-spangled banner, with each point oozing poverty into the social fabric of this nation. The whole assemblage of stars and stripes is set in order and driven by what the perspicacious Emilie Townes calls "fantastic hegemonic imagination."[31] An invidious imagination holds the systemic, structural evil of the poverty and racialization of the economy firmly in place. It politicizes economic statistics to secure subordination, economic impoverishment, and immiseration of minority groups. In short, poverty as a product of racism is a cultural production of evil. There is still a fantastic manipulative imagination aided by trickster Jacob's poplar rod of stripes in the land of the Puritan new Israel of stars and stripes that make one partner rich at the expense of the other.

What are the five points of this star (or streaked rod) that drip poison and poverty, human degradation and strangulation of hope? What are these points that kill dreams and forestall human flourishing?

First, there is the spatial production of poverty. There is a geographical dynamic to poverty in this country. Minorities and people of color are often living in zones and places where there are few opportunities for economic improvement. These zones are also inimical to the accumulation of wealth because of policies such as redlining in the past. As sociologists Mel Oliver and Tom Shapiro have stated:

> Locked out of the greatest mass-opportunity for wealth accumulation in American history, African-Americans who desired and were able to afford home ownership found themselves consigned to central-city communities where their investments were affected by the 'self-fulfilling prophecies' of the FHA appraisers: cut off from sources of new investments . . . their homes and communities deteriorated and lost value in comparison to those homes and communities that the FHA appraisers deemed desirable.[32]

We have often talked about income inequality; it is time to speak about spatial inequality. Economists often consider spaces as "'containers for data' rather than a context for inequality and exploitation to play out.'"[33] There is pervasive inattentiveness to space when theologians or philosophers are discussing the issues of economic inequality. As Gareth Jones argues, even eminent economists pay little or no attention to spatial political economy, more so in the neglect of geographical mobility or geographies of capital and its impact on nations and spaces. "The economic geography of global capitalism for the past forty years shows that capital will seek out a spatial fix to the crises of under/ over accumulation. Fundamental to the power of capital, therefore, is its geographical mobility, to shape-shift from being something fixed to being a flow. The apotheosis of this transformation is finance capital."[34] Black neighborhoods in urban centers have seen devastating declines, and as such the economic well-being of their residents has reduced as unfettered capital and technological innovations in their quasi-random, wind-like movements abandoned them as spaces of surplus populations not immediately relevant to profit interest.

American cities are not designed to disperse economic activities that generate income and provide the wherewithal to all residents, especially those in poor neighborhoods, to have flourishing lives. Rising inequality in the American society and economic disparities between racial groups cannot be totally divorced from the form and intensity of the major cleavages in the fabric of cities. Cleavages are related to spatial demographics. Widening economic disparity between rich and poor neighborhoods means a decreasing trend in integrity and mutuality of a city's parts; the rich neighborhoods are not *present* to the poor ones in a rightly ordered fellowship.[35]

The second point of the star of empire relates to wealth accumulation. Thomas Piketty and Joseph Stiglitz in their recent books have shown alarming growth rates of income inequality in this country.[36] For blacks and other people of color, the condition is worse than portrayed in their studies. The household income of blacks is on average lower than that of whites. The unemployment rates for minorities are higher than that of whites.

Piketty says income inequality will worsen in the future because the rate of return of capital of the richest 1 percent of the American society is growing faster than the economy. He captures this with a fundamental equation, $r > g$ (where r is the rate of return on capital, and g is the growth rate of the economy), which points to a process (force) of divergence in the American economy of the twenty-first century.[37]

> When the rate of return on capital significantly exceeds the growth rate of the economy (as it did through much of history until the nineteenth century and as is likely to be the case again in the twenty-first century), then it logically follows that inherited wealth grows faster than output and income. People with inherited wealth need save only a portion of their income from capital to see that capital grow more quickly than the economy as a whole. Under such conditions, it is inevitable that inherited wealth will dominate wealth amassed from a lifetime's labor by a wide margin, and the concentration of capital will attain extremely high levels—levels potentially incompatible with meritocratic values and principles of social justice fundamental to modern democratic societies.[38]

According to Piketty, we are back in the days of patrimonial capitalism.[39] Minorities have less inherited capital, and generally do not own capital with a rate of growth that exceeds the rate of growth of the economy. Let us relate this to the spatial demographics and racism that we highlighted earlier. Sociologist Elizabeth Jacobs, criticizing Piketty's neglect of politics and racism in his book, makes the connection clear. She writes:

> Because whites were more able to give inheritances or family assistance for down payments, due to historical wealth accumulation, white families buy homes and start accumulating capital on average eight years earlier than similarly situated black families. And because whites are more able to give financial assistance, larger up-front payments typically lower interest rates and lending costs for white families as compared with blacks. Much of this inequality in capital accumulation can be traced back to an early policy decision, which shaped access to capital in important ways.[40]

Given this historical burden and continuing racial discrimination, blacks are not watching the gyrations of Piketty's now famous formula, $r > g$—rather $r > g$ is watching them, mocking their absence from the orgies of accumulation and exploitation. This reminds me of what Malcolm X said about Plymouth Rock, upon which the first pilgrims landed when they arrived in America: "Our forefathers weren't the pilgrims. We didn't land on Plymouth Rock. The rock was landed on us." Whites are today landing and dancing on the Piketty's rock of wealth; tomorrow Piketty's rock will land on blacks. And the day after tomorrow, rocks from the hands of the poor will fly on the streets of America. Taking to the streets to strike for equality and social justice may well be the last recourse for the poor and impoverished seeking a way to feed their families. Piketty has repeatedly stated that the increasing divergence between the rate of return on capital and the rate of growth of the economy is threatening the values of social justice in democratic societies:

> The inequality $r > g$ implies that wealth accumulated in the past grows more rapidly than output and wages. . . . Once constituted, capital reproduces itself faster than output increases. The past devours the future. The consequences for long-term dynamics of wealth distribution are potentially terrifying, especially when one adds that the return on capital varies directly

with the size of the initial stake and that the divergence in the wealth distribution is occurring on a global scale.[41]

The third point of the star that drips its poison into black lives is a failing school system. Blacks, minorities, and children of the poor in this country are not given the kind of education that will prepare them for the economy of tomorrow. Add to this the digital divide between minorities and whites, and between the rich and the poor, and you catch a vision of the children of the barely breathing members of the permanent underclass being suffocated to economic death. All this means that the cruel income and wealth gap between whites and blacks—a veritable indicator of the racialization of the economy—will only widen in the future.

The fourth poisonous point of the five-pointed star is the prison-industrial complex. We have a criminal system that appears to target minorities, either to kill them on the street, judicially execute them, or imprison them in mass as a way of "keeping our streets" safe for the rich class and triumph of capitalists.[42]

Finally, we must direct attention to the differential in the human development index of the various racial groups in this country. The HDI measures critical indicators of human welfare such as life expectancy and human capital. There is a huge discrepancy between whites and blacks, between the rich and the poor. The 2015 HDI values (scaled from 0 to 10) for the various racial groups are: Whites: 5.43; Latinos: 4:05; African Americans: 3:81; Asians: 7:21, U.S. average: 5:03. The United Nations *Human Development Report* for 2016 states:

> [Regarding] human development among African Americans in the United States . . . African Americans' life expectancy is shorter than that of other ethnic and racial groups in the United States. African Americans also trail Whites and Asian Americans in education and wages: Whites earn 27 percent more on average. In some metropolitan areas the disparity is particularly striking. The life expectancy of African Americans in Baltimore, Chicago, Detroit, Pittsburgh, St. Petersburg and Tampa is now close to the national average in the late 1970s. The reasons are complex but linked to a long history of legal and social discrimination. Policies that improve educational achievement can expand opportunities for African Americans

and other racial and ethnic minorities in work and other areas. Equalizing educational achievement could reduce disparities in employment between African Americans and Whites by 53 percent, incarceration by 79 percent and health outcomes by 88 percent. Differences in wages between African Americans and Whites are also related to discrimination in the job market. Discrimination accounts for an estimated one-third of wage disparities, all else (including education) being equal. This indicates that policies are needed to ensure that skills and education are rewarded equally. Social pressures within the African American community can limit choices and later life chances among adolescents. Being labelled as "acting White"—whereby high-achieving African American students are shunned in some contexts by their peers for doing well academically—can discourage good performance in school. Reducing the stigmatization of academic achievement among African American youth could be a step towards reducing inequalities in human development outcomes.[43]

The preceding analyses go to the heart of the politics of inclusiveness and exclusion and the distribution of citizens to assigned places. African Americans have been treated in the American economy, polity, and society as a surplus, and not a plus: the "part which has no part" in the established social order. They inhabit this group that has no part with others in the American society, but a split traverses this group itself.

Gap in Potential Equalitarian Politics: The Splitting of the Part of No-Part in America

Following French philosopher Jacques Rancière, we can easily surmise that African Americans are in the part of no-part in American society, the part that belongs to the whole but does not count. For them, America (and even the part of no-part in it) is really not the site of the logic of emancipatory democracy and the radical, universal equality of all citizens. The part of no-part in the United States is subdivided into two opposing parts, locked in one zone of no-count. While Rancière calls the distribution of people into assigned places according to the police logic "the distribution of the sensible," I will call the distribution of the subparts in the part of no-part, the *distribution of responsiveness*.

This is about the lived reality of being a subject (African American) either included as not fully human in the *part of no-part* or excluded from it as *non-part-of-no-part*. No doubt, blacks as a group in the United States are regarded as the part of no-part. The part of no-part as a whole definitely includes whites, but the black person is (often) not included in the group as fully human. This means that, in the eyes of white supremacists, a black person, a member of the part of no-part, is either inhuman or nonhuman, a new space beyond humanity and its negation that is opened up. To say a black male "'is not human' means simply that he is external to humanity, animal or divine, while 'he is inhuman' means something thoroughly different, namely that he is neither human nor not-human, but marked by a terrifying excess which, although negating what we understand as 'humanity,' is inherent to being human."[44] This perceived terrifying excess not only excludes blacks from the general count, but also from the count within the part of no-part. Racism, the bone that is stuck in America's throat as she shouts democracy and freedom to the rest of the world, is the underpinning of the double exclusion (erasing). Racism as a source of fundamental disagreement in the United States either goes beyond Rancière's notion of politics as disagreement or attaches itself to it, complicating matters for his otherwise neat theory.

Let us name the two parts of the part of no-part object and dynamic order.[45] Object endures over time, existing over time. Dynamic order arises and passes away. A dynamic order is not an enduring being always coming to its identity within the whole and within the part that has no part. The part that is coming to itself, to its identity in and through the part of no-part, is subject to the fate (nonrecognition, assigned place) of the part of no-part. The dynamic group such as blacks in the United States is always (or from to time) attempting to establish itself as an object through the medium of the institutions, to establish and repeat itself as an enduring being recognized as part that can become proper, full members of part of no-part.

While Rancièrian politics of the *part of no-part* arises as a struggle between the whole (the part that counts) and the part that does not count, the *politice* (police and politics = *politice*) arises from dissonance between the dynamic order (of the part of no-part) and the institutions of inclusion. The part of no-part is a cover for the non-part; the one who is not speaking is a cover for the one who cannot speak. The part of no-part is one who has a recognizable, protected identity erasing the identity of the non-part of no-part. The state and its citizens respond differently to the hegemonic identity embodied in the part of no-part and to the marginal identity represented in the *non-part-of-no-part*. This part that does not even count in the part of no-part constitutes a different, more fundamental dimension of political disagreement; it is simultaneously the part of the otherness (part of no-part) that prevents the American political whole from coinciding with itself and the foreign body within the part of no-part that even obstructs its completeness.

In the political struggle, there is the politics itself (or the point of politics), and what the politics negates. According to Rancière, the point of politics of the *part of no-part* is to make itself count, assume the universality of the whole. The politics itself is about articulating the fundamental disagreement that undergirds the distribution of the sensible, and what it negates is the logic of the police state. The dynamic order is the gap in the *part of no-part* that keeps it from reaching full self-identity. The dynamic order is the unassimilable element in the *part of no-part* that resists symbolization in the whole or in the part of no-part. Because the dynamic order is there in the part of no-part as that which cannot be assimilated, its appearance constitutes a trauma, a reminder of the rip in the self-identity of the part of no-part. The part of no-part is split against itself, and the dynamic order is the kernel around which the part of no-part is internally constituted. The part of no-part is not only constituted by the external denial of the count in the whole, but also by its own internal antagonism and conflict. The part of no-part, which constitutes the internal and determinate negation of the part that counts, the police state, is itself constituted by or it harbors its own internal and determinate negation. The dynamic order is an analogue of the very drive of the dialectic that erupts as politics.

If the dynamic order is a mode, a subspecies of the *part of no-part*, that is, if the difference between dynamic order (identity politics) and *part of no-part* is inherent to the *part of no-part*, what then is the difference between universal identity of the *part of no-part* and particular identity of other parts? Is universal identity (politics of *part of no-part* in America) ultimately not merely a more police-mediated form of dynamic order?[46] The politics of the *part of no-part* is suspended over the world of dynamic order. The occasional rip or break-forth of energetics in the symbolic cover over this world—such as the Black Lives Matter movement—is not a failure of this or that minority group to align with the universal or universal identity, as Rancière would have us believe; rather, it is magma lava of political reality showing through the rip. This break-forth may well be a universal politics of another kind: the universal or primordial lie that undergirds not only *the part of no-part*, but also *politics* and *police*, which all parts in America want to hide.

Social Justice and the Healing of the Split

Another thorny issue in the working of the fundamental antagonism of society is social injustice and how to respond to it. There is a proper and improper way to construe social justice in capitalism when we have the logic and dynamic of the split economy in view. Social justice (as redistribution or giving every person his or her due, or the pursuit of full jouissance beyond the law, the removal of all obstacles or prohibitions on the path of full enjoyment) cannot be about mediating synthesis of the two "sides" of the economy. It will actually be done by the radical assertion, affirmation of the split, and the abyss between the economy and the empty place it occupies in our lives. Justice is society's way of oscillating between the different sides rather than confronting the split.

Social justice as a way of covering the gap is a gesture of utopian unification or illegitimate short circuit. The gap cannot be removed, and the two sides can never merge, because the two are one, two different surfaces of one element. The gap is a parallax tension. The gap itself acts through human beings. The proper way to change the situation, to interrupt the negative impact of the split on human flourishing, is not to directly intervene in it, but to turn back to ourselves, to recognize it as a split within being-human, to target ourselves.[47] As Todd McGowan argues in *Capitalism and Desire*, we ought to quit buying the dissatisfaction that capitalism sells us and turn away from its promise of better and greater satisfaction around the corner. Under the influence of capitalism causing us to desire the commodity, we are caught up in new ways to sacrifice ourselves for an economic system, for that new commodity, which never quite satisfies us.

The proper way to begin is to show how an excessive love for, or attachment to, the economy makes us follow the path of the void. The trick here is to see how the very gap that separates the economy from its place in our symbolic order is inherent to either the economy or the symbolic order, and so the very feature that separates us from the economy is what will eventually turn out to unite us with the economy. Rather than seeking to overcome the gap through "justice," we give body to it, ground it as a way of understanding an underlying principle of a new social formation. We do not remove the gap by reducing the difference between the material reality of the economy and the envisaged justice-drenched society, but by reducing the economic reality to *nothing*. It is to move from the economic reality to the void of its own place, the immanent gap that separates the economy from itself, which always shows it as incomplete, *non-all*.

This is not the dream of having capitalism without capitalism, the utopian dream of having the self-revolutionizing, perpetual motion of capital without exploitation. We cannot eliminate exploitation without ruining capitalism. The capitalist form—the expropriation of surplus value—is the necessary condition for the revolutionizing motion of capital.[48] The mistake here is to see the gap as between the revolutionary potential of capitalism (economy) and the possibility of a new common—a common predicated on a vision of a better form of social relations or relations of production, a society free of exploitation that is the obstacle to human flourishing for all and surplus enjoyment. Justice in this view is seen as the act, procedure, or the practice to free, to actualize the possibility of the new common. What is overlooked in this reasoning is that the "condition of impossibility" of human flourishing for all is simultaneously the "condition of possibility" of the revolutionizing potential. "If we abolish the obstacle, the inherent contradiction of capitalism, we do not get the full unleashed drive to productivity finally delivered of its impediment, we lose precisely the productivity that seemed to be generated and simultaneously thwarted by capitalism—if we take away the obstacle, the very potential thwarted by this obstacle dissipates."[49]

The place the economy occupies in our lives is the "essence" of the economy. What we see as gross domestic product (GDP), statistics, income distribution, and so on is the "appearance" of the economy. So many scholars assert that there is a difference between essence and appearance. Where does this difference come from? The split between essence and appearance is internal to appearance. It is not that the essence of the economy externalizes itself and the result is the appearance, which falls short, but what we regard as essence is the gap, the cut within appearance. We see appearance, and we imagine there is a hidden core that needs to be expressed. We have the distinction between essence and appearance of the economy not because there is something beyond the object, a curtain (in this case the economy as we see/read it), but because appearance does not fully coincide with itself.[50] We look for essence when we ignore the irreducibility of an economy's appearance and look to its "substantial support" that is not the economy as it appears to us. The so-called "real economy" is the gap between different modes of appearances, different ways of experiencing the economy, or different domains of representing the economy to ourselves. The essence of an economy is the pure difference that separates an economy from itself. Instead of discovering a hidden secret or huge reservoir of pure potentialities or some terrifying master behind the veil of appearance, we encounter the lack of difference, and confront the same facts as those of the mask of appearance.[51] The economy is not an agent, entity, or substantial reality that acts, but one that has no reality outside its acting (transactions), which is its activities, fully coinciding with its transactions.

Let us return to our issue of justice or proper justice as the radical affirmation of the split, the abyss between the economy and the empty place it occupies in our lives. We must accept the fundamental obstacle that makes harmony impossible, rules out utopian unification, and accede that it is our very psychic investment in capitalism's promises of a better future that is the key problem of not being our brother's keeper. One of the best ways to relate the logic of the split in late capitalism is through an ethics that embraces unpredictability, play, and becoming. This means that we accept that emergence of the new is neither a matter of necessity nor of pure contingency. It is a dialectical mixture of *contingency of necessity* and *necessity of contingency*.[52] In every economy there are laws and economic activities that necessarily occur according to them.[53] How these laws emerged was utterly contingent, as the famous economist and Nobel Prize winner Friedrich Hayek has taught us.[54] This is the *contingency of necessity* in the economy. On the other side of the coin is the freedom of human actions, which stands for the *necessity of contingency*. This freedom is not just sheer contingency; rather, it is a free act, which retroactively presupposes its own immanent necessity, its own reason, thereby creating its own objective condition. The subject's contingent decision is simultaneously the contingent constitution of its necessity.

This assertion of radical affirmation of the split, far from throwing us into radical individualism that rejects cooperation, is a turn to radical mutual dependence or intersubjectivity. The situation of contingency and indeterminacy that an embrace of the split connotes

> . . . might itself reveal an altered social state, one wherein [others'] claims are experienced differently, mean something

new, are more directly necessary for me to lead my own life, to give it sense, to assess, and judge. The key issue in morality might not be the rational justifiability with which I treat others, but the proper acknowledgment of, and enactment of, a dependence on others without which the process of any justification (any invocation of common normative criteria at all) could not begin. . . . This uncertainty and doubt and profound ambiguity, unresolvability about meaning . . . makes possible and even requires a form of dependency, a dependency even at the level of possible consciousness itself, and some "lived out" acknowledgement of such dependency, that now makes up the new moral experience, the claims and entitlements of each on others, that [James] is interested in.[55]

Concluding Remarks

We have examined in this chapter the various forms or guises of the split economy in the United States. We won't summarize all of our findings here, but will focus on five. These five signify five types of uprootedness, or existential disconnection: (a) the uprooting of finance from its connectedness to the general economy; (b) the uprooting of an active, relational presence of human beings with one another (inequality); (c) the uprooting of blacks and other minorities from the core dynamics of human flourishing, a displacement from enjoying the fruits of American democracy and prosperity; (d) the uprooting of economic reports from concrete lives; and (e) the uprooting from space (differentials in availability of opportunities across neighborhoods).

First, we named the economic-finance split, which is the fundamental one, as we have argued in this book from the outset. The second type of split is the one between the rich and poor. America is a deeply divided society. Third, there is the deep racial divide in America: minorities are dislocated from the path of economic parity. Add to this the gender gap in pay that hits women of color—a double whammy. One crucial effect of racism is that black lives are valued less than those of whites, creating what Eddie Glaude calls the "value gap."[56]

Fourth, there is the split between economic statistics and real human lives. We learn a great deal about the working of the economy, what the great measuring devices are in technical terms, cold abstractions embodied in reports, but little or nothing about the concrete experience of ordinary folks. The economy represented by statistics and stock-market liveliness now appears as *something* greater than human beings, a mysterious power hovering over human life. This power appears cut off from how human beings in a given geopolitical space relate with one another, how they manipulate their world and their economic relationships. For most Americans, the reported economy does not seem to emerge from their concrete experience, their way of living in the world with others, and how the future might open up to them and their neighbors.

Finally, we have the spatiality of life opportunities. We argued that the gigantic flow of economic activities in this country should be viewed through the crystal of space. When a ray of light hits a crystal, it splits into spectrum to reveal its true color. The celebrated flow of economic transactions reveals its true color when it hits the crystal of space, assuming different forms to express the underlying opportunity gaps in the complex reality of human spatial existence. Space is not just a set of possibilities as possibilities. It is the possibility as *already* presented, tasted, and experienced.[57] The web of possibilities is lived as concrete embodiment of past life opportunities and dynamic expression of the presence of the desired new that is desired now. What makes space open-ended is not the coming segment as a future segment of time, but the excess of the here that overflows the here and now. Space as a web or ground of possibilities is never lived in all its fullness.

Let me turn to a different meditation on a different space. Imagine Saint Paul arriving on Wall Street as an ethnographer studying the ethics of the players in the financial industry. He would recognize the struggles mentioned in Romans 7, but he would need some doses of Kant's ethics and anti-ethics of Sade to interpret the normative spirit of Wall Street, which is a form of life luxuriating between the graveyard and the sea. Paul would instantly notice the dialectics of law and its inherent transgressions in the life and work of the players on the Street: "I would not have known what sin was had it not been for the law. For I would not have known what coveting really was if the law had not said, 'You shall not covet.'"

The Apostle to the Gentiles would quickly notice that Wall Street is not performing its duty to the American public in the spirit of Kant's "pure jouissance of the Law" and the exact demands of Sade's philosophy of total disconnection between law and desire/transgression in celebration of "pure law of jouissance." Wall Streeters do not want the "obliteration of the space for inherent transgression, which is coextensive with any morality," for without such a space it would be impossible for them to function.[58] Wall Streeters have never rejected their need for a Master. They need a master they can dominate or manipulate. A master figure who can set limits for them, prohibit them from doing certain things, only to see such limits and prohibitions provoke them to cross boundaries and point the way to attaining what they want. On Wall Street, prohibitions must be in place in order for people to enjoy their violation.

When Paul confronts Wall Street, he might not be too surprised by the greed or crass materialism of its players, but what will violently confront him is that truth and meaning are no longer harnessed together. Truth and meaning have been split, with truth no longer grounded in meaning. The truth of signs in language, market values, and meanings are only interplays of multiple words, values, and meanings; there is no grounding in global meaning that can undergird an all-encompassing truth, no global truth to ground all or any meaning. If Paul were to insist on grounding their understanding of the truth of individual actions, or the market as a whole in any horizon of meaning, he will be laughed off as an obscurantist. Paul on his own will interpret all these as the disappearance of God and religion in the capitalist system that came after him. As Alain Badiou puts it: "the simplest definition of God and religion lies in the idea that truth and meaning are one and the same thing. The death of God is the end of the idea that posits truth and meaning as the same thing. . . . Today we may call 'obscurantism' the intention of keeping them harnessed together—meaning and truth."[59]

Paul is right to think that capitalism has a lot to do with the condition of disjunction of meaning and truth. As Slavoj Žižek explains:

> Capitalism is the first socioeconomic order which de-*totalizes* *meaning*: it is not global at the level of meaning (there is no global "capitalist world-view," no "capitalist civilization" proper—the fundamental lesson of globalization is precisely that capitalism can accommodate itself to all civilizations, from Christian to Hindu and Buddhist); its global dimension can be formulated only at the level of truth-without-meaning, as the "Real" of the global market mechanism.[60]

Given this enactment of rupture between meaning and truth, there have been two major types of reaction or resistance to capitalism among religious practitioners, religious ethicists, and philosophers. There are those who want to "re-enframe capitalism into some social field of meaning, to contain its self-propelling movement within the confines of a system of shared 'values,' which will cement a 'community' in its 'organic unity.'"[61] The others interrogate "the Real of capitalism with regard to its truth-outside-meaning."[62] In this book, our approach is not only to understand the Real of capitalism, especially finance capital, without confining the Real within the bounds of any meaning system, but also to interrogate the future capitalism offers to all citizens. Later, in chapter 6, I offer the idea of a future outside the framing within which the future as capitalism designs it appears. It is to think of the capitalist future as split within itself, involving an inherent gap, and the true task is to withdraw from both sides of such a formatted future and to dwell in the gap between them. "Far from perpetuating the fantasy of meaning's eventual realization, the [withdrawal] comes to figure the bar to every realization of [capitalist] futurity, the resistance, internal to the social, to every social structure or form."[63] Not a sovereign, triumphalist capitalism, not a limited capitalism, but only a futureless capitalism can still save us. We are not searching for a false harmony between capitalism (precisely, the Real, the self-revolutionizing movement, of capitalism) and a totalized universe of meaning. The next chapter offers a critique of the fantasy of harmony that often beclouds thinking about economic ethics or a possible response to the workings of finance capital.

PART II

Particular Subject
Logic of the World of Finance

Chapter 4

The Fantasy of Harmony

The problem with twenty-first century philosophical and social-ethical analysts of the modern economy is that they are still attached to a pre-critical worldview. They are plagued by the fantasy of preexisting harmony between economy and finance, industrial circulation of money and financial circulation of money, and Main Street and Wall Street. This primordial fantasy continues in philosophical/ethical scholarship in form of the hope that a harmonious relationship might be possible between the industrial sector (so-called "main," "producing" economy) and financial sector. So philosophers and social ethicists look forward to a future state of economic development when a perfectly harmonious state will be reached in which Wall Street (finance capital) will take on the economy as an end-in-itself, and not as a means to an end, or as a partial object. This is a mistaken view to harbor about our contemporary economy, and one of our objectives in this book is to eliminate such an age-old fantasy, purge economic ethics of prescientific assumptions, and punch a hole in theoretical conception of a harmonious whole.

The fantasy of harmony between economy and finance has a long history and can be traced back, at least since the twentieth century, to the work of John Maynard Keynes. As per this view, in some historic past, economy and finance, the productive sector and financial sector, and industrial and financial circulations of money were integrally connected. Finance worked to promote the growth and development of the real sectors. In this reckoning, finance did not pursue an autonomous, incestuous line of self-aggrandizement; instead, finance and economy constituted a harmonious whole. The two were not split; they had a preexisting harmonious relationship. This respected fantasy does not reckon with the primordial history of economy: that the economy has *always* been cracked. It was never a harmonious whole. But reasoning about the economy has been dominated by efforts to harmonize all of its elements or parts into a consistent narrative. Consequent to this, when we conceive of the crack and antimonies we see in the economy as All, we attribute them to the limitation of our reasoning and techniques or to the inordinate greed of Wall Streeters. We have failed to locate them in the economy itself, which is failing to conceive economic reality as cracked and antinomic. Every economy, every sector of it, has an imbalance, a crack at its very core. When we properly look at the economy with the necessary Roentgen apparatus, we will see its crack, its antinomy, and its antagonism, "the traces of its future death," that will cause it to fail.

What appears as the perennial inability of finance to fund and adequately correlate with real production indicates a crack in the economy itself, so that the very failure to engage with real production is the indicator of the truth of the nature of the modern economy. The problem (inability) here is part of the solution. The very inconsistencies, antagonism (if you like), and anticorrelation between finance capital and industrial (real) capital bear witness to the truthfulness of the working of the modern economy.

In order to constitute itself as a monetary economy, the economy appears to have separated itself from finance, or from itself. Finance is the symbol of that separation, the crack, the *lack* of the economy. Finance thus becomes the desire to gain entry into a world of surplus enjoyment promised by the economy. More importantly, it is the separation of finance from the whole economy that unites finance with it, since this division or separateness is immanent to the economy. Finance, or indeed the economy, emerges when the economy divides itself from itself. The division, the gap between economy and finance, is there even when (if there was ever such a time) finance relates to the real productive economy in a self-identical manner. The so-called 100 percent correlation of finance and economy is possible because the economy opposes itself to finance, separates itself from itself. But in spite of separating and opposing, it relates to finance as the same, only on its opposite side. (This is to say that finance is both the economy—or in the economy—and what opposes the economy. This is so because finance embodies the economy's logic of split and its dynamics of making provision for the future.) We must ask how the same or self-identical is a perfect (appropriate) correlation. The economy is opposed to itself, so identity is not a uniting of the real economy and finance that takes place perfectly or absolutely. Thus, identity, or absolute relation, is not that of a functioning economy.

The finance-induced distortions and deficiencies of the modern economy that we do observe report on the nature of the modern economy. The form of the economy has been contaminated by its finance content. Finance is inscribed into the economy as its uncanny distortion; so economy and finance share the same logical form.

Financial excesses are in the distortions of the economy. The distortions of the economy are directly rendered to observation by the form of finance. They express themselves in finance. Finance also displays the logical form of an economy. What appears as the financial form, no matter how fragile and ephemeral it may seem to us, is the form of the economy. There is more truth in the appearances of finance form than what may be hidden in the real economy or what may be hidden beneath them, if there is such a thing. The real economy or real production is not the hidden reality beneath financial appearances. Economic (productive) structures are nothing but the very form of financial structures, the very form of appearance of money (monetary system). So concern about the unstable and deceptive nature of finance capital misses the point, which is that finance is the appearance of the whole economy, no matter how unstable and "unproductive" it may be. Finance is the appearance, *qua* appearance, of the dynamic conjunction of limit and limitlessness of total human productive activities in a given space-time, that is the economy.

Finance emerged as the primal form of the "excess," accumulative excess output or vitality of an economy, an emergent intensity of production that split the limit of the economy into limit and limitlessness. The separation of finance from the economy is the first division between limit and limitlessness, excess in material production. An economy able to divide against itself on the *production of goods and services* and *stored value*, which can finance them, represents a certain intensity of vitality. Once this excess has appeared, what will the economy do with it? It must be sent in search of material prosperity.

Society is immediately put in a double bind: either this excess is directed to the extant, limited production that will result in feverish inflation of asset value—which is a bad thing—or it must go searching for "economies" that make it insouciant to the good of the extant economy and given the ability to undermine any authority to control it. This is also a movement away from collective activity to support happiness. No wonder that since its beginning (or close to it) finance has turned its energies toward private satisfaction, individual withdrawal into the realm of private leisure, creating escalating demands of private happiness on society by those who have harnessed finance's accumulated vitality.

This is the paradox of finance as a reign of economic excess. The excess signifies the development and transformation of an economy, and also its potential ruin. (Modern public, state economic management has largely been about how to square this circle.) We need to quickly add that this excess, or the reign of excess, is not foreign to the economy. Finance bears the desire of the originating (primitive) economy to be limitless, beyond the limits of immediate satisfaction. Today, technology as limitlessness proper of human existence has made common cause with finance to further this tendency.

In addition to the appearance of the division between limit and limitlessness, the birth of finance signifies the emergence of two principles in the economy: kinship and self-generation. This is the basic division of the economy into parts that are faithful to the whole (a child's bond to its mother) or parts that are not. Organization of productive and reproductive activities of wealth can no longer proceed on a massive scale without "insemination" by finance capital, but finance can grow by self-engendering. An economy is a regime of exchange that is not united. Finance is its founding power of heterotopy for a monetary economy. This effectively happens when the monetary economy commences: when the principle of economic reproduction is separated from the law of kinship, nearness, or naturalness. This is precisely what irks Aristotle and the scholastic theologians: that money (metal), which they regard to be barren, can reproduce. Once finance has been birthed, economic relations cannot be confounded with relation to blood, soil, or religion. And within this, the excellence specific to it emerges: the limitlessness concern to gain, which is actually the absence of concern. This is what it means to be ruled by chance. Finance is all about risk taking, calculation of risks, and the "favor of heaven and fortune," which have no foundation. The excesses of finance capital have nothing to do with supposed madness for profit. "It is simply the dissolving of any standard [of concern by which nature or human convention] could give its law to communitarian artifice via the relations of authority [and harmony] that structure the social body."[1]

For finance to exist, the order of economy must be connected to the construction or emergence of economic "parts." Finance is more than a contract between those exchanging lendable funds limited to *arithmetic equality*; it is an expression of economic "parts" submitting to *geometric equality*, the determination of the worth of each part in the economy for common functioning. But this submission for proportion or common functioning is always already rendered problematic by the count of economic parts or parties that need to hold a share of the community-wide economic power. Finance "arises from a count of [economic] parts," which is always a false count, double count, or miscount."[2]

An economy that has grown beyond the household and has become a monetary one has three parts: production (goods and services), money, and finance. Production brings material wealth to the community; money brings facilitation of exchange; and finance brings the freedom to move from production to money and vice versa (M–C–M). Each of them is threatened by the other. The fluctuation in the value of money (inflation and deflation) threatens the economy and also the value of financial assets. Money's value somewhat depends on the size and prospects of the production of goods and services, and also on the dynamics of the financial markets. Finance (financial assets and liabilities) are linked to monetary values, and also to the economy. What is the quality or proportion of each of these parts, and how can they be compared to produce a common harmony? What does the freedom of finance bring to the economy? What is peculiar to it? This is where we begin to see the false count or miscount of the parts of the economy.

The simple act of money multiplying itself in exchange, and transforming and augmenting itself by passing through production, becomes a positive property of the divided economy, as part of the economy. But it is precisely this that makes it identify with the whole economy. It appropriates the quality of the economy as its own. What it brings to the economy is freedom. This needs to be understood in two senses. Freedom does not really belong to finance, but strictly speaking arises out of the division of the economy from itself. Finance identifies with the whole economy in the name of the internal split of the economy. Besides, it is through the existence of finance that an economy exists as a monetary economy, as one divided against itself for freedom. Finance is not just one part among others; it is the part that separates the economy and establishes it as a monetary economy of financial and industrial circulations of money that can move free from each other.

Here we see another miscount of the "parts" of an economy. The freedom of finance does not allow itself to be determined by its founding economy, and it is not even proper to finance at all. Finance is nothing more than a group of *rights* that has no positive qualification in the transformation of nature into wealth (as production does) and currency of participation (as money does), but nonetheless attributes to itself the qualities or properties necessary to belong to the whole economy. This is the nature of its freedom, that improper property that establishes finance "simultaneously as both part and whole of the [economy]."[3] It is this ability to identify with the whole while enjoying its separative freedom, not being a part of production and money qua mere exchange facilitation, that creates crisis. It is this part of the economy that "cannot in fact have any part other than all or nothing" that periodically sets a limit on arithmetical equality.[4] It is the freedom of finance that splits (interrupts) the play of profits based on exchanging goods and services. "On top of this, it is through the existence of this part [of the economy which] has no part, of this nothing that is all," that the economy exists as a monetary economy.[5]

So the struggle between Wall Street and Main Street, between the two circulations of money, is the economy itself. It is not a monetary reality that the economy has to deal with, but the institution of monetary economy itself. The split that causes monetary economy to occur is also what establishes each part of the economy as different from itself, and the economy as a whole as different from itself. Finance is not so much a part as the merging (remerging) of all parts, and this is what constitutes its penetrative, encompassing power. Finance is the setting of an internal dispute between parts of an economy that are not really parts. It identifies itself with the entire economy while declaring "itself to be the radical exception" to the economy.[6] It is by this exception that it also disconnects all parts of the economy. Economic crises like the crash of 2008 are not primarily a war of finance against Main Street. They reflect the very difference of the economy from itself and difference of each sector of the economy from itself (as a sector). The crash is an expression of the very structure of the modern monetary economy.

There is a monetary economy, a modern economy, when there is a part that is part of no-part, which has no part in the economy. Crisis exists when the institution of a part of the economy that has no part interrupts an economy of exchange. "This institution is the whole of the [economy] as a specific form of connection."⁷ It defines the economy as divided against itself.

While finance periodically interrupts the arithmetic exchange of goods and services, it never sets up geometric equality of proper shares or proportion necessary for the common good. Finance has no space-time other than what is required by its own principle of interiority. The empty freedom of finance sets only the equality of every space with any other space. This is the sheer contingency of its location at any specific time. This is the equality of craving for more space to occupy and abandon; the freedom makes real the ultimate spatial and temporal equality (or contingency) on which every monetary order rests.

Finance has no objective reality apart from the economy. Its complete objectivity is within the economy. All that really exists in the society as economic is the economy: finance is not anything that adds itself to economic things. Finance is not something that preexists or exists apart from an economy that somehow "externalizes" itself (acquires reality) in the economy, and then re-appropriates this "alienated" economy. Finance is the processual movement of the economy in its becoming and the performative result of the economy's own activities.

Finance has the economy as its presupposition. It is simultaneously the truth of the economy and, as such, the absolute first; thus, the economy "vanishes" in its truth, and is "sublated" in finance's self-identity.⁸ This is how we should understand this statement: finance's self-identity "emerges through its negative relationship (sublation) of its [economical] presuppositions and this negativity is 'absolute' not in the sense that it negates [the economy] 'absolutely,' that [the economy] 'absolutely' (totally) disappears into it, but in the sense that the negativity of sublation is self-related, in other words that the outcome of this work of negativity is [the finance's] positive self-identity."⁹

It is in this sense that I want us to interpret the role of finance in the modern economy. The gap of negativity between real economy and "unreal" economy that finance represents is not really a problem; it is instead the very split within the economy that allows it to function. Wall Street causes anxiety on Main Street or Washington not because the finance sector is too far from reality, but because finance that represents the abyss of capitalist economic freedom is too close for comfort. Finance, or Wall Street moral hazard, is not some external power tearing apart the organic unity of the economy; it is the very economy at work. It is the economy split into itself and itself, and there is no third or alternate medium that can guarantee the constant harmony or consistency of its parts. The state, which depends on economic power for its survival and is embedded in the economy, cannot be *the big Other* to guarantee the love of finance for its economy. This split is the "Real" of economic existence, and crisis occurs when economic agents stare into its face and are scared by its gyrating speculative madness.

We often fail to see that finance represents the authentic nature of the modern capitalist economy because we think in evolutionary terms. But if we are to take on the anti-evolutionist motto of Hegel and Marx, which holds that in order to understand the anatomy of a monkey, we must first understand the anatomy of a human being, then we would understand that the most developed form of a social formation provides the key to its earlier forms. The economist knows that all economies, however underdeveloped they may look, or however crudely their monetary system functions, are in faith and truth, inwardly circumcised financial economies. Primitive economies do not need to have an actual Wall Street, the obvious parting of ways of financial and industrial circulations of money, because they are already "inwardly circumcised," since a monetary economy only emerges when an economy cuts, alienates itself from its natural self, when it negates (mirrors) itself. Finance is the site where the economy is linked to its own image. It is where the economy creates its appearance as well as discovers its image. With the emergence of finance, the economy becomes its own spectator, anthropomorphically speaking. "The [economy] is present at the spectacle of its own division and duplication, acquiring in the process, the ability to separate itself from itself. The [economy] that views itself has a sharp awareness of the fact that what it sees beyond the screen is indeed itself or, in any case, a reflection of itself."[10] In this specular play of object ("self") and its appearance, the economy is both here and elsewhere, itself and itself behind a surface, material and spectral. Now there is a gap between the economy and its fugitive double, between self and itself, the economy and its representation.

We know that a mirror does not just reflect appearances and return images. A mirror, as Jean-Pierre Vernant argues, "opens a breach in the backdrop of 'phenomena,' displays the invisible, reveals the divine, and lets it be seen in the brilliance of a mysterious epiphany."[11] Similarly, finance does not merely reflect the image of economy; it also opens a crack in the backdrop of the collective phenomena of economic activities to display the "divine" that is tearing apart the economy. We look into finance to see what is invisible in the economy elsewhere. Indeed,

The Fantasy of Harmony 107

to understand the "anatomy" of the economy, we must first understand the "anatomy" of finance.

In addition to the hold of evolutionary thinking, the split nature of the economy (modern and premodern, past and present) is not easily grasped partly because of the lure of accounting and the easy availability of its deceptive knowledge. Accounting (as language of business and in its basic adherence to the fundamental equation of asset equals liability and credit equals debit) concerns totality, harmony, defining the identities and boundaries of all economic transactions. The basic question that animates fundamental accounting is, what kind of equality is adequate to encode the forced self-identity of the economy? Accounting purports to provide a universal grammar so that everything can be discerned, named, classified, and counted. But this "power" of discernment, the capability to express totality, is itself always already disrupted by the unnameable element of claims and encounters between persons.

There is no finance prior to accounting, that is, the radical homogeneity of credit and debit. Accounting is the fundamental scene where the constitutive difference of finance is made accessible to thought. Everything finance begins with the relation of credit and debit, with the crude demarcation of asset and liability. Finance (as an abstract thought of the primordial split) did not preexist the encounter (discovery) of credit and debit, particularly not before the duality of money and came to be money. (Money is simultaneously a credit [asset] and debt [liability]. So if a credit [debt] is created between any two economic agents, and no third party wants to hold it as an asset, it is not money.) Inasmuch as finance is thinkable as an abstract phenomenon, or entity, it is so only from the point of the first and fundamental scene of the split in money. The split, by the way, did condition the emergence of debit and credit. Debit and credit is the originary power of the split, of money. All forms of money are claims on society; they are credit money, and hence always credit and debit, asset and liability.[12]

The fundamental accounting equation of asset equals liability encodes and maps the universal network of credits and debits, causes and effects of claims in the society. Everything must be rounded off, encoded, and delimited in a universal whole. This is the great and fundamental idea of the accounting equation. But claims by their nature are dispersed, divisible, errant, and created and sustained by aleatory human creativity and social energy, which cannot be one with the symbolic system of accounting. There is always a crack in the system of the economy, money and finance, and fidelity to this crack as amoral refusal of the "morality" of the accounting equation demands an "ethics" that is indifferent to "some substantial or extra-subjective good (pleasure, virtue, civic harmony and so on)."[13]

Lack of Harmony and the Political Economy of Split

Let us summarize our findings or arguments so far. The economy is fundamentally split. Money is split. Finance is also split. There is an internal split in the modern economy. The split refers to the primordial *crack* or *lack* at the birth of the modern economy that both causes and traces an inherent imbalance at the core of any economy. This split is constitutive of the modern economy. There is always an internal gap within the economy, and finance capital is the form of appearance of both the economy and its inherent gap. Contrary to popular opinion, finance or finance capital has no separate existence of its own; it is part of the spatial-temporal processes of the economy. The notion of split economy captures the thinking that for an economy to exist as a monetary economy it must be divided against itself. The basic insight here is that the "external" opposition between Main Street (real production) and Wall Street (mere financial activities, so-called casino capitalism) is grounded in the modern economy's immanent self-opposition.

Often economists, politicians, and other public commentators argue that financial crises or poor industrial developments are caused by the separation of financial activities from real, material productive activities. In more technical terms, they maintain that there is separation between the financial circulation of money and the industrial circulation of money. They attribute the separation to either financial greed (excesses, speculation) or crass profit motivation of bankers, financiers, and stock operators. Consequently, the commentators argue that the solution to financial crises is to bring the two principal sectors together, believing that the separation is not original, not integral to the functioning of the modern economy. They see the separation as an artificial phenomenon arising from the distortions and contortions of modern capitalism. My argument is that the separation is original. The separation is merely indicative of the incompleteness of reality itself, incompleteness of the monetary economy system itself. The separation, which I traced to the beginning of the economic system in the march of human civilization, is the primordial crack in the initial wholeness of providing for human economic needs across time and space. Finance is not the external operation that resists being harmonized with the real economy, but the crack within the real economy itself. If we do not understand this separation or crack as constitutive of the reality of the modern economy, then we would not be able to forge adequate strategies to resist the negative impact finance capital unleashes on human flourishing and inclusive economic community.

Finance is the economy's "earliest and also indirect form of self-knowledge."[14] The emergence of finance is the split of the economy and its "self-objectification" or self-alienation. By finance, we know the economy, and by the economy, we know finance: the two are "identical." Finance explains an economy to itself, and by understanding finance as a self-portrait, a *selfie* of the economy, the antithesis between the economy and finance is broken. The differencing of economy and finance, with which theological analysis usually begins, is a differencing of the economy and its nature (logic). Go ahead and strip an economy of finance, and what is laid bare is not the pure, unsullied, innermost, authentic core of an economy but a pure void, the gap of negativity bereft of the protection that reformers or critics guarantee.

How can the dialectic of economy and finance (the economy radically divided from itself) be broken? Finance (the split) dwells within the fabric and interstices of the "members" of the economy; yet finance and economy are not two things, but two halves of the same thing, which is divided against itself. Finance is that part of the thing, entity (economy) doing what the other parts (of "economy") do not like and thus seen as evil. If the economy were to acquire a *voice* like Paul, it could say something like this in the wake of the 2008 meltdown: it is no longer I that does it, but finance that dwells within me. I see another law at war with the law of material production and inclusive prosperity. Who will rescue me from this body of death? And our answer will be that redemption is not something that can come within you—it cannot come from the economy itself. The economy cannot be delivered by refining economic policies by the so-called experts who think they can create harmony between the parts of the economy. It happens only through politics, the praxis of democratic egalitarianism. Politics, especially in the sense of Jacques Rancière's notion of democracy, offers possibility.

In the praxis of such politics for this purpose, the key act is neither to add anything to finance nor to take anything away from it, but to make a cut, a break. This will not be a break between "economy" and "finance," as hasty thinking would suggest, but to divide finance from within. This is to excise finance from its place beside the "economy" for the sake of freeing large portions of the economy from the fragility it imposes on them, for the sake of inclusive prosperity, to create a narrow space between the "economy" and finance for human flourishing.[15]

As we learned earlier, finance is the "part of no-part" of the economy. In the political system there is a real "part of no-part," those who have no stake in the present organization of society, in the extant distribution of the sensible, and as such directly represent the universal dimension of the social totality. What does it mean for those who have no determined place in the system to confront the monstrous singular universality that is the financial sector? What does it mean for the singular universality of concrete social existence to confront the singular universality of the spectral, abstract world of self-fecundating economic-financial operations? It means to divide, split, cut across the entire body of the financial sector from within, to identify those practices, products, and institutions that have no specific place within the existing global order of finance, although they belong to it. To put it differently, the point of the struggle is not finance versus non-finance, which will keep the current logic of empty formalism and pervasive domination intact; it is rather the difference of *demos/non-demos itself*, "too-muchness of life"/ dead drive, *which as a difference, is universal*, that is, which cuts across" the entire financial sector, splitting, dividing from within every identity, operational logic financial product.[16] As loans are cut into demos and non-demos, as are trade and payment systems, are they inclusive or exclusive of the interest of the "part of no-part"? Is this not the kernel of some of the ideas of grassroots movement for LETS (local exchange trading system), alternative local currency system, zero-interest central banking, interest-free and endogenous equity money, or equity financing that is floating around in heterodox economic circles? The late Nigerian economist Peter Alexander Egom wrote a series of books advocating a commodity payment system instead of an interest-based, debt-driven, seigniorage-laden monetary system for African economies so as to create that narrow space of alternative thought and practice between the laws of economy/finance directed toward "money of micro-finance" and laws toward "money of macro-finance." What he calls money of micro-finance is interest-free and private sector equity or commodity money "that distributes work and its rewards, social and material, evenly and fairly in spaces and across generations, among all of its members of gender, creed, and tribe."[17] Money of *macro-finance and empire/serfdom*, however, is interest-based and public sector debt that "distributes work and its rewards, social and material, unevenly and unfairly, in spaces and across generations, among all of its members of gender, creed and tribe."[18] Egom based his thinking on the efficacy and beneficial potentials of micro-finance instead of the large-scale global financial system on his faith on commodity payment standards.[19]

I do not want us to get carried away by unnecessary hope after all the discussions about politics of the part of no-part and an alternative currency system. For they leave unaddressed some crucial background questions. Will any of the alternative systems provide a means to step beyond the global order of finance capital? Will finance capital (capitalism) not absorb any alternative subsystems or acts of political emancipation? The answer is Yes and No. Yes, because capitalism does well with what has been asserted here: it has extraordinary capacity to absorb and neutralize, and even profit from, alternatives, which from the outset do not fundamentally rearrange the given constituents of the capitalist situation. And No, because there could be grace, "which is a radically external interruption into the realm of [Being, order, law]"[20] to indicate the possibility of a new beginning and to point to the idea that "theology can provide one of the most complex ways of speaking about revolution" or *event*,[21] as Alain Badiou has shown us in his *Saint Paul: The Foundation of Universalism*.[22] Badiou's concept of event is laicized grace. The answer is No, because there could be a Badiousian *event* (an unexpected revolutionary moment), materialist grace (something that cannot be accounted for in terms of the coordinates of a given order), grace—laicized and politicized—that destabilizes the order of Being and establishes foundations for a new political practice. What will then be required is fidelity to the truth event and the hard labor of constructing the new order (society).[23]

Three paragraphs above where we mentioned the name of Paul (the economy anthropomorphically voicing a Romans 7–type complaint), we suggested that the redemption of the economic system cannot come from within it, meaning it must come from outside. It is from this standpoint that we proceeded to discuss the politics of the part of no-part, and all the fine talk about *event*. Now there are two sore points in the whole argument: (a) there is the implicit assumption that the ethics of capitalism (or finance capital) in particular is incompatible with the ethos of equalitarianism and human flourishing that the Rancière's part of no-part upholds, and (b) the redemption needs to come from an outside. What is this outside? What will be our response to these sore points?

Let us begin with the common observation that capitalism is not compatible with any ethics that accents equality and human flourishing for all. At its core, it is beyond good and evil; it cannot work out the good of society from itself. The ethic of capitalism is an instrument to dominate the good and disfigure or appropriate all values, institutions, and traditions that do not support its dynamics. Thus any ethical framing of its logics, dynamics, and outcomes must come from outside, a deliberate imposition on its operations, trajectory, tendency, and disposition.

Where exactly is this outside? The inner logic of capitalism, as we have laid bare in this book, is not compatible with the ethical substance—as geared toward human flourishing for all, equality, justice, and justness of social relationships. Yet the logic (precisely, ethics) of capitalism is not completely foreign to our ethical heritage or human drives or inclinations. As we have noted, no external power, no consideration of the welfare of the other, and no tradition is a law for capitalism, its "will" to dominate, to conquer the good. Capitalists deem themselves free; the system of capitalists considers itself free when it obeys its only law—when, like the Kantian autonomous self, it obeys only what it imposes on itself. Capitalists regard themselves above the good or authority of communities because capitalism's only judge or authority is the law it imposes on itself and freely acknowledges.

The autonomous "will" of capitalists or capitalism is not, however, exactly the rational will of the Kantian ethics. It is situated somewhere between Kant's rational will and Schopenhauer's Dionysian will. Kant conceived rational will as freely subjecting itself to the law of the good, the universal moral law. Schopenhauer's irrational will makes no distinction between good and evil, does not submit itself to the law of reason or the law of the good. Schopenhauer considers the irrational will beyond good and evil. Does the Kantian stance of rejecting the consequences of one's actions in the real world, of considering as "pathological" the use of consequences as criterion for moral value (or decision), not amount to the same thing?

These two inclinations (rational will and irrational will) also mark the ethical substance of societies; the ethical life of societies is always perched somewhere between the ethical vision of Kant and Schopenhauer/Nietzsche. Do we also not find a split between the individual and the ethical substance of her community? There is no guarantee of established harmony between an individual and the ethical substance. From another angle, is the subject's actions not split from her ethical substance or pure will (reason) anytime (when) it irreducibly relies on her situation?

The logic of capitalism dwells in, insinuates itself into, the split in our ethical substance. The ethical substance of any society does not coincide with itself; always incomplete, there is always a crack in it. Capitalism represents the crack, dwells in this crack, and indeed cracks all that is solid and which we hold dear. Capitalism is the otherness that is integral to the body of the (pre)modern ethical substance, the bone that is stuck in its throat, so to speak: the inherent point of failure (the gap) in the ethical substance. The social mechanism, logic, promise, and fantasy of capitalism prevent the ethical substance from establishing itself as a consistent field. So capitalism is incompatible with the liberal notion of ethics (or even Christian ethics broadly defined) not because it is unethical, but because it is disintegrating the ethical substance of our communities, which is not ultimately based on rationalist, or utilitarian, calculations or exercise of pure will.

This assertion raises two questions: first, are the social relations, mutual relatedness, and the commodity economy that transforms relations between human beings into relation between things—all founded on capitalism for centuries now—not part of America's ethical substance? Indeed, as put by Japanese Marxist/continental philosopher Kojin Karatani, "one can no longer be so naïve as to insist that the originally healthy and organically connected relational world has become reified by the intervention of capitalism. This is an ex post facto perspectival perversion. It overlooks the most crucial fact that it is capital and nothing else that organized *social relation* in the first place."[24]

Second, does ethical substance preexist the activities (contingent or not) of individuals in a community? If the ethos, values, of capitalism has permeated and informed our actions today, does it still make sense to argue that capitalism is not compatible with our ethical substance? Has the inherited ethical substance not lost its substantial character? Has its status not changed under the hammer of capitalism and desire? Hence, "it is no longer experienced as a firm foundation given in advance but as fragile symbolic fiction, something which exists only insofar as individuals treats it as existing, or only insofar as they relate to it as their ethical substance. There is no directly existing 'ethical substance,' the only 'actually existing' thing is the incessant activity and interaction of individuals and it is only this activity that keeps it alive."[25] Is capitalist ethos not this foreign body in the social substance that splits it and overdetermines it? Is this intersubjective space in which there is no inherited ethical substance as big Other not also calling us to invent new rules of behavior to undergird human flourishing and civility? We shall return to such questions in chapters 6 and 7.

Meanwhile, let us bring to close the discussion of the theme of this chapter—the absence of harmony between finance and economy—by examining it through the lens of sexuation. This approach was foreshadowed in chapter 3 in the section "The Gap between Finance and Industry." We want to shed light on a very complex relationship through the Lacanian perspective of no direct relationship between men and women (self-declared positions of male and female subjects not based on their biology, genitalia, or genetic makeup, that is, their positions from a psychoanalytical perspective). Women and men are split differently by/within the symbolic order, the phallic function, which "refers to the alienation brought about by language."[26] Bruce Fink sums it up in this way: "While men are defined as being wholly hemmed in by the phallic function, wholly under the sway of the signifier, women . . . are defined as *not* being wholly hemmed in. A woman is not split in the same way as a man: though alienated, she is not altogether subject to the symbolic order. The phallic function while operative in her case, does not reign absolutely. With respect to the symbolic order, a woman is not whole, bounded, or limited."[27] The net result of these different positions that they occupy in the symbolic order is that there is no direct sexual relationship, no sexuation between man and woman. There is only a non-relationship between them. How now do we translate this into our notions of economy and finance? How are they positioned in relation to the ethical substance, the symbolic order?

Admittedly, this is going to be a crude translation, but it might help to further understand the relationship between finance and economy as conveyed by our concept of split economy. The attempt is to show how finance and economy are alienated by/within the ethical substance. In adapting the Lacanian formula, I position finance as "woman" and economy as "man." Finance, though split, is not wholly subjected to the ethical substance of society in the way the economy is. There is *no direct relationship* between finance and economy insofar as they are finance and economy. In other words, they do not "interact" with each other as finance to economy and economy to finance. "Something gets in the way of their having any such relationship; something skews their interactions."[28] They have different kinds of relations to the ethical substance, different ways of being split by *communal demand*.[29]

The whole of the economy falls under the restriction of the ethical substance, that is, under the symbolic castration (renunciation, the giving up of some jouissance) of the nomos. As it goes with any universal claim, there is usually an exception that proves the rule. There exists some part of the economy that the nomos appears foreclosed, that denies the symbolic castration. Every subsector of the economy harbors the structural potentiality of not being subjected to the demands of the ethical substance; carries the ideal of ethical boundaries.

Not all of finance comes under the ethical substance, the norms of the community. Yet, you cannot find one financial market player for which the ethical substance, the norms of society, is totally inoperative. Every player is at least in part determined (conditioned) by the ethical substance, and submitted in part to symbolic castration.

Economy and finance are alienated in and by the ethical substance in very different ways, as witnessed by their submission to the norms of society. Each of them is defined separately with respect to the ethical substance. Economy and finance are split differently, and this difference accounts for their non-identification, non-relationship. Each of them plays different roles in the ethical foundation of human productive activities. The economy (ostensibly) plays the role of giving "meaning."[30] Finance has effects outside of meaning or meaning making, separated from meaning, an empty signifier.[31]

The motor forces of the economy and finance are different. The motor force of finance is *objet a*, and not the economy as such. The financial sector may benefit from the innovations, developments, or the funds requirements of the economy, and so forth, but this is only insofar as the economy arouses its desire, and it stands as an object of its desire. The economy—the real economy at best—is only a prop, a medium for this object of desire, but it is never the partner of finance. On the side of the economy, it is also true that the economy (industry) is not a partner of finance. For industry, it is human flourishing (narrowly defined) that serves as the partner and finance is the prop for human flourishing for industry/economy. Given this dissymmetry of their partners, we cannot theoretically postulate a relationship or identification between them— there is no "sexuation" between finance and economy.[32]

Concluding Thoughts

Given all this, how should we approach the study of economic ethics? The question of economic ethics is to be articulated from the perspective of human existence, the split between credit and debit, the *real* of the economy. This fundamental antagonism, the weight of it, is actualized through the financial system. In order to grasp how the fundamental split between economy and finance drives the whole modern economy and conditions the "pure ethics" of economic existence, we must press into the Lacanian concept of *objet petit a*.

Chapter 5

The Ethical Form of Finance

Finance is the *objet petit a* of an economy's demand for goods. Wall Street finance today is the pure form of the demand for *accumulatable excess output*, expansion of value, the intensity of vitality, the desire of the originating (proto-)economy to be limitless beyond the limit of immediate satisfaction and self-generation. The present globalized casino-styled finance is the pure form of the absence of "content" in accumulatable output, the void around which desire for the originating economy led to the emergence of limitlessness. The primordial demand is satisfied neither by the need for production of goods (expansion of gross domestic product) nor by the need for profit; rather, limitlessness continues on its own. It is the marker of what the primordial (the economy before its split) does not have and will never have. Finance represents what always remains of the desire for the originating (primitive) economy to be limitless when every object that could possibly satisfy it is in place. It is the very separation of finance from economy, the primordial split that produces a *remainder*, which now drives Wall Street finance. Wall Street finance is the primordial void of the economy: the original split between debit and credit, through which the economy and finance has acquired a form. But it is not a form separated from content. Form becomes its own matter (as both Kant and Lacan taught us. More on this below). Finance acts exclusively for itself, functioning as a *pure drive* for itself. Form now functions as its own "matter."

> Here we come across a form, which is no longer the form of anything, of some content or other, yet it is not so much

empty form as a form "outside" content, a form that provides form only to itself. In other words, we are confronted here with a surplus, which at the same time seems to be "pure waste," something that serves absolutely no purpose.[1]

Why does finance, the working of Wall Street finance, conjure the Lacanian notion of the *objet petit a*? Historically, wealth accumulation has "form" and "content." The *will to wealth* ("form") has an external motive that drives it, an object that eggs it on. Today, form appears to be doubled: as itself and content, that is, form drives itself. "Form itself must be appropriated as a material surplus, in order to be capable of determining the will . . . converting a mere form into a materially efficacious drive."[2] It is in this revealing light that we need to understand the logic of wealth creation in the global financial system.

Wealth creation has turned into some form of "pure wealth generation." It is no longer aimed at any particular object or goal, but for the "act" of wealth creation. We should not construe this to mean that the key major players have denied themselves the goods and comforts that money can buy. In this state of "pure desire" for wealth, the pleasure of wealth, though still available for such people, loses its attractive power. Wealth is generated or pursued not only in accord with wealth accumulation, but also exclusively for the sake of wealth. Pure wealth generation requires that not only the players' actions conform to wealth accumulation, but also that this conformity be the only incentive, the motivating force of the "content" of their actions.[3]

We are now in a position to understand the Lacanian image of *objet petit a* as it relates to Wall Street. I have planned our route to understanding the Lacanian notion by going through the territory of Kantian ethics, as the insights of the wise man of Königsberg, which most ethicists are familiar with, make Lacan psychoanalysis easy to swallow. Kant explains that we can do our duty in obeying the law in two ways: *morality* and *legality*, two distinctions in the categorical imperative. A citizen acts only in accord with duty (legality); her right action is motivated by personal benefit, by the pleasure principle. However, she can also act exclusively for the sake of duty. In *The Metaphysics of Morals*, Kant explains the difference between morality and legality: "The mere conformity or nonconformity of an action with law, irrespective of the incentive to it, is called its *legality* (lawfulness); but that conformity in which the idea of duty arising from the law is also the incentive to the action is called its *morality*."[4] If you read this quotation carefully, you will see that the ethical for Kant is an excess, a surplus. In Kant's view, a legal action represents a correspondence between action and law, but in ethical action, there is *something* that goes beyond the conformity between law and action. This *something* is not some extraneous content coming to the form of the law; it is the form itself, the form of the moral law, and conformity with the law is the only "content" or motive force of ethical action. Let me explicate this with the insights of Alenka Zupančič. She divides the fundamental distinctions Kant made in the categorical imperative into two theses:

"In conformity with duty (the legal)."
"In conformity with duty and *only* because of duty."

You now see that what Kant asserts as the ethical is a supplement. The subject's actions or comportment is the same in both cases, legality and morality, and the result in terms of obeying the law, doing her duty, is also the same irrespective of the difference in her motivations. The "extra" that is required for ethical actions serves no purpose insofar as in both situations the subject has done her duty. The extra, at the level of form, is "pure waste." This is a "form that provides form only for itself . . . a surplus which at the same time seems to be a 'pure waste.'"[5] The significance of acting exclusively for the sake of duty, as Zupančič argues, is wasteful excess; yet, at the same time it makes a world of difference, separating the ethical from the unethical.[6] It appears the very separation of the ethical subject from all pathological contents that leads to "nothing" leaves a "remainder" that is "less than nothing," to use Slavoj Žižek's term. This is a remainder, a positivity, a material weight that can influence the subject's action; it's an "absence" that functions as an "incentive." "The subject's separation from the pathological produces a certain remainder, and it is *this* remainder that constitutes the drive of an ethical subject. But this implies that it is the process of separation from the order of the pathological that produces the very thing which makes it possible."[7]

This pure form as a surplus, this surplus of form, is what Lacan calls *objet petit a*. For Lacan, this pure form arises from the workings of demand and drive. The subject demands something, but in the process demand becomes desire when it is directed at something beyond what is demanded. The demand has been satisfied, but the desire continues because the satisfaction did not terminate the satisfaction of the demand; hence, desire now circulates around the void created by the lack, the absence of an object. The satisfaction of the need, in its inability to extinguish the desire of the object of demand, creates *objet petit a*. "Desire can be defined precisely as the *pure form of demand*, which remains of demand when all the particular objects (or 'contents') that may come to satisfy it are removed. Hence the *objet petit a* can be understood as a void that has acquired a form."[8] Casino capitalism, Wall Street's incestuous insemination of finance capital, is the unintended long-run effect or the void presupposed by demand for stored value by the primordial economy or the primal split that engendered the economy. From the beginning, there was the fantasy of full and final satisfaction, the ultimate satisfaction of the subject's desire, fantasy of completeness and harmony in the primitive society. Of course, such a place or level of attainment of desire does not exist (*objet a* does not exist), and subjects are thus always disappointed. "Objet *a* is no being. Objet *a* is the void presupposed by a demand. . . . *That's not it* means that, in the desire of every demand, there is but the request for objet a."[9]

The Kantian ethical subject is split between fulfilling her duty only because of duty and serving some supreme good.[10] Kant in his ethical thinking does not start with or presuppose any notion of the good; the good is defined only by the formal structure of action. Besides, the ethical law in Kant's hand does not command the subject to do a particular thing, does not name the duty, only commanding the person to do her duty. In a certain crude or twisted sense, the logic of Wall Street, the global financial system follows the ultimate logic of Kantian ethics. The collective actions of Wall Street actors do not presuppose any sense or notion of the good; rather, the formal structure of their actions defines it. In the formal logic of accumulation, it is to act not only in conformity with wealth generation and accumulation, but also exclusively because wealth generation and accumulation says nothing to the financial players in the name of presupposed good of society to "do this" or "do that." Wealth accumulation is the only incentive of actions. This is the inherent conflict between market, the invisible hand, and the visions of philosophers and ethicists about creating a flourishing society. Philosophers or indeed societies presuppose a certain notion of the good (such as eudaimonia) to found and define the ethic of the market or global financial system, but sadly, like the Kantian moral law, the ethic of the global financial market, the unconditional moral law of the market, is founded only in itself.

Subjects in the global financial marketplace act toward this moral law with appropriate "respect" or "anxiety." This "moral law" *affects* them, feeling its "presence" (its traumatic proximity) in the daily encounters of person-to-person transactions, determining their will and driving their actions. They feel its presence not in the sense of the law providing representation of certain objects of desire or the ultimate goal of satisfaction for their actions, but the perpetual journey to the goal—the endless repetition of circular movement toward satisfaction of the goal. This gap, which represents the nonaccessibility of the nonexistent *objet a*, is the condition of the financial ethical subject. The financial player is constituted by a loss she never had, and as such the capitalist subject never coincides with herself, but rather with her loss; it is this "alienation" that drives the subject to more accumulation.

They feel the market's presence insofar as they view themselves as being subjected to the market, often humiliated by it and sometimes terrified by it. What Kant writes about the moral law applies to the relationship between the financial market and its key operators. According to Kant, there comes a point in the relationship between the moral and the ethical subject when the person subjects herself to the law and this subjection provokes a consciousness of humiliation and terror. This is the representation of the effect of the law, which in the past directly determined the will of the ethical subject.

> There is something so singular in the boundless esteem for the pure moral law . . . whose voice makes even the boldest evildoer tremble and forces him to hide from its sight [gaze], present it to us for obedience—that one cannot wonder at finding this influence of a mere intellectual idea on feeling quite impenetrable for speculative reason. . . .[11]

The market operators do not forever remain humiliated, terrified, and powerless before the market. Just as the Kantian subjects recover from the feeling of anxiety, powerlessness, and displeasure before the spectacle of the moral law and move on to the feeling of the sublime, the market operators also gain their sense of superiority, their sense of having minds capable of comprehending the market. Powerlessness and displeasure give way to consciousness of unlimitable rational ability (aided by computers) capable of making sense of the market. The market is (seemingly) apprehended, and the players "elevate" themselves above it. Alternatively, the failure of their perceptual abilities leads them to resignify this limitation of their perceptual capabilities as a testimony to the omnipotence, omnipresence, and omnivoyance, the transcendence or greatness of the market: the "supersensible" collective of millions of individual transactions, the "sublime" truth of capitalism.

Let me make a quick clarification at this point so the reader does not read too much meaning into the analogy we have made between Kant's analytic of the sublime and the market. In the Kantian scheme, a subject fascinated by, say, the heaving boundless ocean does not view herself as part of the ineffable forces at work in the overflowing presence of the body of water. But this is not the case in the market. The players in the market, their drive for *objet a*, and the market form a reflexive loop. The inclusion of the subject in the very encounter with (what we have called) the moral law of the market, in the very scene of the endless expansion of value for its own sake, is a distortion that in turn affects the encounter or the loop. Political scientist Jodi Dean expressed this reflexivity in the area of speculative finance in this way.

> If I think that you think CDOs [collateralized debt obligations] are a good investment, then I should make and sell you some. This confirms to you that they are good investments (or else I wouldn't be selling them); consequently, you purchase more, which tells me I was right to think that you thought these were a good investment. I then share this news with others, who want to buy some, which again confirms my expectations and your savvy as an investor, etc. Rather remarkably, this reflexivity has actual market effects; deals are made (insuring payment for the brokers) and prices rise.[12]

We have earlier demonstrated that both in Kantian ethics and ethics of the global financial market, form acts as its own "matter;" form acts as its own efficacious drive, appropriates itself as a material surplus, as a "pure waste." There are now many financial products that have assumed the formal structure of the market's law of morality. Not only is the subject acting in an "ethical" manner in the market, but products do exactly the same thing in the restricted sense of pure ethics, the notion of empty form. Before now, financial products arguably had this structure: (a) an instrument that encodes contents of future streams of payments, materiality, asset, and (b) the risk that attends the stream of payment or assets. We may liken the projected stream of cash flow as the "matter" of the financial commodity and the risk as the "form." But with the development of CDOs such as credit default swaps, risk has become its own content; risk now occupies the position formerly occupied by content, asset; form (risk) functions both as matter and form, as a drive, and as a kind of material surplus of empty form.[13]

Consider how credit default swaps (an insurance on bonds) work. A financial institution lends money to a corporation, and the borrower is expected to make a stream of payments to service the loan. The borrower, the issuer of a corporate or sovereign debt, insures the lenders (buyers of the bonds) against possible default or "credit event." Usually, an insurance company or bank steps in, after an exchange of fees, to guarantee the buyers of the bonds against nonpayment by the issuer of the bonds. The payment of fees (premiums) to the insurance company ensures that the buyers of the bonds get the necessary protection of their investments. If all goes well and the debt issuer does not default, the buyers will lose only the annual fees (premiums) that they paid to enjoy the protection. If the debt issuer defaults and the buyers do not have credit default swaps (CDS), they will lose varying proportions of their original investments.

Note that the buyers of credit default swaps are protecting their investments against the typical risk of constrictions in the flow of cash payments in the servicing and repaying of principles. The seller of the CDS to the buyers of the corporate bonds are making money on the risk assumed by buyers of the bond, who in the first place carried the risk of default by issuers of the bonds. From the late 1990s, many bankers quickly discovered they did not need to bother lending to corporations and earn 6 or 7 percent interest, when they could just issue CDS and collect endless premiums from buyers of corporate and municipal bonds on the promise of paying something to the holders of the CDS in the event of default. No need to put money down, but they can make profit limited only by how many CDS as a bank you can sell.

The market has become so sophisticated that those who have no stake in the original investments or loans will buy CDS. These types of CDS are known as "naked credit default swaps" and serve to give speculators a chance to take positions on the credit worthiness of the original issuers of bonds. (The value of naked CDS derives from mathematical estimations of the value of a third person's ability to keep its promise to pay.) This class of speculative traders is betting on the risk that supervenes the original risk of those who hold the bonds of the reference entities. Simply, they bet against the original loan. Naked credit default swaps now constitute the largest portion of the outstanding portfolio of CDS. In the words of Katerina Kolozova: "Contemporary finance capital, or the so-called finance industry, relies and profits from the operations of circulation as a process *per se* and as tautology, divorced from any grounding in the material basis of capital."[14]

On the whole, risk has curved in on itself. Risk on Wall Street is now reflexive. Form (risk, self-referentiality of risk) appropriates itself as an asset, as content in order to be the *drive* for investment (ethical) action. Financial product such as naked CDS stands as the commodity of the lack of the commodity, the content as the lack of content. Naked CDS as a signifier of the lack of underlying asset or future cash flow also came to function in the wake of the 2008 financial meltdown as "the signifier of the lack of signifier."[15] It came to stand for the unknown, the void that exceeds the existing causal network. Derivatives like CDS repeat the structure of form becoming its own content in Kantian ethics. Ethics of the global financial system demands that investment action not only conform with risk consciousness (pricing), "but also that this conformity be the only 'content' or 'motive' of that action."[16]

We have so far examined two ways actors in the market, acting from the demands of the ethical form of finance, exhibit the motive of respect for the "moral law of the market": (1) the feeling that arises from consciousness that their actions are being "morally" required by the empty form, that is, the logic of the market having an effect on the will of the players. There is a consciousness of being motivated by the market. It is an effect of the law of the market on the players and, (2) the market as a sublime object. The market is also present to the players in the form of an ever-present command of debt, capturing and shaping subjectivities. Debt "represents the economic and subjective engine of the modern-day economy. Debt creation, that is, the creation and development of power relation between creditors and debtors, has been conceived and programmed as the strategic heart of neoliberal politics."[17] With this development, there is a change in the place of debt in the economy. In the current mode of debt governance of the whole socioeconomy, debt no longer serves the banks as its Master. It is no longer debt that the bank desires to impose on corporations, the "real economy," or the rest of the society. Debt occupies the place of the banks; there is no longer the dichotomy of originating sector of credit and consuming sector of debts. Banks are both debtors and creditors, and corporations are also both debtors and creditors. Debt is the Master. The economy affirms nothing but debt. Debt is all-knowing not in the sense that creditors know everything about everybody, but in the sense that debt aspires to fully incarnate the future, the repayment of debts and interests, attempts to capture, neutralize, or close off many of the future possibilities of debtors. The "souls" of citizens and institutions have been trained to accept the creditor-debtor relationship of finance capital. As Maurizio Lazzarato puts it in his stimulating 2015 book, *Governing by Debt*:

> Contrary to an opinion everyone from anarchists to neoliberals seem to share, the debt of today's capitalism is unpayable, unreimbursable, and infinite. The function of credit is expressed still more precisely in the literary, rather than economic, terms of Kafka. They apply particularly well to our condition as debtors, for, like Joseph K., we are all presumed guilty even if we have done nothing wrong. The form contemporary debt takes resembles at once an "apparent settlement" (we go from one debt to another, take out credit and repay, and so on) and an "unlimited postponement" in which one is continually indebted, and the debt is never (and must never be) honored. Credit has not been given in order to be reimbursed but rather to be in continual flux.[18]

The creditor-debtor relation, which is the encompassing nature, logic, and dynamic of today's economy, which is the fundamental power relation of our modern-day society, also enforces its demand on those who benefit from it more than any other group. A bank is "free" to pursue its way of making profits (transform money into debt, to exploit consumers and industrialist, appropriate surplus labor of society) as long as it is able to honor its debt, keep its promises to its creditors, and working on its "self" (the configurations of its assets and liabilities, and human resources) to make itself fit to play in the market. Financial institutions—just like every person in society—are included in the universal power relation of debt of modern-day economy. They are caught in the endless circuit of capitalism that is beyond their control. They always face the power of the market to create or destroy capital. Only debt and debt repayment counts. When debt is in the position of the Master, when it is "the political operator of global governance,"[19] or when debt becomes the "debt of the existence of the subject themselves,"[20] debt can neither be mastered nor fully settled. It is Master. Debt works as a command: it keeps on accumulating more and more. It is a drive shaped by the "self-propelling circulation of capital."

Debt as master is especially devastating for American workers and students. Any talk about Saint Paul going to Wall Street must endeavor to mention the groans and cries that hang over the profits of banks that he would hear walking the space between the grave yard of Trinity Church and the sea that is Wall Street.[21] (A street that got its name from the wall early Dutch settlers built to keep out Native Americans.) If Christianity in the past has helped to shape people for capitalism, as Max Weber taught us, capitalism is now shaping citizens' fundamental identity, "formatting" their souls through indebtedness to make them willing to do for personal, intimate reasons what capitalism requires of them. As eminent theologian Kathryn Tanner recently put it:

> The whole of one's person is a target for profit-making in these changed conditions of work (such as job insecurity, flexibility in job requirements, downward pressures on pay, overwork, or near impossible demands for performance) and debt. In constantly assuming debt, for meeting of almost every conceivable need, one obligates oneself to manage one's whole life in ways that are compatible with paying it off. All decisions one makes as a worker and consumer come to be affected, into an indefinitely extendable future—the need to be indebted never seems to cease.[22]

Let us briefly focus on student debt, which currently stands at over one trillion dollars, to illustrate the crushing weight of indebtedness on ordinary Americans.[23] Anytime I walk on the streets of the university where I teach, I see hundreds of students—blacks, whites, Asians, Latinos—rushing to their classrooms, and my heart breaks. I ponder what American society and its economy are doing to them, to their future. America has caught them in a web woven by the paradox of capitalism, and they know not what they do. On the one hand, the market gives a sense of freedom and power to student-citizens. They shout, "I can do it!" On the other hand, late capitalism renders them fragile. Their social fabric is vulnerable, their inherited social institutions precarious. Debt has neutralized or closed off many future possibilities. The huge debt bearing down on students threatens to undermine their freedom and right to be active participants in the social life of their time.

"I can do it"—that shout, that belief, embodies the perennial exuberance of youth, yet the souls of too many young people have been captured and reformatted by capitalism's ceaseless push for profit.[24] The American financial apparatus and its university system have inscribed the promise to repay "infinite" debt on the minds and bodies of the students who walk up and down the streets of America. Students are branded! Together, capitalism and the university marketplace have burnt a creed into the souls and memories of these young adults, a creed that says good citizens keep their promise to repay debt, no matter how severe the burden.

The system has enormous, unbalanced power over students. What undergirds this economic dynamic is a relationship not of free, equal exchange but of debtor–creditor, a power relation that not only imposes particular modes of future behavior on students, but also renders them "guilty" even before they act, like Josef K. in Kafka's *The Trial*.[25]

Reinhold Niebuhr once stated that anywhere there is an imbalance of power, there is bound to be injustice. The injustice of the crushing debt burden on American students today—more than $1.1 trillion—reflects a harsh asymmetry. American colleges in cahoots with late capitalism no longer promote only the nurture of skills and moral values fitted for life in capitalism, but also directly advance the production of student indebtedness.

We have entered a period in which debt peonage is coterminous with college education. The labor of students after graduation is now inevitably *serf labor* that feeds the wealth of creditors, rendering the student's life and existential condition increasingly fragile. The college–student relationship is being reshaped by the dictates of finance capital's creditor–debtor relationship, which informs and contaminates other social relations. What Deleuze and Guattari warned generally about the ascendancy of debt is now happening to the American college student: "Debt becomes a *debt of existence*, a debt of the existence of the subjects themselves."[26] In such a scenario, the debtor never quits repaying. The duty of debt becomes never-ending.

Those of us who teach in expensive universities are seeing debt redefine the education of the heirs of American civilization. In the past, college education endued students not only with an ethos of effort and reward, but also with a sense of obligation to serve the common good. Today, the pressing obligation that looms over them is to honor their debts, perhaps also to assuage the guilt of having incurred debts. If in the past graduating students threw their caps into the air to signify freedom and the hope of soaring to greater heights, today they are "free" insofar as they can live their lives in ways that ensure the reimbursement of their loans.

From the eighteenth to the early twentieth century, the poster children of exploitation under merchant capital were the degraded, subjugated, enslaved people of foreign lands by such trading and colonizing firms as the East Indian Company and the Royal Niger Company. In nineteenth-century England, in the early years of industrial capitalism, the showpiece of oppression and exclusion were the enslaved African Americans in plantations and the heavily exploited factory workers, the proletariat whose surplus value was expropriated by the bourgeoisie. Today, the face that represents the oppressed—the person whose soul is trained to accept the creditor-debtor relationship of finance capital, the citizen whose future possibilities are expropriated before she even starts her life—is the American college student.

A sad irony in all this touches American churches. Many have been so engrossed in fighting battles for the other dire poster children that they have in most cases neglected the huddled masses of students yearning to breathe free.

What can the American churches do to stop the neglect of the debtor children in their midst? Let me suggest four economic reforms that churches should support.

First, congregations should press for the abolition of the charging of interest on student loans by all lending institutions. In the place of loan and interest repayments, every indebted student will agree, for five years, to pay back 10 percent of any personal income that is above the national median personal income level.

Second, churches should urge institutions to declare *jubilee* for a college graduate if by age fifty, because of years of below-average earnings, she has not been able to complete five years of payments of the 10 percent of personal income that is above the national median personal income. At this point she is set free from student-loan obligations. The excessive level of students' debts has brought the debtor–creditor relationship to its extreme and now threatens it. Historically, when debts become excessive and undermine the survival of the financial system itself we have restored to cancellation or forgiveness; this is what we did in the 2008 financial crisis. There is no point holding on to student debts that cannot be repaid, but can only expand in their own self-reproduction and indefinite subordination of citizen-debtors.

Third, congregations should support a national drive to set up a social education fund whereby every citizen of working age pays 2 percent (or an appropriate progressive rate) of his or her annual income to help subsidize students' education.

Finally, churches should mount a sustained campaign to put pressure on all colleges to decrease their tuitions and fees, and on governments to provide free education in all public colleges. Alleviating the burden of student loan debt is the prime duty of all social justice–committed citizens and institutions. Doing so will generate wealth for all. Doing so will make America greater.

Truths and Afflictions of the Modern Economy

In this chapter, we have been working to understand the ethical form of finance capital on its own terms. That is, we have attempted to grasp the pure kernel of the ethics of finance without presupposing a notion of sovereign or supreme good. We learned that in the global financial market form acts as its own "matter." This is both at the level of the actors, and at that of the commodities themselves. Products, commodities, have evolved into a fully-fledged and all-absorbing "form" of ethical actions and "drive" (*objet a*) of the players in the financial industry. This is because "they repeat in their own structure and relations the circulatory regime of global capital."[27] Thus, "derivatives [such as naked CDS] should be understood as commodified forms of drive. Products of the perceived need to protect investors against the risks involved in complex speculative financial transactions, derivatives make these transactions possible, thereby producing retroactively, their own conditions of emergence."[28]

The bottom line of our findings from these two observations is that the Void is constitutive of the whole operation of the global financial system. We are to view Wall Street as a pure being-for-itself. It is like what is left of a subject after it is freed from all positive content. The true source of what many liberal critics consider as Wall Street's "evil" is not the public good the financial industry sacrifices, not the contents emptied from products, and not the pursuit of *pure value*, but the very form itself.[29]

This is the impossibility, the constitutive lack, the incompleteness around which "substantial" Wall Street, the financial industry's network of substantial truths, structures itself. As we saw in chapter 4, the economy is always already *financialized* (as in finance being the constitutive hole of the economy); the substantial economy is the same thing as path in/to/into itself, which emerges or is phenomenalized as finance. The idea that we can keep the "evil" of finance at a safe distance from the "good economy" is an error. This idea misses the truth about how the modern economy works because the truth of the economy is constituted through the financial sector. Thus, the so-called "evil" of the financial sector might not be the form of the moral law of finance but the perspective that perceives the financial sector as external to the economy—and regards such externality as evil.[30]

Finance is an *affliction* to the economy. This is in the sense that it is not an external pressure imposed or pressing on the economy. Finance is *extimate*; it is what is in the economy more than the economy itself, a foreign body at the very heart of the economy.[31] The idea that we could simultaneously have a sophisticated modern economy and remain at an objective distance from the "evil" of finance ignores the way in which the split between economy and finance is part of the economy itself. Finance is that which was in the economy itself when it is not yet the economy. Far from being a "pathological" outsider, finance emerged precisely at the point when the primordial economy transcended basic production for daily consumption to stored value, when society produces today what it will consume tomorrow. Finance emerged at the point when excess-over-daily-needs emerged as the motive force for production, at the point where "surplus" became the cause of desire. Today, finance occupies the position of motive, and over time its empty form becomes its own end in itself, standing in for the surplus jouissance that our ancestors always wanted in our productive activities.[32]

The point I am emphasizing is that "evil" is inscribed into the very nature of the financial sector—more precisely, into the timeless character of the economy. Finance is a fissure at the core of the economy; its blind drive exists from the beginning, from the absolute zero point of the economy's prehistory. The economy's prehistory began with the split and made itself into a totalized whole. It sort of moved from a "place" of limitation, tranquility, and annihilation of surplus with tendency to fold back on itself to the potential "placelessness" of the void of limitless expansion.[33]

The exciting philosophic question here is not whether finance is evil or not, but how does the modern economy achieve or maintain consistency so as not to lose itself in the void of limitless expansion? Another question is: why did the economy "create" the financial sector? Far from being an invasion, inversion, or subversion of the economy, finance is the economy's most faithful companion, a form shadowing or driving content. Not only can the working of the economy not be understood without finance, but it would not be an economy if it did not bear finance within itself as the void of its limitless expansion.[34]

The crucial lesson to learn here is that it is wrong to think of the otherness of the finance sector as alienation of finance from the economic whole. The alienation of finance from the economic whole is simultaneously the alienation of the economic whole from itself. The economy is an assemblage of disparate elements (transactions) and traversed by gaps and inconsistencies. The economy is structured around the fundamental impossibility of the *futureness* it tries to cope with.

There is the fundamental impossibility of knowing (mastering) the future. It is the obstacle to the future that sustains the future. The future is the *a-present*; the negation of the present, and this negation is strictly immanent to economic transactions. The present never attains its goal or finds satisfaction within itself. In this case, the present and the future are not two segments, but the present and its impossibility (its failure) posited as separate; the present and its impossibility of existing as master of the future is externalized as the other. The future is the abyss in which present human economic activity that never reaches its goals performs its repetitive gesture and finds satisfaction in the very repetitive failure. Owing to the invocation and provocation of the future, the present never coincides with itself. Futureness is "nothing but a split between two forms of otherness"—the unsatisfactory present as other and the uncertain, uncontrollable future as the other. The split is not only this structure, it is also in excess of structure.[35]

Let me make this point clear with an example from Wall Street. Finance functions on impersonal trust and convention. Both trust and convention are specific forms of emotions. Trust is needed in the first place due to uncertainties and the insecurity of money as a future claim of society's wealth and promise.[36] Decision making about claims and promises rely on "future-oriented emotions." These emotions are often mistakenly considered to arise solely out of greed, fear, or personal desire, but as the research of Australian sociologist Jocelyn Pixley has shown, they are born out of "the unknowability of the future [that] drive economic life as much as does rational calculation."[37] Given fundamental uncertainties, expectations about the future value of assets are formed through conventions, emotions, and imaginations.

Financial products in a certain sense are trust that is packaged and sliced, diced, sold, and bought. More precisely, they are parcels of future hope and promises based on emotions of past performance and trust. Trust in a particular parcel alone is not enough to price, buy, and sell financial products. The market needs convention to price or evaluate any specific package of trust offered for sale. The convention (which is essentially a bet that the future will resemble the present and a way for rational investors to save face) is also engendered by uncertainty.

Normal finance prides itself on rationality. But in the midst of these inevitable uncertainties and insecurities there is an "emotional serpent in the Eden of assumed rationality."[38] Rationality about the future that is unpredictable and essentially unknowable requires emotions, future-oriented emotions. The importation of a "future" into the present is what enables investors or decision makers to act. As Keynes informs us, the grip of emotion, which he dubbed "animal spirits," is explained by uncertainty about the future.[39]

Todd McGowan in his book *Capitalism and Desire* argues that Keynes's description of economic reality in his books and essays is incomplete, missing some hidden depth, and cannot reach the "noumenal reality" of economic behavior in themselves, which is enjoyment, psychic investment in capitalism.[40] He chides Keynes for failing to penetrate the depth of "enjoyment" that allegedly sustains capitalist subjectivity or boom-bust cycle of production. What if there is no depth, but only the temporal and spatial separation of one transaction from another that produces a certain remainder that constitutes the drive of the ethical subject? This may imply that "it is the very process of separation that produces" the very future which makes it possible and which must be enjoyed and circled around.[41] More importantly, what if the failure McGowan highlights is the very sign that Keynes has touched the Real of the economy: the animal spirits? What if the very epistemological incompleteness is inscribed into the assemblage of economic transactions (economic reality) as their own ontological incompleteness? In fact, what undermines futureness (enjoyment) is the inscription of the subjective excess—which Keynes calls "animal spirits" and it may well indicate contact with the Real that eludes complete symbolization. Slavoj Žižek is accurate when he writes, "The Real coincides with the very obstacle to itself, the very thing that obscures access to the Real is the inscription of the Real. This is why in a proper dialectical approach, we should abandon the entire rhetoric of penetrating through deceptive appearances to the way things really are in themselves."[42]

In Keynes's conception of the "animal spirits" there is a coincidence of opposites. The highest and lowest orientations in human economic activities are conjoined. Out of the animality of human instincts, the greatest boost is given to production, but out of this also comes the obstacle to economic production. There are moments when capitalists overcome their "animal humanity" and turn into optimistic investors. But at other times their animality interrupts the continuous immanent flow of investment decisions. The highest and lowest tendencies of the animal spirits are like the two sides of a Möbius strip: if you move from the center of inclination you will discover that you have progressed into the heart of the other, the opposite. In this sense, the "animal spirits" is somewhat homologous to the penis (organ of insemination and urination), as Hegel conceptualized or analogizes it in his *Phenomenology of Spirit*:

> The *depth* which Spirit brings forth from within—but only as far as its picture-thinking consciousness [representation] where it lets it remain—and the *ignorance* of this consciousness about what it really is saying, are the same conjunction of the high and the low which, in the living being, Nature naively expresses when it combines the organ of its highest fulfillment, the organ of generation, with the organ of urination. The infinite judgment, *qua* infinite, would be the fulfillment of life that comprehends itself; the consciousness of the infinite judgment that remains at the level of picture-thinking [representation] behaves as urination.[43]

There is an economy because the economy is in itself *non-all*, traversed by antagonism, tracked by the animal spirits and marked by the constitutive impossibility of futureness. Put differently, there is an economy because it cannot be stabilized or exist fully. There is a void at its very core, which it is always trying to master.

A close reading of Keynes's animal spirits actually reveals that our economic system (reality) is a result of a double failure, the incontinence of the penis that is the animal spirits. We have economic growth, excessive boom, because of the failure to restrain the capitalist penis from executing its highest function (secreting sperm, the juice needed to engender new products and expand the production possibilities frontier). On the other hand, we have contraction, the inability of the same capitalist organ to restrain itself from peeing (raining) on its parade. Thus, the premise of Keynes's understanding of the capitalist business cycle is that the economic reality (system) is "the outcome of its redoubled failure."[44] The economy emerges and lives "out of its own impossibility, i.e., it is the obstacle to [the economy] which sustains [the economy]."[45]

Concluding Thoughts

From our discussions in part II it is clear that Wall Street has reduced every transaction, object, commodity to their dead components, leaving only "mechanized forms." But it is precisely through this mechanization that the spirit of the community (or genuine) ethics can arise and assert itself in contrast to the deadness and *kenotic* (economic kenosis, emptying of content) life of exchange.[46] By this I mean that it is precisely through the freedom and singularity of the individual, the *ex-position* of self to other selves, contradictions of social mechanism (wherein parts or sectors are indifferent to the welfare of other parts or the whole) of a split society, and not through a return to premodern organic harmony, unity, or essence, that our ethics needs to thrive, as Jean-Luc Nancy argues in his *Inoperative Community*. There are two ways of asserting this split (the social mechanism), instead of trying to avoid or "overcome" it. One way is to confront the future that capitalism promises and sells to all of us and alternatively think of another future within it. This is to think of the capitalist future as split within itself, involving an inherent gap, and our true task is to withdraw from both sides of such a formatted future and to dwell in the gap between them. We will explore this option in chapter 6. In chapter 7, we explore the second option, that of pluralism that emphasizes singularity, freedom, and mutuality. Here we will explore

Nancy's theory of exposition of beings as way of identifying with ruptures (split) as a mode of being. A community entails the exposition, the presence of each self to all. The presence of self to self precludes thinking of the community as an essence or effectuating its own essence as something beyond the exposition of self to self. An economy is this exposition: the co-appearing of finite selves, ensembles of selves, and each self is exposed to an outside. This outside is only an outside of another ensemble of selves. The "being" of community is the exposure, exposition of selves, which "are themselves constituted by sharing, they are distributed and placed, or rather *spaced*, by the sharing that makes them *others*: other for one another," and "whose relationship—the sharing itself—is not a communion."[47] Thus without this exposure and sharing, the community would not exist. But before we engage the beauty of Nancy's thought in chapter 7, we need to first explore what it would mean to abolish a capitalist-formatted future so as to release the "ecstasy of sharing" as a basis of pluralism.

PART III

Singular-Plural Subjects
Deactivation of the Capitalist Future

Chapter 6

Abolish the Future

Introduction

We have learned throughout this book that subjects are invested in the capitalist narrative of dissatisfaction, which it claims to be uniquely situated to address under its promise of future enrichment or fulfillment. Although, the orientation to better (future) satisfaction predates capitalism and was present at the birth of finance or the split of the primordial, Todd McGowan has a point when he states in his book *Capitalism and Desire* that citizens do not realize that the repetition of failure to find full satisfaction is key to capitalism's psychic hold over them.[1]

The primordial tilt to the future—which capitalism inherited and "weaponized" under its commodity form of production—has power to discipline or transform behavior or sustain desire for higher levels of satisfaction because it is a fundamental gesture of promise, the hope of a more complete satisfaction of desire, and enjoyment, which tomorrow (next time) holds. If one could only deny oneself a part of present consumption (and invest), then tomorrow would open up a variety of levels of satisfaction that are not possible today. But this promised land of complete satisfaction is never completely attained—it is always at the edge of realization. The denial of consumption, which is in turn the investment of the saved consumption, turns in on itself as the promise to accumulate, becoming an endless path to ultimate satisfaction. So, the promise of the future never loses its power. In the logic of this fundamental fantasy of the economy, the present is always not fully satisfying; in the face of the future-to-come, the next present is to arrive. The "substantive" content of the present must be declared hollow or hollowed out for the promise of the empty form of the next time (tomorrow), which the subjects of the economy will successfully fill up.[2] The future becomes surplus-future, a stand-in for something sacrificed in order to create more satisfaction, *surplus-jouissance*. The future becomes what can be grown and accumulated.

Of course, neither our ancestors nor we have quite gained that extra future, as more (better) future is always the enemy of (present, attained) future. This surplus-future, the pursuit of the gain-of-future, is caught up in the compulsion to repeat. Because the gain-of-future operates through repetition: "one misses the goal and repeats the movement, trying again and again, so that the true aim is no longer the intended goal but the repetitive movement of attempting to reach it."[3] At the end, the gain-of-future is "attained" by the repeated performance to reach it. The surplus-enjoyment is derived by working (driving) toward it, and not actually by reaching the intended goal.

Therefore, the major ethical challenge set before us is how to *abolish the future*, abolish the mesmerizing future formatted with capitalist promise that incites consumers' desire for desire, inflames our dissatisfaction with the consumption of every commodity, and constricts our freedom. The abolition of the future is not simply a rejection of the future or an indifference to futurity; it is to go against the future of capital and its politics of preprogrammed ends. The aim of this stance is to exit from the capitalist mechanisms of the future, psychic investment in the governing fantasy of the future, the liberation of our future from the commodity form it has been made to assume.

Once again, to abolish the future is not a romantic embrace of the present because of its jouissance or pagan rejection or closure of the future or because of any belief in beyond-history afterlife, but because it is a way of interrupting our drift into a formatted capitalist future, which might be catastrophic for general human flourishing. Following Slavoj Žižek, the abolition of the future means to take upon ourselves "the risk of giving birth to some radical Otherness 'to come.'"[4] The abolition of the future at a deeper level "does not designate the closure, the impossibility of change, but what we should be striving for—to break the hold of the catastrophic 'future' and thereby open up a space for something New 'to come.'"[5]

To enact this move we must learn to separate from the capitalist machine of jouissance and learn to be "omnipotent" before the harsh face of late capitalism by reckoning with our *impotentiality*.⁶ Human freedom is fast losing its *impotentiality*, that is, being able to abstain from doing what capitalism demands. The world of markets now constitutes a state of exception where the distinction between human freedom and the freedom of capital are rendered inoperable. Human potentiality (disconnected from its impotentiality) is subservient to the actuality of capitalism. Human freedom is made to serve predetermined ends of capital. We must relearn how to live in the present without the perpetual pursuit of abundance in the name of a better future. My argument for abolishing the future is similar to that of German philosopher Frank Ruda, who argues for the abolition of freedom—we must act as if the end time has come, as if there is no tomorrow-to-come, no capitalist future.⁷ This maneuver allows us to see the capitalist future as if it has already happened, a fate we can now retroactively change to create new possibilities. Ruda asks: "Assuming that this catastrophe [of formatted future] is our destiny might then retroactively change the conditions of possibility of this very destiny. It may retroactively make it possible to change what appears to us as fate."⁸

This way of being in the world takes the future not as something ahead of us, but as something that has already happened. If we can assume this stance, our sense of acquired release may give us the courage to alter the certainty of the programmed capitalist future, or at least to nudge it into a different path. Perhaps, Micaiah's vision (prophecy) of Israel's defeat in 2 Kings 22 hinted at this idea of inversion of the future, turning it into something that has already happened. King Ahab of Israel had invited Micaiah to prophesy whether Israel would win its impending war with Ramoth Gilead. To cut a long story short, after much drama and hesitancy, Micaiah pronounced these words to Ahab and Jehoshaphat, the king of Judah, who was visiting him: "I saw all Israel scattered on the hills like sheep without a shepherd, and the Lord said, 'These people have no master. Let each one go home in peace'" (v. 17). Micaiah did not say he *sees* or *shall see* defeat; rather, he says he *saw*. He saw the future before it arrived. The king did not like this prophecy, and sent Micaiah to prison. Ahab did not get the hint of the inversion of the future or fate in Micaiah's prophecy. Ahab's goal should have been to change the conditions that would lead to the prophecy coming true, thereby altering his destiny. In the religious culture of ancient Israel, Ahab could have deployed technologies of the self, communal prayers, and other cultic practices to change the destiny of defeat, and thus move to split the prophetically formatted future. He could have split the patterned future before him and his nation in two: a future of catastrophe, and a future that could birth something new to come—some "radical otherness to come." In this way, he could choose to indwell the crack between the past trajectory of life, the new future to come, and the fate ahead of him. King Hezekiah before him, when confronted with a prophecy of death, acted to split the future and saved his life, as reported in 2 Kings 20.

Below I offer some ideas of a future outside the framing within which capitalism has encased our future. These ideas encourage us to think of the capitalist future as split within itself and learn to dwell in the gap of split. This is about enacting, performing, imagining a new temporality by which humans insert themselves between the present and the formatted capitalist future, thereby exercising their uniquely and supremely human capacity to begin something anew and display their distinctiveness as individuals, as Hannah Arendt has taught us. This is about enacting or recognizing ruptures of preexisting temporal conditions, that is, contemporary social orders—ruptures that must be created and sustained by *actors* in every generation. This requires that the actors or subjects be faithful to and propagate the rupture in historicization initially caused by them or generations before them.

Splitting the Future of Capital

To the split logic of the capitalist economic system, the political (where being is staked, contested, and ruptured) must equally respond with an ethos that matches it—or at least understands how it works. The political today must, among other things, be "man's release from his self-incurred tutelage," as Kant put it. And this "tutelage" is the insufficiency of the audacity in tracking, using, and following the self-assured guidance of the logic of split independently of the capitalist trajectory of history. The contrast here is between an incipient fullness of freedom (the reconnection of potentiality and impotentiality of action, as argued in chapter 3) that is self-assured by the boldness of a novel *living into the crack of capitalism* to resist its formatted future, and the lethargic inherited trajectory of a capitalist formatted future now oppressive, and being evaded if not completely surpass-able.[9]

How do we begin to imagine a future that is outside the preformatting of capitalism? One way is to think of the capitalist future as split within itself, involving an inherent gap, but the real task is to withdraw from both sides of such a formatted future and dwell in the gap between them. To use the words of Lee Edelman from a different context, "far from perpetuating the fantasy of meaning's eventual realization, the [withdrawal] comes to figure the bar to every realization of [capitalist] futurity, the resistance, internal to the social, to every social structure or form."[10] Not a sovereign capitalism, not a capitalism without its self-revolutionizing power, but only a futureless capitalism can still save us. Put differently, only a split future will save us.

This is a future that exists as a companion of the capitalist formatted future, a "companion to the movement of capitalism, yet an oppositional movement created by capitalism itself."[11] The potency to constitute this alternative future comes from capitalism itself. Karl Marx had a similar idea of communism: rather than being an outsider or a replacement force, it is what splits capitalism from within. Instead of communism being a *constitutive idea* (ideal), it is a *regulative idea* that offers an alternative perspective to critique and contest the reality of capitalism. In an addendum to *The Germany Ideology*, co-written with Friedrich Engels, Marx states that "communism is . . . not a *state of affairs* which is to be established, an *ideal* to which reality [will] have to adjust itself. We call communism *the* real movement, which abolishes [*aufhebt*] the present state of things, the conditions of this movement result from the premises now in existence."[12]

The capitalist formatted future flows out of the self-reproductive futurity in capital's auto-replicating movement. An internal split rips capitalism, and its promise of a better future is its way of dealing with this inherent antagonism. What Todd McGowan identifies as the process or means capitalism uses to capture the libidinal lives of consumers, the sword that wounds and destabilizes the structures of psychic stability of subjects, is the same that heals capitalism. Capitalism lashes out and grabs citizens into its orbit of formatted or ever-more promising future because it ever needs the future to heal its own wound. In this relationship of exchange, which is inescapably dependent upon the future, there is a form of fear: capitalists are afraid of products not being sold, workers are afraid of not selling their labor-power or being discharged, and consumers are afraid of being deprived of the latest satisfaction, which appears in the guise of desire.[13]

There are two kinds of future in the movement represented by M-C-M¹ (M-C/ C-M¹), as M-C (buying of labor-power) and C-M (selling products) are split spatially and temporally via money. If this two-part movement is disrupted, capitalism cannot sell its bill of formatted future. In buying labor power as a commodity (M-C) to potentially produce products, capitalists depend on recouping their investments in the future. This expectation is actualized when surplus value is realized in circulation (selling of products), that is, when M-C becomes C-M¹. This exchange process upon which capitalism depends, this capital's movement of accumulation, has two parts, two critical moments: production and circulation (consumption), and this split constitutes capital (also its destiny and the source of its crisis) and forms the basis of its promise of a better future.[14] Kojin Karatani teaches us:

> Here let us reconsider the meaning that industrial capital is based upon labor-power commodity. This implies not only that industrial capital hires workers to make them work, but also, and more importantly, that surplus value is attained only by workers, who in *totality* buy back what they produce. (Although what workers buy are consumer goods, if they were not sold, neither could producer's goods be sold.) That is to repeat that the accumulation of capital is realized not only in the production process, but also, and ultimately in the circulation process.[15]

He goes on to argue that workers as consumers can disrupt this split process of capital's movement of accumulation, if labor movements can form alliances with consumers' movements, "not as a political coalition between existing movements but a totally new movement itself."[16] According to him, capitalism must be engaged on two fronts: by those selling to it their labor-power, and by those buying its products in the form of movements of consumers' boycotts. "As long as our minds are split between process of production and process of circulation, it is impossible to resist capital's accumulation and the relation of production inherent in capitalism. The opposition to a capitalist nation-state should be neither a workers' movement nor a consumers' movement; this should be a movement of workers qua consumers, and consumers qua workers. The movement must be a transnational association of consumers/workers."[17]

The specific notion of a split future, which has driven our analysis of opposition to capitalism, appears to be an antinomy. Karl Marx appears to have dealt with a similar antinomy when he argues that surplus value is attained from the process of circulation and the same cannot arise from the process of circulation.[18] "Capitalism cannot therefore arise from the circulation, and it is equally impossible for it to arise apart from circulation. It must have its origin both in circulation and not in circulation."[19] In the same vein, and given the ability of capital to absorb alternatives into itself, we can say that the split future therefore cannot arise from capitalism and equally cannot arise apart from capitalism. The emergence of the split future "must, and yet must not, take place in the sphere of [capitalism]. These are the conditions of the problem. *Hic Rhodus, hic salta!*"[20] Split future within capitalism is an antinomy. This antinomy is solved when we invoke an alternative value system to the one created by capitalism. The problem is solved (addressed) when we grasp the split future in the difference between value systems.[21]

When we say "abolish the future," we are not saying attain a future that is outside the relations of capitalism, or reach a future that comes from an external point to them, but instead a future at the very limit of the relations of capitalism—at the point it cannot absorb.[22] "The" limit does not exist, but there is a "limitness." What this means is that the character or quality of the future that marks the limit of capitalism cannot be described ahead of its arrival. It cannot be predicted. Though we cannot say whether we have reached the limit or not, we can bring it under our judgment of ethics or justice without being able to describe it in any substantial way. There is no metalanguage that we can access that will completely interpret all phenomena and enable us to see the capitalist mode of production, the late capitalist society, as completely revealed in our analytical model. The truth about the limit of capitalism "will always be located outside of knowledge, anyone's knowledge," but capitalism is limitable.[23] Its patterned future can be scattered and a new future "beyond" (at its limit) its trajectory ushered in. The new future is also without predicate. The future never stops coming, unfolding, and continues to be formed and re-formed over time. The *limitness* that exists within the capitalist future, that split, gap within the capitalist future itself, is the edge, the eschaton of capitalism. So, in a certain sense, *limitness*, which is at the edge of the space-time of capitalist trajectory of formatted future, is the true *eschatos* (in the original meaning of a spatial or temporal end/edge). This alternative future will take place at this edgy and porous boundary. The effort to live into this gap or at this edge is not only about relating to the world as it *is*, but also *as it can be* given a particular vision of unexplored possibilities. In this venture of mediating the worlds of "is" and "as," the subject inserts herself between the capitalist preformatted future and a new possible future of the time spectrum. From here she seeks to break with social institutions and shared human existence and force them toward a new horizon of possibilities. Suspended between (or subtracted from) the "no more" (or no longer acceptable) and the "not-yet," she must fight two antagonists, resisting one and dragging in one. She may have the dream of jumping out of the struggle. But this is not possible for her. The *place of limitness of capitalist future* is our unavoidable site of struggle against the dark forces of past, present, and future. We cannot afford to elude this battle if we want to create a flourishing economy for all God's children. We must step into capitalism's continuum of time to create a gap between its formatted future and an alternative future where we change the meaning of the past and the present, and stop or redirect their oppressive trajectory in order to help life better flourish.

We must learn or re-learn how to live in the cracks, in the splits in the contemporary order of being. All those committed to redirecting the oppressive trajectory of capitalist time need to insert themselves into the cracks in the order of being without jumping out of capitalist time altogether. In this gap, they form coalitions and create new context, rather than waiting for the capitalist formatted future to carry them along as flotsams in a swift current. These kinds of citizens as committed subjects are marked by *fidelity* to the discerning of possibilities visible from a particular context of capitalist time. Subjectivation is basically a process of striving for the very limit of the relations of capitalism, creating and actualizing possibilities, which remakes social coexistence for the sake of human flourishing. Subjectivation is living in the splits, cracks, or ruptures that disrupt the extant orders of beings.

Split, the bane of ruptures in being "is fast becoming the banality" of late capitalism.[24] In the twenty-first century capitalist economy, we can have splits without emancipatory disruption because we can have disruptions in our lives without real changes. In a world without emancipation, both change and disruption yet abound! The more things change under capitalism, the more they remain the same. The (pseudo) splits are assertions of capitalist power, not ruptures in the order of being.

Capitalism is recasting split into a normal, usual phenomenon integral to our socioeconomic existence or as its historicity. As a result, split ceases to be something *evental*, losing its disruptive and transformative power, "and becomes instead simply a rather banal characterization of the human situation."[25] Split appears to be divested of its power to rupture ongoing social automatism, along with its power to upturn the givens of a situation, to reveal the new, and to shock or surprise. But we must resist this banalization of split, reject turning it into its antithesis, and affirm its power to question our existence.

Let us pause to address a possible objection to the whole idea of finding a limit within capitalist time as a conception of resistance. The critic may quarrel with the idea of abolishing the future, and yet not attaining a future that is outside the relations of capitalism or reaching a future that does not come from an external point to them, but from the very limit of the relations of capitalism—at the point it cannot absorb. The critic might contend that a proper alternative to capitalism should be to completely abandon the capitalist relations of production and retain its self-revolutionizing power. This is a fantasy that Marx in some moments harbored. This is the dream of having capitalism without capitalism, the utopian dream of having the self-revolutionizing, perpetual motion of capital without exploitation that we mentioned in chapter 3. As Slavoj Žižek puts it in his usually blunt and irreverent style, we cannot eliminate exploitation without ruining capitalism. The capitalist form—the expropriation of surplus value—is the necessary condition for the revolutionizing motion of capital.[26] Any limit to growth will destroy capitalism. In order to reproduce itself, it must constantly increase, and produce. Capitalism depends for its survival and vitality on endless expansion; therefore, it is always integrating into its process, goal, and direction any external limit before it. Every barrier is only a challenge to be overcome, as it does not constitute an absolute boundary. Thus, we cannot have capitalism without its self-revolutionizing power. This is where our concept of limitness comes, as an internal split within the future time of capitalism. We need a concept of limit that is within the infinite drive of capitalism's self-revolutionizing power—this will be a limit it cannot integrate.

This is where Hegel's notion of *bad infinite* and *true infinite* comes in handy. A bad infinite has no external limit. But a true infinite makes its limit constitutive of itself. Its limits are not external, but internal. Hegel describes bad and good versions of the infinite in this way: "The image of progression in infinity is the straight *line*; the infinite is only at the two limits of this line, and always only where the latter (which is existence) is not but *transcends itself*, and in its non-existence, that is, in the indeterminate. As true infinite, bent back upon itself, its image becomes the circle, the line that has reached itself, closed and wholly present, without *beginning* and *end*."[27] The crux of the conceptual issue here is that this idea of limit within limit (that is, *limitness*) enables us to envision an alternative to the formatted future of capitalism without reverting to a finite logic of capitalism's self-revolutionizing power, an alternative to an oppressive capitalist future "that nonetheless remains within the spirit of modernity" and not regress to "the finite logic of traditional society."[28] As McGowan states it: "The limit that capitalism cannot integrate is that of the true infinite. This limit is internal, a self-limitation of the socioeconomic system itself [or more precisely, of the subjects themselves]. A self-limiting system, precisely what Hegel theorizes with his concept of the true infinite, is the only tenable alternative to capitalism. It does not pose an arbitrary limit that the capitalist system can quickly subsume but clings to the limit as constitutive of the system itself. To subsume the limit thus becomes unthinkable."[29]

In my 2014 book, *Economics in Spirit and Truth: A Moral Philosophy of Finance*, I put forward the idea of unpredictability of human behavior as an internal limit to capitalism.[30] Here I conceived finance (economic transactions, for that matter) as the self-externalization of the human spirit. I was searching for a way to nudge citizens to recognize their participation in capitalism's bad infinite, and thus force the system to come to terms with its constitutive finitude. The human spirit was articulated as the inherent yet contingent obstacle to finance capital. I thus conceived human spirit not as an external limit to finance capital, "but as the internal limit of human society," or the social order.[31] Finance capital requires the predictability of human behavior to function, but the unpredictability of human ethical commitment or orientation will throw off its progress. This social, ethical unpredictability "can become an internal limit of the social order, the basis for a true infinite. By starting with this unpredictability as the limit, social production would orient itself around addressing this limit without any possibility of ever transcending it."[32]

In the same vein of thinking of the true infinite as the possible destiny of finance capital, let us dare to say its logic of bad infinite might lead it here, that is, to the internal, constitutive limit. Its pursuit of emptying of content (as we saw in chapter 5) will bring it to encounter the limit of void as its own internal limit. As Marx once said, "the *true barrier* to capitalist production is *capital itself*."³³ The unrestrained emptying of content as a means of increasing production and profits will undermine capital accumulation, which spells its failure. The endless progress of bad infinite will eventually trip finance capital to stumble on its true infinite rather than reach the fantasy of unrestricted unleashing of forces of production and complete absence of any limit or barrier.

Behavioral unpredictability alone will not do the trick. McGowan also recognizes that citizens must limit their desires, as capitalism depends on our material desires to function. Thus, in addition to the ethics of unpredictability, I also suggested that citizens regard their existence as a potentiality, a way of resisting (finance) capitalism. This is to say citizens should identify with their incapacity to satisfy all their desires or to act precisely in the way the economic system wants them to act, and learn to derive satisfaction from failure to meet all the demands of capitalism's bad infinite or their material desires. In making this suggestion, I turned to Giorgio Agamben's definition of potentiality: "To be potential means: to be one's own lack, *to be in relation to one's own incapacity*. Beings that exist in the mode of potentiality *are capable of their own impotentiality*; and only in this way do they become potential. They *can be* because they are in a relation to their own non-Being."³⁴

This account of impotentiality, for Agamben, gestures to an orientation to interrupt the productivity or potential productivity of capitalism, as citizens accept their own incapacity to realize all their material desires. Of course, we need to add that "the political valence of impotentiality is never cut and dried . . . Withdrawal from the capitalist system energizes the system by providing it with a new potential that it must work to actualize."³⁵

This idea of self-limiting brings us to crucial connections in the thoughts of Saint Paul and Hegel. The specific nexus of their thoughts in the area of love of neighbor offers us a lens to look into how to live in the crack of capitalist future, in the split of capitalist time. Let us now borrow theoretical provocations from Saint Paul and Hegel. Paul splits time between now and the eschaton; time into the time now (messianic time) and the end of time and eternity, and time into time that remains between time and its end, as Giorgio Agamben teaches us.³⁶ He also splits Jesus's notion of love into love of God and love of neighbor, conveniently deemphasizing the former.³⁷ Hegel also splits Paul's notion of love into the empty form of an "ought" directed to individuals (a mere "ought" that is contingent and contentless) and as value realizable as an activity of the state (that is, governmental institutions, civil society, laws, and practices of a given community). Hegel argues in §425 of the *Phenomenology of the Spirit*[38] that the love of neighbor without the activities (practices) of the state (ongoing relationships and social practices of "reciprocal recognition") is meaningless and contentless.[39] For Hegel, any talk of love of neighbor without power analysis, without considering if members of society recognize one another as loci of authority and accountability, is incomplete.[40] Hegel's point is that we need contextual social practices that will make the command of love determinate, which reason alone or individual sentiments alone cannot do. We need institutions and social practices in order to love our neighbors well—*actively* and *intelligently*.[41]

In the overall context of our interest in this chapter, Hegel's theorization of neighbor's love offers an insight into how to live in the crack of the capitalist future. To work this out in the purview of Pauline theology, let us start by comprehending Paul's splitting of Jesus's command to love. In Romans 13, Saint Paul radically reduced Jesus's understanding of the Word, the law and the prophets. "No dual commandment, but rather *one* commandment. I regard this as an absolutely revolutionary act," writes the Jewish philosopher Jacob Taubes.[42] Paul, claiming to stand in the messianic time inaugurated by Jesus, reinterprets Jesus's understanding of the law and political ethics of believers in ways that appear to circumscribe it (Romans 13:8–14). In response to a question from the lawyer about which commandment in the law is the greatest, Jesus answered, "'You shall love the Lord your God with all your heart, and with all your soul, and with all your mind.' This is the greatest and first commandment. And the second is like it: 'You shall love your neighbor as yourself.' On these two commandments hang all the law and the prophets" (Matthew 22:35–40). But Paul in summing up the law omitted the command to love God: "Owe no one anything, except to love one another; for the one who loves another has fulfilled the law. The commandments: You shall not commit adultery; You shall not murder; You shall not steal; You shall not covet, and any other commandment, are summed up in this word, Love your neighbor as yourself. Love does no wrong to a neighbor; therefore, love is the fulfilling of the law" (Romans 13:8–10).

Paul sublates the command to love God into the love of the neighbor without even the force of the divine mandate, as in Leviticus 19:18: "You shall not take vengeance or bear a grudge against any of your people, but you shall love your neighbor as yourself: I am the Lord." As New Testament historian L.L. Welborn puts it: "Without the divine mandate, it is scarcely possible to imagine that one could undertake something as unreasonable and difficult as loving the neighbor as oneself."[43] Paul's call to mutual love, not even backed by the force of a divine mandate as in Leviticus, is quite radical. The neighbor in Paul's injunction—unlike that of Leviticus 19:17–18—is not a brother, sister, or kinsperson, but the *other* by reason of class, race, ethnicity, gender, and so on.

> The obligation of mutual love not only traverses these distinctions, but embraces "the other," as the embodiment of difference. Paul's choice of the word "other," rather than "neighbor" or "brother," was no doubt intended to short-circuit the widespread assumption in Greco-Roman society that true love depended upon sameness, affinity, and familiarity, and that the true friend was a "mirror of the self." The sweeping nature of Paul's formulation suggests that Paul had in mind not just particular cases, but the ethic of the community: a community that practices love of "the other" can never be a totality—that is, a group closed upon itself. A people that practices love of "the other" is perpetually incomplete.[44]

Why would a Christian undertake a task as difficult as loving "the other," or the neighbor, without a divine mandate? Even with a divine mandate, it is a very difficult task, as Freud informs us in his commentary on Leviticus 19:18. He evaluates the injunction to love the neighbor at different degrees of propinquity to the recipients of our love. He starts from the case of a neighbor who is not a perfect stranger.

> We will adopt a naïve attitude towards it, as if we were meeting it for the first time. Thereupon we find ourselves unable to suppress a feeling of astonishment, as at something unnatural. Why should we do this? What good is it to us? Above all, how can we do such a thing? How could it possibly be done? My love seems to me a valuable thing that I have no right to throw away without reflection. It imposes obligations on me, which I must be prepared to make sacrifices to fulfill. If I love someone, he must be worthy of it in some way or other. . . . He will be worthy of it if he is so like me in

important respects that I can love myself in him; worthy of it if he is so much more perfect than I that I can love my ideal of myself in him.[45]

Freud brings his objection to Leviticus 19:18 to a crescendo when he writes:

> The bit of truth behind all this—one so eagerly denied—is that men are not gentle, friendly creatures wishing for love, who simply defend themselves if they are attacked, but that a powerful measure of desire for aggression has to be reckoned as part of their instinctual endowment. The result is that their neighbor is to them not only a possible helper or sexual object, but also a temptation to them to gratify their aggressiveness on him, to exploit his capacity for work without recompense, to use him sexually without his consent, to seize his possessions, to humiliate him, to cause him pain, to torture him and to kill him. *Homo homini lupus*; who has the courage to dispute it in the face of all evidence in his own life and in history?[46]

Where did Paul get the courage to dispute such a story of humankind? How did Paul embrace or assume away the strangeness of the neighbor who in Freud's term cannot be loved? What new communal consciousness did Paul think himself capable of awakening in Christians that could work the magic? How do we seek to clarify "Paul's eschatological faith [that] enables his confidence in a community capable of obligating itself to mutual love"?[47] More importantly, why did Paul lift the burden of loving God from the new messianic community, from the new people of God?

Following Welborn, I argue that Paul lifted the burden of the love of God because he believed he was in the messianic time. For those who have experienced the calling of the Messiah to a new community are those who now recognize that while they were still sinners God commended his love toward them and the Messiah died for them: the weak, ungodly, and enemies (Romans 5:5–11), and for them there were no longer two imperatives, but one—to love the one for whom Christ died. This is at once recognition and affirmation of the kenotic movement of the divine love, which not only led to the sacrificial death of

God, but has also "sublated the first commandment."⁴⁸ Welborn brings his reflection on Paul's radical reduction of the dual commandment to a close by drawing an inference: "One who has awakened to the messianic nature of his or her own existence is empowered to do the most difficult thing—the thing that Freud, as Paul's spiritual heir, rightly judged to be unreasonable and impossible in human terms: to love the neighbor."⁴⁹

It is based on the Pauline sensibility that those who are called into messianic community have only one imperative: to love the other as themselves. As per his reasoning, Christians' commitment to their membership, the messianic calling, their gratefulness to God's offering of Jesus to the world and Christ's suffering for them, and their awareness of their embodiment of God's tender care for all humanity, compel in them the love of the neighbor. This is all about grace, as can be easily understood from Romans 5. In this reckoning, the grace of God that was shed abroad on all God's children calls them to the love of the other. In the new community of Jesus, the love of God by its members is presupposed. The love of neighbor (the other) is implied in the love of God—as its presupposition. The love of God (as in both God's love for people and people's love for God) is the constituting power of the community. The first part of the dual commandment is the *constituting love* of the second part, the *constituted love*. The first is the violence of passion, so to speak, that posits the law of neighborly love.

This awakening to the messianic foundation of Christian social ethic for Paul does not have the individual as the solitary subject, but the community, the individuals within a community. Paul in Romans 13:8 has a *collective subject* in mind, an "awakened communal consciousness," as both the verb and the pronouns are in plural form in the original Greek.⁵⁰

Now a question quickly arises: how does Hegel understand this collective subject, the communal consciousness that has grasped the full import of God's tender, loving care? This is not exactly how Hegel would have put the question. He has no such explicit resort to God's tender love as a presupposition for splitting love of neighbor into the two parts of empty individual love and love via community practices in §425 of the *Phenomenology*. But luckily, the Hegelian split not only has its presupposition, but also some kind of *collective subject* as Paul. Hegel's idea of love of neighbor that is realizable only through the state assumes that members of the community have mutually agreed to recognize one another; they are invested in a network of "relationships and practices of reciprocal recognition that binds us to one another in the midst of ongoing difference and conflict."[51] American philosopher Molly Farneth argues in her brilliant book *Hegel's Social Ethics* that Hegel's philosophy of conflict and conflict resolution or social ethics presupposes a community held together by members (fallible human beings) who recognize everyone's authority to make truth-claims and give reasons for his or her actions, and everyone's actions and reasons are accountable to the judgment of all others; that is, they are justifiable in a publicly accessible manner.

Just as Paul felt it necessary to talk only about loving the neighbor, foregrounding the love of God, let us also focus on Hegel's notion of the love of neighbor that foregrounds "reciprocal recognition." In this way, we do not have to assume that all citizens worship one God or must only honor one type of moral vision flowing from one particular religious tradition. The presupposition—which is Hegel's—is that members (bourgeoisie and workers, or Wall Streeters and Main Streeters) of the American society are committed to humans living together with their differences.

Given Hegel's account of neighborly love, in order to live in the crack of capitalist time, to create and sustain love amid the capitalist/commodity form of love, "we're going to need a socially and politically attuned account of what love is and what it requires of us. And we're going to need concrete relationships, practices, and institutions that make it possible for us to love our neighbors well."[52] These are practices and relationships of reciprocal recognition that can set internal limits on the working of the bad infinite of capitalism, on the behaviors of individuals on Wall Street. As Hegel demonstrates in his analysis of the wicked consciousness (akin to the arbitrary capitalists who follow only their own consciences or convictions) and the judging consciousness (akin to the liberals who think that they are following the objective moral law, the good of society) in §666–670 of *Phenomenology*, reconciliation between the two subjectivities is possible insofar as no one party wants to humiliate the other or claims to be a carrier of perfect moral rectitude. Rather, each party acknowledges that his or her actions are only an expression of particular commitments or beliefs.[53] The point is to have a political praxis that insists that as citizens we acknowledge our subjective responsibility or accountability, that we have something to say about each other's commitments to the project of living together; we acknowledge "the *social practices* through which individuals' commitments, including intentions and judgments, can be evaluated, challenged, and shaped by others."⁵⁴ This is a necessary political dimension to any economico-psychoanalytic conception of setting internal limits to the capitalism as a bad infinite. The idea of unpredictability of human behavior as an internal limit to capitalism must be made concrete, actualized as social practices, institutions, and relationships that go beyond individuals or sentiments of religiously pious citizens. In Hegel's thinking, without this, love is nothing; without splitting love into individual sentiment and love made concrete in politics of reciprocal recognition, the command to love thy neighbor is a mere ought, an empty form of a universal law like Kant's *Sollen*. Once again, let me pull back and say I am not holding my breath waiting for the politics of reciprocal recognition to provide the internal limit to capitalism. Nonetheless, I believe that the political is the best option we have to restage the formatted future of capitalism.

Concluding Remarks

It is in the light of having necessary limits and avoiding being trapped in the logic of capitalism's bad infinite that we must now raise the issue of theology of abundance for serious reconsideration. The usual (liberal) theological image of society's abundance that eviscerates all limits and restraints on productive forces (Marx's fantastic image of communism) is only a theorization of capitalism's bad infinite. To be sure, liberal theologians are anti-capitalist and are staunch advocates of equality and human flourishing for all, yet they betray their critique of capitalism and buy into the psychic appeal of capitalism of always imagining and promising a better future. Their own well-meaning and sincere anti-capitalist stance and commitment are ways of leading them to capitalism's bad infinite via their disdain for conceptions of limit and scarcity. Their grave error is to misunderstand the logic of equality. As McGowan puts it:

> The logic of an egalitarian society is not that there is nothing missing, that society has reached self-realization. It is not a society of unleashed and unlimited productivity, as it is for Marx. Instead, the egalitarian order involves a recognition of a necessary limit that will not only function as a boundary to its growth but that will simultaneously constitute growth as a possibility. Rather than attempting to overcome this limit—whatever it is—egalitarian society will nurture it as the

society's own essence. It would be a society that embraced its obstacle as its very condition of possibility.[55]

In chapter 7 we will explore the questions of theology of abundance and scarcity as they impinge on economy theology. Some readers will have already noticed that this book has a methodological intent, and in the next chapter I make this explicit. The arguments about scarcity and abundance are linked with pluralism; scarcity, appropriately conceived, nudges us toward an "ecstasy of sharing," and pluralism ought to be conceived as a way of politically coping with scarcity rightly. The new methodology suggests that economic theologians (ethicists) need to be steeped in political theory/philosophy. The politico-economic analysis of the split economy provided in this book has demonstrated the urgent need for the kind of politics to nudge (compel?) Wall Street to submit to the judgment of others, the community of citizens who recognize their individual and collective responsibilities to submit to reciprocal accountability and authority, and to commit to a model of public discourse that accents relations of reciprocal recognition, pluralism, and debate and contestation.

Chapter 7

Abundance, Scarcity, and Pluralism
A New Direction for Economic Theology

Introduction

What does it mean to think economic theology in the light of the logic of the split economy and politics that takes differences seriously? Throughout this book, we have emphasized the social, ethical, and political implications of the split economy as we were building the theoretical/philosophical framework to understand it. This has been an experimental work: economic ethics that when viewed from a certain angle becomes a political theory of ruptures in the order of being and their ongoing implications in socioeconomic life, creating a politico-economic ethics of the global financial system. The issue now is: how do we think economic theology that takes seriously political theory and the project of human living together in a pluralistic society? Like the economy, the community is split, shot through with fundamental antagonism, and there is no path to common essence/communion or noncontested harmony. I intend to begin framing my ideas about the direction of economic ideology by starting from an analysis of the fundamental neoclassical economic concepts and work out their political and theological implications.

There are four basic and related concepts in economics: scarcity, choice, opportunity cost, and ends. These four are founded on Lionel Robbins's famous definition of economics "as the science which studies human behavior as a relationship between ends and scarce means which have alternative uses."[1] When I began my training in economics decades ago, professors would quickly tell you—and undergraduate textbooks celebrated it—that any serious consideration of the relationship between ends and scarce compels thought to consider the four fundamental concepts of economics. Because resources are scarce to meet all the ends a person desires, the person has to make choices, and making choices means forgoing opportunities or incurring opportunity cost. We do not have the time and space here to analyze the economic-theological implications of all four basic concepts, so we will concentrate on only one.

This chapter focuses on scarcity in order to forge a new understanding of economic theology in its relations to politics, and to lay out a theory of scarcity and political life via the lens of economics. Specifically, I want to examine the connections between scarcity, abundance, and pluralism within the context of economic theology, to show that economics and theology can mutually enrich one another given the logic of the split economy. Theologians are quick to contrast scarcity, which they think is the blind spot of economists, with abundance, which they argue characterizes God's created order. But one thinks that this way of thinking about the relationship between scarcity and abundance is inadequate if we want economics and theology to mutually inform and enrich one another.

In this chapter, I will engage nonsentimentally with established theological opinions on abundance, strive to understand the economists' concept of scarcity on their own terms, and provide an astute theoretical investigation of political praxis that might address the tension between abundance and scarcity in contemporary society. If abundance is about having enough (overflow) to *share resources with others*, then scarcity is about having enough (overflowing) sense to rationally share the tradeoffs that create and sustain the resources. The key word in both instances is share, "to cut"—how economic life cuts into existence, into Being. Sharing always involves others, exposition to others. The central political question in the economic theological examination of abundance and scarcity is how does any community *fittingly* organize (or define the *nomos*) the mutual sharing and exposition of its diverse worlds, spheres?[2]

The economic character of capitalist social life is internally constituted by the relationship between scarcity and abundance. What gets people to produce the abundance of material goods is their rational allocation of scarce means. Rational selection of one's time and other resources is simply the way that abundance (now and in the future) is appropriated and actually enjoyed.[3] We shall shortly demonstrate that rational allocation of resources is a form of sharing that connects scarcity, abundance, and pluralism. The antagonism is not between abundance and scarcity; rather, the true line of division is between their field of opposition and pluralism, a political remainder (or better a subtraction[4]) from the two moments. What is the contour of passage from abundance and scarcity (two moments) to pluralism (the third moment)? We shall show that the distinctions between these moments are principally formal; they have the same content in three modalities: sharing.

I argue that scarcity and abundance are forms of sharing, forms of "being-with," the sharing of Being. They are respectively the "I" and "we" of "being together." Abundance, the "we," does not precede "I" (scarcity), there is a mutual exposure to one another that preserves material abundance. The economic concept of scarcity is the notion of sharing of relations, the touching of singularities at their limits, that gives rise to abundance. In this chapter I want us to think of the mutual abandonment and exposure of abundance and scarcity, an approach that will enable us to conceive of abundance as neither a form of authentic, true creaturely existence, nor a spectacle of costless consumption. We need to conceptualize it as an "ecstasy of sharing." Pluralism is a way of sharing of Being, the being that is at stake in how our lives hang together, the being of our existence that is always a coexistence. Pluralism is a way of sharing our being-with, our coexistence in a common polity, our living together in political space. It is about working out the good and fitting nomos to share a polity's abundant being-with and scarce goods in ways that (can) promote human flourishing for all.

The economic concept of scarcity points us to the cost of producing material abundance, to how end (same) and means (other) share one another to generate or sustain material abundance. There is no end if it is not shared by means (alterity), and not because there is an ultimate means that all ends have in common, but because end itself is the sharing of means. There are no ends whose identity or realization cannot be found in their "relations" to means and other ends. What realizes itself as an end must find itself being exposed to or being in contact with means in such a way that no end can be realized on its own. In the same vein, there is no abundance if abundance is not shared, "and not because there would be an ultimate or first signification that all [abundance] have in common, but because [abundance] *is itself the sharing of Being.*"[5] This focus on sharing will eventually enable us to forge a common philosophical-economic-and-political perspective that enriches our economic theological understanding of scarcity, abundance, and pluralism. Often one does not see scholars drawing the connections between the obvious economic issues of scarcity and abundance and the political issue of pluralism. It is also not common to encounter the argument that the concepts of abundance, scarcity, and pluralism are rooted in the notion of sharing. Sharing (considered here as social and not ontological or metaphysical) is both the point of departure, the presupposition, and the destiny of these three concepts.

A good part of my career over the last fourteen years has been devoted to seeking common platforms of communication between theologians and economists. I have named myself a theological theorist precisely for this reason. As a theological theorist, I principally work to investigate two problems in the task of interpreting and transforming societies: the relatively broad problem of relating theology to economic and political theories; and the narrow problem of bringing economic and political theories to bear on theological and ethical analyses. The goal is to link theological and nontheological thoughts in the creation of better levels of human flourishing.

This is an important part of my understanding of the discipline of Christianity/Religion and Society. For me, this discipline is about relating the visions and energies of Christianity to various spheres of life in ways that promote human flourishing. I take the visions and energies of Christianity to be set in a triadic practice model: an economy of equity, a politics of social justice, and fidelity to disruptive grace and endless renewal. This is a model we also see in God's covenant with Israel.[6] So, for me, any serious work in Christianity and Society—at least from the ethical lens—must attempt to couple economics, politics, and theology by following the promise that is latent in a particular historical situation. In this chapter, my focus on scarcity, abundance, and pluralism conveys this intellectual commitment. I join an economics of scarcity to a theology of abundance to shed light on the politics of pluralism in order to clarify the promise of *revolutionary belonging* in our times. The question I raise in this chapter concerns how the key concepts of scarcity and abundance in economic theology must reckon with the political reality that constitutes the social. The moral and economic questions and their justifications, which theologians raise and address, are ultimately decided in the political system. I am in good company when I argue that economic theology or any serious rumination on economics and theology is incomplete without addressing the political. Kathryn Tanner concludes her book *Economy and Grace* with a call for a communal or political *will* to fight for change, to alter the organization of economic life. Here I go further, to sketch the kind of pluralism that can influence public policy making.[7]

What Is Scarcity?

Theologians in general do not like this word. They think it wrong for economists and policy makers to talk about scarcity. They aver that it is wrong to talk of the benevolent God as a creator of a world of material scarcity. Theologians hold that scarcity and abundance are in binary opposition in God's economy. They question how anyone could talk of scarcity in the face of the plenitude of God's gift of life and the abundance of creation. The problem is that of greed and the unwillingness of human beings to open themselves to the transforming power of love and justice. With this critique they pat themselves on the back, thinking they have delivered a devastating blow to the concept of scarcity. Anyone satisfied with this line of critique has not understood the concept of scarcity in economics. This concept of scarcity differs from scarcity in other contexts or the scarcity mentality. This concept of scarcity says resources are limited but we can through careful allocation and creativity develop new combinations of resources to reduce the gap between perceived needs and available resources or uncover new possibilities for human flourishing.

It is obvious that some theologians are conflating the concept of scarcity with the fundamental accounting equation of credit equals debit; resource inflow must exactly match resources outflow. Christian theologians argue that in the created order of plenitude we can manage an economy of grace, and thus balancing of books is wrong. They are wrong because scarcity as an economic concept is not exactly about balancing accounting books in a double entry system or standing up against generosity. The economic concept of scarcity is not about scarcity mentality. It is neither about hoarding, nor about the peasant mentality of limited goods. This concept works well with nonzero-sum interactions. The history of increasing levels of material production and standards of consumption that rational management, informed by the relationship between scarce means and ends, has generated is evidence enough to convince any open-minded scholar that the concept of scarcity does not create scarcity of resources. It is about something much more fundamental, and I will come to that shortly.

The concept of scarcity in economics does not primarily refer to scarce resources in any absolute sense. Scarcity here is different from scarce resources. The concept pertains to the use of resources, the demands of judicious allocative choices with the attendant forgone opportunities. It complements the exercise of human freedom in the condition of bounded rationality, temporal limitation, and bounded corporeal presence. The concept of scarcity exemplifies the need to allocate by subjects under the constraints of finitude, competing alternative uses of resources, and the demand of resources exceeding their supply.

Scarcity in economics refers to the impossibility of any person to have her cake and eat it too. It means that when a resource is allocated to a particular project, it is not available at the same time to be allocated to another. When I use the dollar in my pocket to buy some oranges, that dollar is no longer available to buy a bottle of Coke. Now this does not mean that money is scarce in my pocket or bank account. This nonavailability of the dollar after I have bought the orange is true whether I am a pauper or a billionaire. In the same sense, a billionaire can allocate a billion dollars to build a factory and may still have many more billions to spare, but that particular billion spent is no longer available.

Before an agent makes a choice or decision, she is potentially at a place of freedom and the infinite. But the moment she acts, or chooses, she negates her original infinite potential, as she must be immediately constrained by finitude in the phenomenal realm. All human activities are constrained by finitude; the concept of scarcity recognizes this fact and directs attention to addressing this fundamental problem of human agency.

Scarcity is not only about being unable to spend a particular dollar twice, but also about the relation between wants and resources. I may have a million dollars to spend, but if my wants are unlimited, I will experience scarcity of resources or money to satisfy them. Because human desires have been conditioned and disciplined in particular ways, there are just not enough resources to satisfy all the wants at the same time (scarcity in consumption). The concept of scarcity does not enjoin us to a world of carefree jouissance, but to that of sustenance with care, with relevant doses of trade-offs. (There is also scarcity in production. This is the inability of a national economic system to produce all the material provisions its citizenry needs for human advancement.)[8]

Abundance, Scarcity, and Pluralism

In their advocacy for abundance, many theologians conflate the concept of scarcity and competition or the ills of capitalism. Even in a society without competitive struggles for goods and prestige, the concept will still operate. Persons with unlimited access to all the resources that they want might still need to allocate resources and to spatially distribute their corporeal presences in order to enjoy them. For instance, they must still make choices about going to the beach or to the opera house. Their physical bodies cannot be at two places at the same time. Even if the way of realizing God's gifts of abundance is communal (as against market), they will butt against the concept of scarcity.

The concept of scarcity is not built on the ruins or in the wake of abundance. No concept of scarcity came along to help capitalism, exploitation, and oppression dissipate abundance or social ties that sustained community. Abundance has never been experienced along the lines of the romantic projections of theologians. It did not take place outside the frame of scarcity as understood by economists. Abundance in the absence of a conception of scarcity did not take place for tribal societies; it did not take place in the age of agricultural communes. (For even in ancient gift economies choices between ends and means had to be made on how to generate and distribute the gifts.) So that romantic abundance far from what capitalism has crushed or dissipated is what happens to our imagination in the wake of the rigors of rational allocation and societal transformation.

I have stated what scarcity is not. So, what is it? Scarcity is the recognition of finitude as the basic condition of existence. It means we cannot always fully realize our aims with what we have at hand. We cannot play God. Our resources are limited, as is our knowledge. We neither have limitless resources to spend as we wish, nor do we have unlimited cognitive competence that will enable us to specify a comprehensive and complete account of life's operations. The *indicative* of finitude gives rise to the *imperative* of sustenance with care.

Coupled with finitude is the implicit concept of immanence. Yes, the economic concept of scarcity evokes the concepts of finitude and immanence. Immanence here means that the economic system, the whole set of decision matrix in a given society, is limited to the system. There is no outside or transhistorical power or system that we can invoke to override the choices or to transfer dollars into our pockets to replace the ones we have spent. The economic system is immanent to itself; the economy is common to itself. It is not even immanent to something, be it even something that is common to all, something that permeates the whole community. Everything exists on the same plane. No natural or supernatural power or machine stands in relation of transcendence to economic actors that can undo expenditures, transactions, or time at will. All transactions and allocations therefore are preserved in immanent relation. No rational or nonrational fool is allowed to smuggle in a magician to cancel or suspend finitude or laws of nature. If such a magician is allowed, then our choices will have no meaning and will not convey information about the exercise of our will and freedom or the condition of our unfreedom.

This understanding of scarcity as a social mechanism of finitude applies even to our political system. The economic concept of scarcity also supports the deep meaning of pluralism. In a democratic society there is bound to be incompatibility of values (or goods), so not all values (or goods) of the various segments can be fully or simultaneously realized. This imposes on us, as in economic transactions, the burden of choice. Choices must be made, and this may lead to conflict in our personal and social lives. The burden of choice overall necessitates forms of settlement of conflict in the forms of markets and politics and a combination of the two. This choice speaks to the political life of a community. One area in which we need to analyze how this choice speaks is in the area of scarcity. Scarcity and choice require some people to make sacrifices for the sake of the whole economy. The question is, who is asking whom to make the necessary sacrifices? Pluralism is one solution to the choices that lead to conflicts. Plurality not only describes the nature of our basic being-with (singular-plural), but a commitment to it in the management of coexistence or the commons may shed light on how the necessary sacrifices could be apportioned among the agonistic parts of a polity.[9]

What Is Abundance?

My approach here is to provide multiple theological interpretations of abundance, and along the way to offer constructive critiques of them. This is done in the hope that we may reach a philosophical conception of abundance that is not at loggerheads with the concept of scarcity.

First, abundance in the language of Genesis 1, Psalm 104, and Psalm 150 is about fruitfulness, overflowing goodness of God, and human gratitude toward God for divine provisions that sustain existence. As

Abundance, Scarcity, and Pluralism

Walter Brueggemann puts it, "Together, these three scriptures proclaim that God's force of life is loose in the world. Genesis 1 affirms generosity and denies scarcity. Psalm 104 celebrates the buoyancy of creation and rejects anxiety. Psalm 150 enacts abandoning oneself to God and letting go of the need to have anything under control."[10]

Many readers of Brueggemann will immediately say that abundance rejects the concept of scarcity. What Genesis 1 rejects is acquisitiveness and accumulation, which create scarcity of resources and not the concept of scarcity. Brueggemann reveals what he means by scarcity when he accuses Pharaoh of introducing scarcity into the world. With Joseph's interpretation of Pharaoh's dream about a future famine, Pharaoh "organized to administer, control and monopolize the food supply. Pharaoh introduces the principle of scarcity into the world economy. For the first time in the Bible, someone says, 'There's not enough. Let's get everything.'"[11] As we learned from Lionel Robbins, the concept of scarcity is about allocative efficiency in the use of material requisites of well-being. It is not about unbridled accumulation and creation of monopoly. Every careful economic theologian should be able to sort out the difference between the power of belief in scarcity and the power of the concept of scarcity as an organizing framework for economic rationality.

This brings us to our second theological interpretation of abundance. We would begin by providing another illustration of the discourse of abundance where the confusion between belief in scarcity and the concept of scarcity is evident. In Isaiah 55:1 the prophet declares that everyone who is hungry and thirsty may come to the Lord to eat and drink without cost. This is a prototypical verse used to supposedly put economists in their place, to show them how the logic of abundance and the care of the poor work in the planetary household of God. Sure, it speaks of abundance, but let us ask a few questions to see if what is portrayed here is against the concept of scarcity. Is the abundance portrayed here signaling an ethos of sustenance without care or an ethos of economic equity? There is no doubt about God's generosity, but to think that eating and drinking without cost means there is no cost attached to the production of the nourishment is to miss a crucial point within today's debate about economic equality. Provisioning for the poor is never a matter of costless transaction, but about how society should legitimately share the burden. Let us call a spade a spade: the real issue of godly abundance on this side of eternity is distribution (*nomos*[12])—it is not about any magical ability to produce material goods from thin air or from the bowels of the earth that bypass the rational principle of care embedded in the concept of scarcity. A close reading of Brueggemann bears out this point:

> In 2 Corinthians 8, Paul directs a stewardship campaign for the early church and presents Jesus as the new economist. Though Jesus was rich, Paul says, "yet for your sakes he became poor, that by his poverty you might become rich." We say it takes money to make money. Paul says it takes poverty to produce abundance. Jesus gave himself to enrich others, and we should do the same. Our abundance and the poverty of others need to be brought into a new balance. Paul ends his stewardship letter by quoting Exodus 16: "And the one who had much did not have too much, and the one who had little did not have too little."[13]

First of all, let us quickly note that the principle of Brueggemann's "Jesus as the new economist" is still within the logic of economics and finitude. Jesus was not known to be materially rich at any time in his earthly life. So, the words "Jesus was rich" must refer to his heavenly life, and on coming to earth, the phenomenal realm of finitude, he became poor. What does it mean to say, "It takes poverty to produce abundance. Jesus gave himself to enrich others"? The poverty of scarce means (finitude) is required in order to produce abundance. Means give themselves to ends to realize and enrich ends. Society uses scarce resources to realize and enrich abundance. The production of abundance and the enrichment of others work by sharing, giving, and receiving.

We should also note how Brueggemann brings down the good news of God's abundance to the level of material existence and calls us to address the structures that keep material well-being far from the places where it is urgently needed. What economic theology needs to emphasize is how the secluded abundance in one part of town needs to be brought into new balance with the open poverty in the streets.[14] After the theology of abundance has done its work of enabling us to subversively re-imagine our economic reality, we must confront the systems of oppression to reorder the system of distribution and mode of exchange. This calls for the praxis of justice, for political organizing whose logic may go against the grain of the present clamor for godly abundance.

The talk of abundance in the midst of so-called scarcity mentality and cutthroat competition is not as benign as it seems at face value. As America's love affair with consumerism blossoms we hear more and more talk about the need for the ethos of abundance. One wonders if all this talk about godly abundance is not one subtle way to avoid confronting the hard realities of transformation of social structures. The economic system we live in has managed to create enough wealth to eliminate poverty, and we can release its wealth to address the social problems of our times without the preachment on bountifulness of creation, if we are willing to organize, resist, and transform the structures of oppression.

We should ask if all this talk about godly abundance in the midst of our enjoyment of the abundance of capitalism is not a clever way of putting a soothing balm on consciences seared by consumerism. We do not really criticize or confront capitalism when we berate the concept of scarcity, which is recognition of finitude. The critique of scarcity is rather an indirect attack on finitude, a display of our anxiety concerning finitude. So we like to think that there is a possible mode of existence where finitude does not matter. In the face of hard material reality, the theological focus on godly abundance, which ignores the real operation of the economic principles and concepts in the lives of people, tends to reduce the necessary social transformation to moral transformation of individuals. But theologians, who are not inclined to understand the fundamental organizing principles of the economy, and inclined only to contrast theological ideas to principles of the wider world that guide its creation of values, downplay institutional and communal changes.

Now we come to our third theological interpretation of abundance. There are scholars who will not accept that the good news about godly abundance boils down to distribution, as I indicated a few paragraphs ago. For them, that is an unnecessary attack on capitalism, and short-circuits the Creator's vision of bountifulness. We just have to wait to create enough wealth for all. If only we can keep up expanding production, we will reach an alternative level of income distribution that will be preferred by all. The reasoning is that to improve the welfare of a group of persons in ways that make another group worse off is not efficient. Such thinkers often associate abundance with a vision of plenty or with limitlessness. Any theology that associates godly abundance as can be experienced in history with limitlessness is faulty.

Is abundance infinite and immeasurable? If the answer is no, then it has a limit. This makes sense because abundance by common understanding is about surplus. The idea of surplus is always related to a defined limit; without knowing the perimeters of a thing we cannot ascertain what is over and beyond it. Abundance does not mean that material resources in the created order have no limit, no point of exhaustion. Abundance is not absolute, as having no relation to anything, not confined to any bounds. I imagine abundance always as a matter of excess over a certain limit. Unfortunately, there are a good number of theologians and pastors who think abundance is the same thing as limitlessness.[15]

Let me illustrate this point with two examples: one from the Bible and the other from nature. Many Pentecostal pastors like to encourage their congregants to give abundantly to the churches. To this group of preachers, abundance is certainly giving without limit. They want their members to give until they ask them to stop. In saying this, they point their listeners to Exodus 35. God commanded Moses to construct the ark of the covenant, and Moses in turn asked the children of Israel to give. They gave so much gold and silver that Moses had to ask them to stop. But when we look at this story more closely, the abundance was strictly defined by Moses's order or immediate satisfaction. The abundance in this case was not pure abundance, but abundance defined by a limit. If Moses had kept on expanding the size of the project or adding more projects as the people freely gave, the abundance would have turned to inadequacy. The excess that constituted the abundance was defined by the limit of the project at hand and not by an "unlimited" number of projects or desires.

The sun gives its energy to the earth in abundance, but no well-regarded scientist has stated that its energy is not exhaustible or its abundance is not relative to the earth or our solar system. Our sun's energy does not fill every space in the universe. The true nature of the sun's ability to give energy abundantly to life on earth is its capacity to replenish the use of energy on earth. Abundance is more a matter of replenishment than unlimited excess. Abundance does not mean that a giving or sustaining source must fill all spaces and spill over. It needs only to create the space to which it can move into. The energy of creation or the big bang is abundant because the universe expands by creating the space it moves into. Similarly, the mark of abundance of a nation's endowment is for it to perpetually replenish the social fabric in which we live, move, and have our social being, and to open new spaces of sharing friendships, justice, and natality into which our community can move.

This way of understanding abundance is not the approach most theologians take. Theologians are often trying too hard to distinguish themselves from economists who are supposedly bedeviled by scarcity. Positing their stance as one at variance with that of economists, they feel compelled to conceptualize godly abundance as limitlessness. The ensuing theological concept of abundance is almost magical and transcendental. Their preternatural concept of abundance does not necessitate decision and choice, so it cannot lead us to meditate on the mechanism or procedure for decision making. It does not confront us with fierce urgency to resist the current system. Theologians may not realize it, but the idea of abundance as limitlessness plays into the hands of the rapacious system that they argue promotes the mentality of scarcity in order to keep its grip on power. Whether these well-meaning scholars like it or not, their language of limitless abundance connotes waste, environmental destruction. The only form of limitlessness worth considering is the capacity of our present set of endowments to continuously replenish the social fabric.

Fourth, in the mood of a generous interpretation, let us say that when some theologians speak of abundance they do not mean to say that there are infinite resources that can be used without care. All they want is for the essential goods of society to be provided as public goods. Examples of public goods include national defense, lighthouses, breathable air, and toll-free roads and bridges. Public goods are goods that can be simultaneously consumed by many people at the same time without rivalry or competition. No one is deprived because another person is consuming a particular public good. One person's consumption of it does not reduce the amount or benefits available to another person. No one needs to appropriate it as exclusive private property in order to enjoy it. Voilà, public goods consumption takes away the competition that deprives some of what they need in order to survive or flourish.

Whoa, this is an instantiation of the godly abundance in a world of scarcity, and theologians celebrate. Before you celebrate this, remember that there is cost to the production and sustenance of public goods. And in its production, someone or an institution made a choice on how to allocate societal resources. There are also potential or actual congestion costs. For example, when a community provides a reading room for its teenagers, two or more persons can enjoy the facility at the same time. But let the number of users rise to a thousand at any one particular time, and you have what economists technically define as "congestion costs." Suddenly, people begin to bump into each other, and the noise level becomes unbearable. One person's consumption is now affected by the consumption of others. Eventually, the librarian steps in to allocate time slots or desk spaces to accommodate everyone. We meet here again the concept of scarcity the moment we think about production and congestion costs.

This brings us to a crucial point. Theologians need not berate and reject the concept of scarcity in order to talk about abundance, non-rivalrous consumption or use of resources. And they do not necessarily need to set abundance against the concept of scarcity to make their point about the well-being of the poor. Besides, even in a world of superabundance, scarcity (in the sense of rivalrous consumption) does not go away. The consumption of certain goods, which are not public goods, exhibits rivalry. Let us imagine ourselves on an island having most delicious navel oranges. We can all have the number of oranges we want, and yet we have to deal with the concept of scarcity. The orange you ate is no longer available to me. Eventually, given a certain population level on the island, the oranges will run out. Kathryn Tanner is right when she argues that a public good "does not have to exist in vast quantities. To serve all the boats floating by, a million lighthouses are not required; one will do. Total demand is often satisfied in the case of a public good through the production of a single unit, since everyone is able to make use of the very same thing."[16] (Never mind that she ignores congestion cost.)

Fifth, there is a version of abundance as material sufficiency that pivots on conditionality of human obedience to God's covenant. This school maintains that abundance refers to God's plenteous provisioning and promise of unbounded prosperity insofar as human beings appropriately respond to God's law. Abundance in this line of argument actually refers to conditional material sufficiency. The "promise of material sufficiency is merely provisional. In particular, it is contingent on humans not impeding the unfolding generosity of God's providence through their moral failures," as Catholic theologian Albino Barrera puts it.[17]

Many theologians, such as Kathryn Tanner, will find trouble with Barrera's argument: the thought that God's giving of abundance is conditional upon proper response to God's commandments.[18] She argues that God's act of giving is not conditional upon proper response or return made by human beings. The conditionality of material sufficiency, contrary to Barrera, is not based on what we owe to God or what God demands in return for God's gifts, but our obligation to one another.

Abundance, Scarcity, and Pluralism   171

"Our good works . . . are not owed to God, but they are to the world. This is an unconditioned obligation to give on our part because God's unobligated or gracious giving to the world is unconditioned by any differences of merit."[19] We owe it to the world to not only be sources of divine beneficence to those in need, but also to rationally appropriate the gifts, to maintain with care.

Does Barrera's understanding of abundance obviate the need for our grappling with the concept of scarcity? Since we all know that human beings are fallen creatures and as such they cannot always remain faithful to God's covenant, it is, therefore, disingenuous to invoke the logic of conditionality as a basis for a theological rejection of the concept of scarcity. Fortunately, Barrera endorses conditionality without rejecting the concept of scarcity. He, to the surprise and possible chagrin of many a theologian, goes on to argue that scarcity and abundance are parts of the fabric of God's deliberate care for humanity. He endorses the concept of scarcity and its complex and intimate relation to conditional material sufficiency:

> God does not provide humans "sustenance without care" but sustenance with active interpersonal engagement. It is a sustenance with struggle, a heroic one, as seen in the exacting demands of living up to the Law and in the statutes' further development. God's vision is material abundance, but that abundance is conditional on human response. God could have mitigated the sacrificial demands of the economic ordinances [in the Old Testament] by attenuating the degree of scarcity in creation. The less severe the material shortages, the less care that is needed for sustenance and the less interpersonal friction in the economic realm. By requiring much deliberate and sustained effort, scarcity deepens Israel's partaking of God's righteousness.[20]

Let me restate the point Barrera is making in my own way. The scarcity or limited degree of faithful commitment means scarcity is ensconced in abundance or at least in the human access to its enjoyment. Insofar as God's gift of abundance is conditioned on covenant fidelity, it is not (easily) accessible. Put differently, owing to our fallen nature, the human self is split against itself; "we are torn apart by the conflict between our attraction to the good news of God's abundance and the power of the belief in scarcity. . . . We spend our lives trying to sort out [this] ambiguity."[21] The political system is one place we sort out this ambiguity collectively as a society. An economic theology that is not at the same time a form of political theology is a vitiation of natality, the initiation of something new amidst ongoing social reality.

Sixth, some theologians compare the distribution mechanism of God's abundance to a blowtorch giving its flame to the lead pipe in a welding process. The torch gives flame without losing the basic properties of the flame. The blowtorch gives without suffering loss, without being in thralldom to "scarcity mentality." What they forget to notice is that the energy of the flame is coming from somewhere and as long as the flame lasts it is a loss. While the theologians of the blowtorch-lead-pipe world celebrate and ignore the concept of scarcity, the citizens of the energy world asked to make the sacrifice will not celebrate. Let us not even raise the concern of other citizens who will question whether it is better to give flame to the lead pipes carrying water to the houses of millionaires than to warm the houses of the poor and huddled masses. What is the best way to allocate the flames that have alternative uses?

Seventh, according to another perspective, abundance is about "the unbounded divine capacity to provide to whomever God, as the Lord of history, chooses is clearly manifested when YHWH gives the Chosen People cities and houses they did not build, wells they did not dig, and vineyards and olive groves they did not plant (Dt. 6:10–11)."[22] This abundant forceful transfer of wealth has a cost to it and perfectly illustrates scarcity. Cost was required on the part of the dispossessed to create the houses, wells, vineyards, and olive groves, and the transfer of wealth created scarcity relative to demand in the land of the defeated. The concept of scarcity forces us to pay attention to cost no matter how hidden it is in any rhetoric. By the way, such a transfer does not create any new surplus or abundance if we consider the possessors and the dispossessed as in one regional economy.

The orientation of the various theological understandings of abundance is that abundance is an innate quality of God's created order. My question to the theologians who advocate the viewpoints of abundance presented above is this: how is this quality or goodness of God communicated as a gift to human beings in their current material reality? How does what is a subjective genitive become an objective genitive? Lest we forget, theologians have neither argued that abundance in creation is self-diffusive, nor posited that the goodness of creaturely abundance on earth is not external to us, but embraces us unto itself. The power of abundance in the public square or the marketplace is not yet self-diffusive and unitive. The political and economic question is how do we allow this power (the innate power of God's created order) to actualize itself in us and through the common institutions of socialities?

Let us even say that the innate quality is received as gifts by human beings in a way we cannot tell. As created beings, humans inevitably and automatically received gifts of material goodness from God to support life. But even at this theologians still must make the necessary distinction between the reception of the gifts of abundance and of human beings acting on them. Human beings must act on the gifts, and acting will bring them in contact with the concept of scarcity. They can squander the gifts or rationally take care of them, knowing that the material supports of life are not infinite. (Thus, any economic theology will also need an eco-theology.)

Economists argue that human beings do not arrogate to themselves the innate wealth of creation. Rather, in production, exchange, and economic transfers—which are governed by the tension between scarce means and ends—they are taken up into it. This economic viewpoint acknowledges that the density and abundance of relations, mutuality, interdependences, and collaborations in a community create economic wealth. Members of a community are always called upon to make sacrifices and carry burdens (that is, choices and opportunity costs) in order to bring forth new creations, new manifestations of abundance and liberation. For economists, the new creation is the diffusiveness of the goodness of the created order. In this overarching framework, the work of the concept of scarcity is not opposed to the goodness of unfolding abundance. Similarly, one can say that theologians and economists are not very far apart in their positions in the tension-soaked terrain of abundance and scarcity. Theologians articulate the ideal of the ethos of abundance and the economists say that the enlivening spirit of the dynamic toward the ideal is borne by the power of the notion of scarcity, a deliberative search for the optimal set of means for the "non-divine" material provisioning of human existence. The theological-economic ethicist would then add that politics of justice must be brought into focus to show how to transform the structures and practices of social, economic, and political systems toward a better approximation of the ideal. One point of departure for thinking such politics is a rethinking of the theory and practice of pluralism.

The theology of abundance, just like the economic concept of scarcity, leads to questions of politics, of pluralism. We cannot adequately address them as economic theologians if we do not resort to the questions they inevitably raise about how social lives hang together in any community. Even those theologians who avoid the thought of abundance as limitlessness and confine their understanding to God's endowment of creation to ensure material sufficiency for human beings or all created beings still must face the same question.[23] What exactly does material sufficiency mean? Do we mean material sufficiency to sustain the goodness of *contingent existence* of human beings? Or should the level of sufficiency include development and sustenance of creaturely activities geared toward human flourishing? If our answer to the last question is yes, then what level of excellences and capabilities truly define the fullness of human life or are proper to the human mode of being and operation? Who is to decide the relevant level? What if we cannot realize all of them at once (meaning we come up against finitude or temporal scarcity)—how do we make the choice? Oh, no, the pristine theology of abundance cannot avoid the economic issue of scarcity and the political matter of institutional procedure for communitywide choices of how we should live together.

The network (field) of abundance, scarcity, and pluralism comprises the building blocks of capitalist sociality, the packets of energy quanta, the helix structure of its economic life. The complementary drives of abundance and scarcity form an interactive structure held together by pluralism (or more precisely the singular-plural). The tension between the animating dynamic of scarcity and abundance, between here and now or the here and the not-yet, is *one* of the abiding features of the capitalist system. The incompleteness within the heart and trajectory of the economic life pushes the common life toward decentered and differentiated participation in collective political effort. It is always a matter for politics how the constitutive units (persons or groups) of a whole should act on each other in order to bring the whole to its dynamic levels of perfection.

What Is Pluralism?

The constructive critiques of scarcity and abundance we offered above as well as the various indications we gave along the way that imbricated them in the politics of pluralism demand that we offer new conceptualizations of these two terms in ways that organically link them to pluralism. This is the task of this section. My arguments will pivot on Jean-Luc Nancy's notion of "sharing" (*partage*) in communities under conditions of finitude.[24] Nancy argues that there is no common substance that characterizes a community. Members of community only share of themselves, share in their exposure to each other. Each member is an other to others because of the sharing; each singular being shares in the sharing of others. It is this sharing that constitutes the community and the members as singularities and resists their fusion into one subject or communion. "Community is the community of *others*, which does not mean that several individuals possess some common nature in spite of their difference, but rather that they partake only in their otherness. . . . They are together, but togetherness is otherness."[25]

Before abundance, there is finitude; that is, I am first of all exposed to limit, exposed to another being, to *singular beings*, exposed to means, means that cannot be appropriated at once to serve my end. When we appear in the world we are already involved in sharing—the sharing of finitude, the means of our social bonds—and we are at the brink of the limit of our being. We do not complete the sharing, but continue to replenish it. The concept of scarcity reveals one of the ways we continue the sharing.

Scarcity is sharing of means around ends. The realization of ends must pass through means. The realization of ends is by consumption of means. End by definition is not present to itself. It realizes itself by exposure to the otherness of means—partaking, sharing in the otherness of means. The means also partake in the end. Means and ends both share of themselves. The concept of scarcity does not mean insufficiency or lack in an originary sense, but the dynamic activity of sharing. The sharing is always incomplete. "Sharing is always incomplete, or it is beyond completion and incompletion. For a complete sharing implies the disappearance of what is shared."[26]

The concept of scarcity points to the articulation of means and ends, their interplay at a juncture, where they touch one another. In order to be, end appropriates means or its own becoming, but the nature of means is to offer itself.[27] End by this appropriation attempts to complete itself, but means in offering itself "incompletes itself," "offering to something that is not it nor its proper becoming."[28] An end is also eventually destined to be shared, to offer itself in its becoming even though it "must appropriate its own becoming."[29] In this overall sense, abundance is both means and end. Scarcity resists it from completely appropriating its becoming to be a permanent or totalizing end. This is to say scarcity opens up, dislocates abundance toward its further potentialities.

The connectivity ("mutual immanence of things") between ends and means as weaved by the concept of scarcity means that there is no actuality (no realization of ends or production of new forms) without relations.[30] The concept focuses—at least implicitly—on how the many means become one end (product, service, occasion) and are increased by one transformation, unfolding actuality. This one actuality becomes a means further down the line. This suggests that every means is in a certain sense everywhere, in every end, in every product (service), if you will pardon my Whiteheadian prose flourish. Scarcity (not a lack, void, or negative) is a process that savors its incompletion. The concept of scarcity gestures to the repetition of difference, the past of means enfolded in a becoming present to yield the future, the novelty of end. The hope of the creative-destructive process of entrepreneurship is that the entanglements of actual means in the production exercise will repeat with a difference to provoke a novelty or give an indication of possibility.

In the space between actuality and potency, scarcity enfolds or invaginates godly abundance in an erotic immanence of relations to yield the novum. Every production occasion or transformation of means into ends is a *contraction*. The process enfolds the universe of the means only to unfold it differently. Scarcity, or rather the economic concept of scarcity, is not a negative but the *fold* between means and end, the relation of difference, the multiplicity of the many that become one and increase it. Simply put, scarcity inhabits abundance. Or we might say scarcity is the immanence of infinite ends in finite means.[31] In the light of all this, the real problem in the economists' concept of scarcity as a pathway to abundance is that it considers the transformative process as a determinate dialectic instead of indeterminate creativity. In this swerve, we catch a glimpse of a road to abundance not taken by economics.

Scarcity in economics also means the infinite (non-*fin*) subtraction of infinite abundance. The concept gestures to the subtraction of something, this something which has to give, which opens a community to its potentialities rather than to its destiny. The prodigality of civilization, rather than that of creation, is made by what is withdrawn.[32] The withdrawn is the other; there are always others who cannot be fused into a collective process or product. There are always alternative means that were forgone to make a product, and they stand as some kind of impotentiality, the means that conserves itself and saves itself in production. The economic notion of scarcity establishes the impossibility of gathering together all means, or the threads of finitude to create abundance.

Pluralism is the sharing demanded or necessary for being-in-common without a common being or essence or common project of community. Pluralism is demanded or necessary for a community without the same identity and background. Pluralism is a matter of a community "incompleting its sharing." Sharing of the members' exposure to one another and the means of negotiating their being-in-common (without being togetherness) is not completable. The completion will imply the disappearance of the community of sharing or the emergence of *fusional communion*. Pluralism is in fact nothing other than the consumption, replenishing, and recreation of the spaces of sharing, the sharing of the social fabric.[33] It is not a work to be completed; "what is shared is the unworking of works."[34] Pluralism is an acknowledgment that society is always divided and sharing; there is no mythic space of communion it wants to recover, create, or discover. Pluralism is the exposure of the common to the fact of politics: that there are agnostic interests that know their places and their meanings in the common as opening to otherness and in relations. Politics is about representation and governance of the common of a bounded, limited community, the site of social existence where being and well-being of a community are at stake, open to contestations by various forces and interests.

This understanding of pluralism dovetails nicely into the concept of scarcity that we have developed in this chapter. The concept of scarcity calls us out, calls us into communication and cooperation. No one person can form a community because, as Hannah Arendt once informed us, "Not man but men inhabit the earth and form a world between them."[35] There is no essence to the community, and what constitutes it is our sharing of our exposure to each other and our dependence on each other for help. This is simply a reflection of the irreducible pluralistic nature of existence. Scarcity is an experience of the finite abundance of sharing. We come to our abundance, beyond ourselves, in the presence of others, by others' finitude.

Abundance is sharing. It is the ecstasy of sharing, the jouissance, enjoyment of sharing. This is the form of sharing a community's extant set of endowments that continuously replenish its social fabric. It is a sharing that *radically* opens new spaces for sharing friendships, justice, and natality. It is the grace (dynamic) of coexistence that disrupts institutions to open new avenues for real, substantial life, opening them up to play as an endless power to begin. The vexing political question is how do we allow this power to actualize itself in us and through the common institutions of our communities? Pluralism is the sharing necessary for abundance in a community without a common being or essence.

Abundance is the indefinite abundance of sharing, an abandonment to the prodigality of sharing, a yielding to the flourishing of all human beings. Abundance is the *with* of members of community sharing, sharing existence. Abundance is not a totality, an ensemble of things in which each member would participate; rather what is shared is the between and the *with* of the members, and it is also what participates.[36] The in-finite meaning of abundance under "human conditions" is scarcity, the very spacing of finite existence. Scarcity is not just the technical means to the end of abundance, but the sharing (spacing is sharing) itself as in-finite end, sharing "as the existence of finite existence in all its brilliance and violence."[37]

Conclusion: The Methodology of the Five-Pointed Star

Let me end this chapter by summarizing my approach to economic theology, which I have detailed in the preceding pages. My methodology could be likened to a five-point star. The first edge shows that the economic theologian is not a mere theologian, but also an economist steeped in political theory/philosophy and ready to deploy his or her skills to examine and reconstruct tradition and inherited wisdom, to formulate lines of critique and protests, and to point us to new spaces of transformative praxis. This way of conceiving the discipline flows from the Tillich-Wariboko tripartite framework (Catholic substance, Protestant principle, and Pentecostal principle; tradition, protest, and new creation) of social analysis.[38]

Abundance, economic concept of scarcity, and pluralism is a triad that maps into tradition, protest, and new creation. Theologians inherited the notion or tradition of abundance, a supposed common bequest from the Creator, which they have raised to the level of the infinite, absolute. In the name of rational allocation and finitude, the economic notion of scarcity critiques or protests against this elevation. The political notion of pluralism gestures to the appearance of something new, to new forms of immanent socialities that can initiate something new amidst ongoing social processes as the "field of opposition" between abundance and scarcity moves forward. It stands against the seeming contestatory relationship between abundance and scarcity to nudge the extant configurations of sharing of Being to new levels of flourishing. Put differently, the intersection of abundance and scarcity at new levels of the production possibilities frontier (or curve) beckons new forms of pluralism (sharing of Being, being-with), summons an alternate frontier of social flourishment, which political praxis must actualize. All serious economic theology must come to rest at the point where it calls for new arrangements for sharing of Being that might realize the just goal of in-finite existence of abundance, the creative superfluity of humankind. Indeed, economic theology today calls for multidisciplinary scholars who can think the thoughts of constructive theologians, practical economists, and political theorists. The multidisciplinary dimension of economic theology constitutes the second edge.

In addition to highlighting the multidisciplinary nature of economic theology, this chapter has also shown that the field is an art of translating economic concepts into philosophical-theological language. For example, I demonstrated above that the concept of scarcity is also about the philosophy of sharing. Indeed, I uncovered the philosophical underpinning of the concept of scarcity. This approach of digging deep into economic concepts and theories to reveal their philosophical, theological, or ontological underbelly constitutes the third angle of the five-point star, and gestures to my more than decade-long endeavor to seek common platforms of communication between economics and theology.

Economic theology encompasses the task of clarifying and refining economic concepts and related theological concepts in order to promote a more meaningful or fruitful conversation between the disciplines of economics and theology. We demonstrated this with the concept of scarcity, abundance, and pluralism. Conceptual clarification is the fourth side of the five-point star.

Finally, through the potential contributions of the already mentioned four sides of the star, the discipline of economic theology advances the aim of properly mapping the ever-changing relationships between Christianity and its society as ethicists seek to promote human flourishing in pluralistic polities.

Overall, these five dimensions of economic theology are necessary for a political praxis that takes seriously the logic of split economy and wants to generate liberative social-ethical analysis relevant for the emergence of new forms of immanent socialities that might engender or sustain an alternative future to the formatted future of late capitalism. As we stated earlier in this book, economic theology (philosophy) must open a space for citizens to make a decision based on a prepared future (that is the new that flows from capitalism's trajectory of the past and present, late capitalism's project of a better future) or a radical future that could arise from the unforeseeable new that asks for, creates, and sustains alternative possibilities—the unexpected, risky path.

Epilogue

Let me begin by summarizing the fundamental arguments of the book. Then, the task becomes elaborating on the arguments, explicating the thought processes that engendered them, and trying to convince readers of their soundness. This book speaks from the interstices between philosophy, theology, political economy, and psychoanalytic theory. From these medial spaces, it tries to understand the fundamental antagonism, the split that underlines and plagues—also gives and sustains the life of—the modern capitalist economy.

The analysis began in earnest by searching the origin of this split. By origin, I do not mean a historicist search for absolute beginnings, the objective context and causes that explain the split. It is also not a search for a cause outside of the immanent network of causality, or a genealogical account of the split. It is not a Hobbesian staging of mythology—the state of nature—as a historical point of departure for subsequent development. It is rather a retroactive recognition that a shift, a bifurcation, happened in the nonlinear evolution of civilization or material existence, which cannot be pinned down precisely but whose evocation helps us to make sense of our current world. The glimpse of the historical past reveals that the economy has always been split, divided against itself, and this division takes the form of finance.

Our concept of finance as the crack in the economy calls into question any thought about the unity or wholeness of the economy. Finance is the structural incompleteness of the economy, the stumbling block of the economy, its inherent contradiction. Finance is the not the economy, but its point of nonrelation, its deadlock. Finance is not simply a deviation from the original (primordial) economy, but also the point at which the primordial economy's own inherent impossibility coincides with itself, gets articulated as such. This way of looking at finance forces us to think of it as a division, a split of *the same economy*. The traditional way of thinking about the economy as financial circulation of money versus industrial circulation of money does not see the finance industry's "difference as difference, but as a question of belonging to two separate worlds, which are 'different' from a neutral bird's eyes description, but otherwise coexisting as integral parts in the hierarchy of [economic] order, the wholeness and unity of which is in no way threatened by this 'difference.'"[1]

Finance arising from this source, from the crack, has aroused itself into a despoiling invader. In reaction, the usual practice of social ethicists is to condemn the players in the financial industry, to portray them as greedy and attacking the value or meaning of their actions. In this book, however, we have avoided the age-old practice of easy condemnation of greed or personal characters, as we have transposed the "source of evil" from the people to the basic *form of the economy*, the fundamental antagonism of the primordial economy that has persisted into our contemporary economy, and this is not because I am naïve and unaware of the many corrupt players on Wall Street. The focus on form is my way of telling readers that crises such as the 2008 financial meltdown are not crises of morality *per se*, but crises of capitalism. We should focus less on individual sin and greed, and endeavor to understand that the logic of the system induces corruption. When we seek the source of the "sin," we find it not in our brothers and sisters, but in capitalism itself.

Thus, in this book the ethical analysis of the major players of Wall Street breaks with the fascination with the telos or hidden meaning of their actions and centers attention on the form, to decipher the key that unlocks the form of their action. The economy—or, precisely, the fundamental split that disturbs the economy from coinciding with itself—is the designer of the form to which the so-called hidden meanings or contents of the players' actions/plays are submitted. Ethical evaluation in this perspective is not about assessing the gap between a universal empty form of an ethical injunction and the contingent contents used to fill the empty form, or about a subject divided between the supreme Good and empty ethical injunction; rather, it is about radicalizing the gap. In this relevant sense of ethical evaluation, it is not about uncovering what separates the subject from the universal form of the ethical demand, but transposing the division between universal empty form and the contingent contents into the content itself, as an indication of an economy that is *not-all*, and where there is a constitutive lack in the economy that disturbs every ethical action. This lack is persistent and repeating in concrete situations. This gap, this fundamental contradiction, is what establishes the form of what Wall Street does, and points to the primordial split, and no matter how much we or the government want to direct Wall Streeters to the supreme good, this primordial split will persist. Our sermonizing or pleas will never abolish this gap; that is, the "abyss of negativity remains forever the unsublatable background of [financial] creativity."[2]

My point is that Wall Street has an ethic that is better grasped in its form, which is the very structuring of the fundamental contradiction of the split economy. At this juncture, it is important to remind the reader of what "fundamental contradiction" means in this book. It serves us eminently well here to quote the succinct definition of the term given by Alenka Zupančič:

> When I talk about a "fundamental contradiction" I am not referring to some contradiction buried deep down in the foundation of things, and influencing them from there. Contradiction is "fundamental" in the sense that it is persistent, and repeating—yet always in concrete situations, on the surface of things and in the present. It is by engaging with it in these concrete situations that we work with the "fundamental contradiction."[3]

Finance rose as an internal disturbance and interruption of the harvest (gathering, killing, production)—of the consumption cycle of the proto-economy—as a gap appearing in the path to immediate *death* of output. Finance is the detour taken from the path and represents the forces that sustain the deviation from the fundamental drive to consume without remainder. Finance is the social practice, "the knowledge (know-how) necessary for the *preservation of this detour* from the fundamental negativity" implied in primordial economic activities, which we can name production-canceling-itself-out.[4] Finance (metonym of early surplus) is the inherent gap on the account of which the proto-economy (production-canceling-itself-out, a kind of being-toward-death) does not simply coincide with itself. No wonder finance is a nightmarish disturbance of the economy, even until today.[5] Note that what is meant by gap, or split, is the "natural economic life path" of the proto-economy breaking into two: one leading to cancellation, and the other inherently deviating from the first, but always headed to rejoin the first (that is, the drive toward cancellation, the path to immediate *death* of output). Note also that there are two drives. The second drive of deviation (*the preservation of the detour*) is part of the logic of cancellation (production-canceling-itself-out); it is the repetition and appearance of the first. The second seems to pave the route of the first. Seen in this light, the theoretical importance of the social-ethical condemnation of the "evil" of the financial sector greatly diminishes. It is a component drive whose function is to assure that the capitalist economy "shall follow its own path to death and to ward off any possible ways of returning to" harmonious existence or society-wide human flourishing other than those which are immanent in the economy itself.[6]

The split, the cut, is not a wound or laceration, but exposure of the inside as an outside, thus, the ex-posing of the *tomorrowness* inside of today, which, without this uncovering, dilation of the economy will not exist or would not have been birthed. It remains, obstinately, in its most intimate logic, the present exposed to the future, satisfaction exposed to dissatisfaction, the entire "inside" of today's production and consumption exposed to the "outside" of the future, and the promise of better enrichment.[7] The split, the breach, is the origin of the economic world.

This fundamental split is simultaneously expressed in various struggles between the sectors of the economy through displacements and distortions and "the very structuring principle of these distortions."[8] The gap separates the economy as the principle of cancellation from the economy in its "oppositional determination" (finance), as the conservation of the deviation, as one of the elements of the whole economy.[9] I have named the distance of the economy from itself as finance, the (original) space that was opened and is still opened by the gap. When this (virtual) principle that structures the whole economic field encounters itself in the guise of the financial sector as a form of its actualization and specific articulation, there is an absolute contradiction. One way this happens is when the economy assumes the character of finance as a whole, the so-called increasing financialization of the economy, a phenomenon that is leading to increasing instability. Viewed from another perspective, from a Marxist one for that matter, we can say the condition of absolute contradiction is always already inherent in capitalism. Indeed, Marxian theorists hold that the sectors of the economy, the industrial branches into which the economy is divided, are basically the subdivisions of capital.

We can approach the idea of absolute contradiction from another perspective. If the name for the split, the fundamental contradiction, is finance, *absolute contradiction* is the name for the split—the fundamental antagonism in which finance, the split, has itself as an object. This is the context in which, on the one hand, finance "intuits" in the economy knowledge of itself as the primordial split or the universal essence of the fundamental antagonism. On the other hand, the economy "recognizes" itself in nonrelation with finance. In this context—usually in an economic/financial meltdown—finance cuts off funding to industry, withdrawing into the trap of inwardness, and clearly manifesting the absence of *direct relationship* with the economy. Industry on its own refuses to generate accumulatable surplus (the original generative source of finance and *futureness* as if it were withdrawing into a mode of *production-canceling-itself-out* of the proto-economy. The reciprocal recognition (self-encounter) of separateness, the universal essence, and nonrelation is absolute contradiction.

Let me conclude by saying that the overarching insight of this book is that the economic unconscious is finance. By this I mean that *finance is economy*. This statement should not be construed to mean that *economy is finance*: the "is" between finance and economy is not reflexive. The *economy is finance* implies the well-known financialization of the economy; it means a reduction of all economic transactions to the content of financial complexes. But the expression *finance is economy* means that the (negativity of) the primordial split, which we have named finance, is formally included in the whole economic field.[10] This is what it means to say the modern economy is cracked.

The economy is split! This is both bad and good news. Bad news because, as we have demonstrated throughout this book, the fundamental antagonism of the post-primordial economy prevents it from identifying with any supreme notion of the good or human flourishing; rather, its logic is technically beyond good and evil. This is so because the event of the primordial split is "demonic." "To call capitalism [the split economy] demonic means that it is a structure of evil characterized by the ambiguous unity of creative and destructive powers. Tillich stresses that the demonic is no individual act of evil based on the free decision of personality. Rather, it is 'a structure of evil beyond the moral power of good will, which produces social and individual tragedy precisely through the inseparable mixture of good and evil in every human act.'"[11] All these point to the tragic quality of the primordial split triggered by desire and economic insecurity. "A situation is tragic in which the very elements which are most valuable by their very value drive it to self-destruction."[12] The split as manifested on Wall Street is driving the economy as a whole toward self-destruction. The economy is a "life" in which separation is continuously posited but cannot be overcome within the logic of the economic system.

The good news is the economy is a site of perpetual politics. Once we accept the perpetuity of antagonism and conflict in the very working of the economy, we then must "reject the dream of displacement, the fantasy that the right laws or constitution might someday free us from the responsibility for (and indeed, the burden of) politics."[13] This will take commitment to perpetual agonistic democratic practices—perpetual revolution, if you like—in order to deal with the perennial issue of humans living together. This calls for a politics bent on attaining the dynamic ideal of transforming communities for human flourishing. This quest should not be limited to the distribution of power in any given society, but should be expanded to include transformation of the coordinates that organize our existence, eliciting an interruption of the flow of social life. This is to say that economic ethics must become (include) a political theory that is not restricted to the creation and maintenance of "a reasonable, just, and stable social order," but one that is a theory of rapture.[14] "Rapture is the occurrence of the impossible, when the very ground under our feet shifts in order to transform the point from which we see" our socioeconomic reality.[15] This calls for a subject that emerges as "a break within time and because of this break, the subject has the capacity to form values that make life worth living."[16] This break within time can only be gestured to and cannot be offered as a capitalist promise of the future. Hannah Arendt writes: "This small non-time-space in the very heart of time [i.e., the break within time], unlike the world and the culture into which we are born, can only be indicated, but cannot be inherited and handed down from the past; each new generation, indeed every new human being as he inserts himself between an infinite past and infinite future, must discover and ploddingly pave it anew."[17]

Notes

Introduction

1. Max Weber, *The Protestant Ethic and the Spirit of Capitalism*, trans. Talcott Parsons (New York: Charles Scribner's Sons, 1958), 138.

2. Milton Friedman, *A Theory of the Consumption Function* (Princeton, NJ: Princeton University Press, 1957).

3. Todd McGowan, *Capitalism and Desire: The Psychic Cost of Free Markets* (New York: Columbia University Press, 2016), 26.

4. Slavoj Žižek, *Incontinence of the Void: Economic-Philosophical Spandrels* (Cambridge, MA: MIT Press, 2017), 219.

5. Georg Lukács, *History and Class Consciousness: Studies in Marxist Dialectics*, trans. Rodney Livingstone (Cambridge, MA: MIT Press, 1971).

6. Žižek, *Incontinence of the Void*, 152.

7. This way of framing my argument is indebted to Žižek, *Incontinence of the Void*, 152.

8. Frank Ruda, *Abolishing Freedom: A Plea for a Contemporary Use of Fatalism* (Lincoln, NE: University of Nebraska, 2016).

9. Giorgio Agamben, *Potentialities: Collected Essays in Philosophy*, ed. and trans. Daniel Heller-Roazen (Stanford, CA: Stanford University Press, 1999).

10. Giorgio Agamben, *Nudities* (Stanford, CA: Stanford University Press, 2010), 44.

11. Agamben, *Nudities*, 43–44; *Potentialities*, 182.

12. Agamben, *Potentialities*, 182–183; original emphasis.

13. Guy Le Gaufey, *Une archéologie de la toute puissance* (Paris: EPEL, 2014), 111; quoted in Žižek, *Incontinence of the Void*, 161.

14. "The commodity is, first of all, an external object, a thing which through its qualities satisfies human needs of whatever kind. The nature of these needs, whether they arise, for example, from the stomach, or the imagination [fantasy], makes no difference. Nor does it matter here how the thing satisfies man's needs, whether directly as a means of subsistence, i.e. an object of consumption, or

indirectly as a means of production." Karl Marx, *Capital: A Critique of Political Economy*, Vol. 1, trans. Ben Fowkes (London: Penguin Books, 1976), 125.

15. Jacques Lacan, *The Seminar, Book XX, Encore* (New York: Norton, 1999), 49.

16. This sentence was inspired by J.P. Clark, "Ibadan," in *Collected Poems: J.P. Clark-Bekederemo, 1958–1988*. (Washington, DC: Howard University Press, 1991), 14.

17. Katerina Kolozova traces developments like this in the financial industry to the capitalist drive for profits "that is grounded in flawed metaphysical presupposition" (p. 55). In the last instance, the self-sufficient and self-enclosed universe of speculation (financial and beyond financial) feeds on the physical world, which it treats as mere material (not matter) for the (re-)production of abstract values. The role of the abstraction in the capitalist world is to (re)produce imperfect matter into numeric perfection (money) and to elevate it to a level where matter transcends itself by being transformed into "materialistic value" or "pure materialism. . . ." It is a pursuit of surplus value, rather than use value, which culminates in the surplus of "pure value." See Katerina Kolozova, *Toward a Radical Metaphysics of Socialism: Marx and Laruelle* (Brooklyn, NY: Punctum Books, 2015), 54–55.

18. https://substitute.livejournal.com/986052.html

19. Slavoj Žižek, *The Ticklish Subject: The Absent Centre of Political Ontology* (London: Verso, 1999), 173–174.

20. Giorgio Agamben, *The Time That Remains: A Commentary on the Letter to the Romans* (Stanford, CA: Stanford University Press, 2005), 108.

21. Agamben, *Time That Remains*, 108.

22. Agamben, *Time That Remains*, 108.

23. Paul Axton, *The Psychotheology of Sin and Salvation: An Analysis of the Meaning of the Death of Christ in Light of the Psychoanalytical Reading of Paul* (London: Bloomsbury T&T Clark, 2015), 70.

24. This way of describing the relationship between economy and finance was inspired by Slavoj Žižek, *The Parallax View* (Cambridge, MA: MIT Press, 2009), 106.

25. Karl Marx, *Capital*, Vol. 1, 769.

26. Thomas R. Blanton and Raymond Pickett (eds.), *Paul and Economics* (Minneapolis: Fortress Press, 2017) and Thomas R. Blanton IV, *A Spiritual Economy: Gift in the Letters of Paul Tarsus* (New Haven, CT: Yale University Press, 2017).

27. This also explains why I have not engaged with Principe's *Secular Messiahs*, as her brilliant book does not deal with this dimension of Pauline studies or speak to the intersection of political economy and Lacanian philosophical psychoanalysis. See Concetta V. Principe, *Secular Messiahs and the Return of Paul's "Real": A Lacanian Approach* (New York: Palgrave Macmillan, 2015). Other

excellent books on Paul are Abed Azzam, *Nietzsche Versus Paul* (New York: Columbia University Press, 2015); Robert T. Fortuna and Beverly R. Gaventa (eds.), *The Conversation Continues: Studies in Paul and John, In Honor of J. Louis Martyn* (Nashville, TN: Abingdon Press, 1990), and John M.G. Barclays, *Paul and the Gift* (Grand Rapids, MI: William B. Eerdmans Publishing Company, 2015). None of these books deals with the subject area of our current project, though they provided me excellent orientation to my research in Pauline studies.

28. Blanton IV, *A Spiritual Economy*, 5.

29. Žižek's *Incontinence of the Void* inspired this way of structuring the book's arguments.

Chapter 1

1. Jacques Lacan, *Le séminaire, livre V: Les formations of de l'inconscient, 1957–1958*, ed. Jacques-Alain Miller (Paris: Seuil, 1998), 218; quoted in Paul Eisenstein and Todd McGowan, *Rupture: On the Emergence of the Political* (Evanston: IL: Northwestern University Press, 2012), 12.

2. Eisenstein and McGowan, *Rupture*, 13–14.

3. Giorgio Agamben, *The Time That Remains: A Commentary on the Letter to the Romans* (Stanford, CA: Stanford University Press, 2005), 49.

4. Agamben, *The Time That Remains*, 50.

5. Eisenstein and McGowan, *Rupture*, 5.

6. Thomas Piketty, *Capital in the Twenty-first Century* (Cambridge, MA: Belknap Press, 2014), 747–748.

7. Francis Ching-Wah Yip, *Capitalism as Religion? A Study of Paul Tillich's Interpretation of Modernity* (Cambridge, MA: Harvard University Press, 2009), 39–40.

8. Paul Tillich, *Theology of Peace*, ed. Ronald Stone (Louisville, KY: Westminster/John Knox, 1990), 52.

9. The definition of economic ethics is inspired by Piketty, *Capital*, 749.

10. Eisenstein and McGowan, *Rupture*, 3.

11. Eisenstein and McGowan, *Rupture*, 4.

12. See below for the meanings of "animal economy" and "human economy."

13. This way of putting across my idea was inspired by Slavoj Žižek, *On Belief* (Oxford: Routledge, 2001), 131–132.

14. Žižek, *On Belief*, 104.

15. Žižek, *On Belief*, 101.

16. Nimi Wariboko, *Economics in Spirit and Truth: A Moral Philosophy of Finance* (New York: Palgrave Macmillan, 2014), 13, 123, 133–137, 143.

17. Žižek, *On Belief*, 105.

18. Sentence is inspired by Depoortere, *Christ in Postmodern Philosophy*, 145.

19. This way of arranging my thesis, the flow of the paragraph from when I first mentioned "the fundamental argument of this chapter" to this point was inspired by Frederiek Depoortere, *Christ in Postmodern Philosophy: Gianni Vattimo, Rene Girard and Slavoj Žižek* (New York: T&T Clark, 2008), 141–142.

20. Leonardo Boff, *Liberating Grace*, trans. John Drury (Eugene, OR: Wipf and Stock, 1979), 168.

21. Gar Alperovitz and Lew Daly, *Unjust Deserts: How the Rich Are Taking Our Common Inheritance and Why We Should Take It Back* (New York: New Press, 2009), 97; quoted in Joseph E. Stiglitz, *The Price of Inequality: How Today's Divided Society Endangers Our Future* (New York: W.W. Norton & Company, 2013), 98.

22. Stiglitz, *Price of Inequality*, 116.

23. Slavoj Žižek, *The Parallax View* (Cambridge, MA: MIT Press, 2009), 57.

24. Slavoj Žižek, "The Real of Sexual Difference" in Suzanne Barnard and Bruce Fink (ed.), *Reading Seminar XX: Lacan's Major Work on Love, Knowledge, and Feminine Sexuality* (Albany, NY: SUNY Press, 2002), 61.

25. Karl Marx, *Capital: A Critique of Political Economy*, vol. 3, trans. David Fernbach (New York: Penguin, 1981), 347.

26. Todd McGowan, *Capitalism and Desire: The Psychic Cost of Free Markets* (New York: Columbia University Press, 2016), 12–14, 37, 49, 85–86.

27. Jean-Luc Nancy, *The Inoperative Community*, trans. Peter Connor, Lisa Garbus, Michael Holland, and Simona Sawhney, foreword Christopher Fynsk (Minneapolis: University of Minnesota Press, 1991), 25.

28. McGowan, *Capitalism and Desire*, 183.

29. Wariboko, *Economics in Spirit and Truth*, 79–80.

30. Nimi Wariboko, *God and Money: A Theology of Money in a Globalizing World* (Lanham, MD: Lexington Books, 2008), 195–103.

31. "Prosumer" is a term coined by Alvin Toffler, *The Third Wave* (New York: Bantam Books, 1981), 36–39, 117, 266. Toffler is prescient in identifying split causes in the human psyche and society by the various phases of economic development. But he traced the problem of today's society to the fundamental split initiated by the industrial revolution (36–45, 117, 231, 266), forgetting that the split is much older than that. He discusses the effect of the split on politics, sexuality, and the psychic and personality of human beings. Toffler, however, notes that the most fundamental split occurred when production was separated from consumers, the splitting of prosumers into producer households and consumer households—the emergence of the market that now coordinates the interdependency and mutuality of households. Contra Toffler, our analysis shows the split first occurred in the same household as subjects split their own harvest into two portions: consumption now and consumption tomorrow. Intertemporal splitting preceded the spatial split of production and consumption. It

is also important to note that Toffler does not conceptualize the split as related to the self-division of being as we have done here.

32. Jan-Olav Henriksen, *Desire, Gift, and Recognition: Christology and Postmodern Philosophy* (Grand Rapids, MI: Eerdmans, 2009), 338–339.

33. The commentary that follows is adapted from Nimi Wariboko, *The Split God: Pentecostalism and Critical Theory* (Albany, NY: SUNY Press, 2018), 33–36.

34. F.W.J. Schelling, *Abyss of Freedom/Ages of the World* (Second Draft, 1813), trans. Judith Norman (Ann Arbor: University of Michigan Press, 1997). In this section of the chapter, I am going to combine my reading of the second and third drafts of Schelling's *Ages of the World* and Žižek's interpretation of the second draft to provide a succinct summary of its main ideas as bear on our purpose here.

35. Andrew Bowie, *Schelling and Modern European Philosophy* (New York: Routledge, 1993), 105, quoted in Žižek, *Indivisible Remainder*, 37.

36. The next four paragraphs are indebted to Wariboko, *Economics in Spirit and Truth*, 134–135.

37. For a simple discussion of PPF, see Sean Masaki Flynn, *Economics for Dummies* (Hoboken, NJ: Wiley Publishing, 2005), 38–44.

38. It is important to add that points on the curve considered efficient by economists may not always be ethical, moral, or good for workers. Managers might have attained positions on the efficiency frontiers by paying very low wages or externalizing the cost of environmental pollution or ecological degradation.

39. This way of putting across my ideas was borrowed from Paul Tillich in a very different context. See Paul Tillich, *The Religious Situation*, trans. H. Richard Niebuhr (New York: Henry Holt, 1932); see also Yip, *Capitalism as Religion?*, 30, 32, 45–46.

40. Eisenstein and McGowan, *Rupture*, 28.

41. Hannah Arendt, *Between Past and Future: Eight Exercises in Political Thought* (New York: Penguin, 2006), 13.

Chapter 2

1. Todd McGowan, *Capitalism and Desire: The Psychic Cost of Free Markets* (New York: Columbia University Press, 2016), 113–118, 123–130; for a discussion of the concept of the big other.

2. Alain Badiou, *Theory of the Subject*, trans. Bruno Bosteels (New York: Continuum, 2009), 8.

3. Paul Eisenstein and Todd McGowan, *Rupture: On the Emergence of the Political* (Evanston: IL: Northwestern University Press, 2012), 72.

4. Lacan, *The Ethics of Psychoanalysis*, 83–84.

5. Frank Ruda, *Abolishing Freedom: A Plea for a Contemporary Use of Fatalism* (Lincoln, NE: University of Nebraska Press, 2016), 94.

6. Giorgio Agamben, *The Time That Remains: A Commentary on the Letter to the Romans* (Stanford, CA: Stanford University Press, 2005), 47.

7. Agamben, *Time That Remains*, 49.

8. Slavoj Žižek, *Event: A Philosophical Journey through a Concept* (Brooklyn: Melville House, 2014), 94–95. This is an adaption of Žižek's ideas from a different context of Hegel's understanding of "absolute knowing." A truth needs time to make a journey through illusions to form itself. One should put Hegel back into the series of Plato-Descartes-Hegel, corresponding to the triad of Objective-Subjective-Absolute: Plato's ideas are objective, Truth embodied; the Cartesian subject stands for the unconditional certainty of my subjective self-awareness. And Hegel, what does he add? If "subjective" is what is relative to our subjective limitation, and if "objective" is the way things really are, what does "absolute" add to it? Hegel's answer: the "absolute" does add some deeper, more substantial, dimension—it includes (subjective) illusion into (objective) truth itself. The "absolute" standpoint makes us see how reality includes fiction (or fantasy) . . . (94–95).

9. Here I am playing with Derrida's words: "The double did not only add itself to the simple. It divided it and supplemented it," Jacques Derrida, *Writing and Difference*, trans. Alan Bass (Chicago: University of Chicago Press, 1978), 299; quoted in Jean-Luc Nancy and Aurelién Barrau, *What's These Worlds Coming To?*, trans. Travis Holloway and Flor Méchain (New York: Fordham University Press, 2015), 8.

10. On this crucial point, it bears to quote Ward Blanton at length: "In the text of Romans, notice the way in which the dialectical standstill or suspension of agency within the juridical economy does not simply operate in the splitting or doubling of the inner man/wretched man of this scene, fissuring his agency into antagonistic strategies (cf. 7:21–24). Much more striking than this Platonic splitting of agencies, I think, is the way there is here clearly a matching split or duplication of *nomos* as well, as if the agency of *nomos* itself appears as *both* prohibition *and* transgression of the same. In this passage there is apparently hit upon a 'law' of law itself, as if having 'discovered' a law within law or a code inside of code, a little shadow of law producing its opposite, resistance to it, active rebellion and criminality rather than docile acquiescence to appropriate limitations. 'So I find this law: when I want to do good, evil lies ready to hand. . . . [That is] I see in my members another law (*heteron nomon*) at war with the law of the mind (*nous*)' (cf. 7:21f.). Here the very impasse or obstruction within the otherwise smooth functioning of power in a system of juridical compliance itself comes to name *another nomos*, namely, the *nomos* of the way the arrival of commandments is always a repetition of the 'springing to

life again of sin' (cf. 7:9), a return of the repressed which displaces the 'I' from itself, effectively 'killing' it (cf. 7:10). And this displacement and splitting of the I, we should not miss, emerges from a 'chance' that is susceptible of being grasped as a 'production' (cf. *kateirgasato* 7:8) of a surplus capable of inverting the value of the intentions of the actor in question." See Ward Blanton, *A Materialism for the Masses: Saint Paul and the Philosophy of Undying Life* (New York: Columbia University Press, 2014), 171.

11. Žižek, *Event*, 101.

12. Slavoj Žižek, *The Ticklish Subject: The Absent Core of Political Ontology* (New York: Verso, 2008), 173–174.

13. Žižek, *Ticklish Subject*, 175.

14. Paul V. Axton, *The Psychotheology of Sin and Salvation: An Analysis of the Meaning of the Death of Christ in the Light of the Psychoanalytical Reading of Paul* (London: Bloomsbury T & T Clark, 2015), 116, 200; Slavoj Žižek, *The Monstrosity of Christ* (Cambridge, MA: MIT Press, 2009), 273–275.

15. Slavoj Žižek, "The Abyss of Freedom," in F.W.J. Schelling, *Abyss of Freedom/Ages of the World* (2nd draft, 1813), trans. Judith Norman (Ann Arbor: University of Michigan Press, 1997), 7.

16. McGowan, *Capitalism and Desire*, 228.

17. McGowan, *Capitalism and Desire*, 230.

18. G.W.F Hegel, *The Phenomenology of Spirit*, trans. A.V. Miller (Oxford: Oxford University Press, 1977), 377.

19. This sentence is a slight rephrasing of McGowan's analysis of Hegel's ethics transformation of Kant's morality. See McGowan, *Capitalism and Desire*, 230.

20. McGowan, *Capitalism and Desire*, 11–12.

21. Karl Marx, *Capital: A Critique of Political Economy*, vol. 2, trans. David Fernbach (New York: Penguin, 1981), 199.

22. McGowan, *Capitalism and Desire*, 244.

23. McGowan, *Capitalism and Desire*, 236.

24. McGowan, *Capitalism and Desire*, 235.

25. McGowan, *Capitalism and Desire*, 47.

26. Jennifer L. Koosed. *(Per)mutations of Qohelet: Reading the Body in the Book* (New York: T&T Clark, 2006), 19.

27. Jacques Derrida, *The Post Card: From Socrates to Freud and Beyond*, trans. Alan Bass (Chicago: University of Chicago Press, 1987), 39.

28. Nimi Wariboko, *Economics in Spirit and Truth: A Moral Philosophy of Finance* (New York: Palgrave Macmillan, 2014), 38–55.

29. Wariboko, *Economics in Spirit and Truth*, 63–68, 133.

30. Joan Copjec, *Read My Desire: Lacan Against the Historicists* (London: Verso, 2015), 205.

31. Copjec, *Read My Desire*, 205.

32. Jacques Lacan, *The Seminar of Jacques Lacan, Book XVII: The Other Side of Psychoanalysis*, trans. Russell Grigg (New York: Norton, 2007), 107; I have adapted Lacan's words from a different context for my own purpose here. "Discourse begins from the fact that here there is gap. . . . But, after all, nothing prevents us from saying that it is because discourse began that the gap is produced."

33. Slavoj Žižek, *The Year of Dreaming Dangerously*, 28.

34. Jacques Rancière, *Disagreement: Politics and Philosophy*, trans. Julie Rose (Minneapolis: University of Minnesota Press, 1998), 13.

35. Jacques Rancière, *Dissensus: On Politics and Aesthetics*, ed. and trans. Steven Corcoran (London: Continuum, 2010), 35–36.

36. Rancière, *Dissensus*, 36.

Chapter 3

1. Paul Eisenstein and Todd McGowan, *Rupture: On Emergence of the Political* (Evanston, IL: Northwestern University Press, 2012), 68.

2. Michel Foucault, *Society Must Be Defended: Lecture at the Collège de France, 1975–1976*, trans. David Macey (New York: Picador 2003), 10–11.

3. Max Weber, *The Protestant Ethic and the Spirit of Capitalism*, trans. Talcott Parsons (London: Routledge, 1992).

4. Eisenstein and McGowan, *Rupture*, 74.

5. Roland Barthes, *Camera Lucida: Reflections on Photography*, trans. Richard Howard (New York: Farrar, Straus and Giroux, 2010), 26.

6. Barthes, *Camera Lucida*, 57.

7. Kojin Karatani, *Transcritique: On Kant and Marx*, trans. Sabu Kohso (Cambridge, MA: MIT Press, 2003), 157.

8. Slavoj Žižek, *The Parallax View* (Cambridge, MA: MIT Press, 2009), 61.

9. Žižek, *Parallax View*, 61.

10. Potentiality, as Aristotle taught us, consists of potential to-do and the potential to not-do, which is called impotentiality.

11. Žižek, *Parallax View*, 202.

12. Giorgio Agamben, *Nudities*, trans. David Kishik and Stefan Pedatella (Stanford, CA: Stanford University Press, 2010), 44–45.

13. Human beings as *argōs*-being. There is a certain purposelessness at the core of human beings. Let me explain what I mean by *argōs*-being because it holds a key to comprehending the argument I will be making here. Aristotle wonders if nature left man without a function or work (*ergon*) that is proper to human beings or if they are essentially workless (*inoperoso*), functionless (*argōs*).

> For just as the goodness and performance of a flute player, a sculptor, or any kind of expert, and generally of anyone who fulfills some

function or performs some action, are thought to reside in his proper function [*ergon*], so the goodness and performance of man would seem to reside in whatever is his proper function. Is it then possible that while a carpenter and a shoemaker have their own proper function and spheres of action, man as man has none, but is left by nature a good-for-nothing without a function [*argōs*]? (Aristotle, *Nicomachean Ethics* 1097b, 25–30)

The translation is from *Nicomachean Ethics*, trans. Martin Oswald (Indianapolis: Liberal Arts Press, 1962). Aristotle quickly retreated from this thought and supplied the answer: "Activity of the soul [is] in accordance with virtue." This is the essence of human beings, at least and insofar as she is in the *polis* and it is the end she pursues. Today, we are no longer quick to identify what is the proper timeless function of human beings. And we even regard community as *inoperative* as it is only the experience of *compearance*, as Jean-Luc Nancy has taught us. Community or the notion of the community, according to Nancy, is not based on some essence, idea, or project. As he argues in *The Inoperative Community*, the community is not about communion, an essence, but about being-together, being *ex-posed* to one another. See Jean-Luc Nancy, *The Inoperative Community*, trans. Peter Connor, Lisa Garbus, Michael Holland, and Simona Sawhney (Minneapolis: University of Minnesota Press, 1991). So, and rightly, Giorgio Agamben argues that human action cannot be regarded as a means that makes sense only with respect to an end. See Giorgio Agamben, *Means without End: Notes on Politics*, trans. Vincenzo Binetti and Cesare Casarino (Minneapolis: University of Minnesota Press, 2000), 115–116.

14. Žižek, *Parallax View*, 84.
15. Žižek, *Parallax View*, 122.
16. Giorgio Agamben, *The Kingdom and the Glory: For a Genealogy of Economy and Government*, trans. Lorenzo Chiesa (Stanford, CA: Stanford University Press, 2011), 99.
17. This way of rendering my ideas was inspired by Slavoj Žižek, "The Real of Sexual Difference," ed. Suzanne Barnard and Bruce Fink, *Reading Seminar XX: Lacan's Major Work on Love, Knowledge, and Feminine Sexuality* (Albany, NY: State University of New York Press, 2002), 73–75.
18. Kenneth Reinhard, "Toward a Political Theology of the Neighbor" in Slavoj Žižek, Eric Santner, and Kenneth Reinhard, *The Neighbor: Three Inquiries in Political Theology* (Chicago: University of Chicago Press, 2006), 58; original emphasis.
19. Slavoj Žižek, *Incontinence of the Void: Economico-Philosophical Spandrels* (Cambridge, MA: MIT Press, 2017), 89.
20. Slavoj Žižek, *The Fragile Absolute, Or Why Is the Christian Legacy Worth Fighting For?* (London: Verso, 2008), 12.
21. Žižek, *The Fragile Absolute*, 13.

22. See Nimi Wariboko, *God and Money: A Theology of Money in a Globalizing World* (Lanham, MD: Lexington Books, 2008), 24–37.

23. For a discussion of teleoeffective structure, see Theodore Schatzki, *The Site of the Social: A Philosophical Account of the Constitution of the Social Life and Change* (University Park: Pennsylvania State University Press, 2002).

24. Bruce Fink, *The Lacanian Subject: Between Language and Jouissance* (Princeton, NJ: Princeton University Press, 1995), 134.

25. Fink, *Lacanian Subject*, 42–44.

26. Fink, *Lacanian Subject*, 44.

27. Fink, *Lacanian Subject*, 140.

28. Daron Acemoglu and James A. Robinson, *Why Nations Fail: The Origins of Power, Prosperity, and Poverty* (New York: Crown Business, 2012), 376.

29. Joseph E. Stiglitz, *The Price of Inequality: How Today's Divided Society Endangers Our Future* (New York: W.W. Norton & Company, 2013), xxi, 3.

30. Stiglitz, *Price of Inequality*, 24–25.

31. Emilie Maureen Townes, *Womanist Ethics and the Cultural Production of Evil* (New York: Palgrave Macmillan, 2006).

32. Mel Oliver and Thomas Shapiro, *Black Wealth/White Wealth: A New Perspective on Racial Inequality* (New York: Routledge, 1995), 18, quoted in Elizabeth Jacobs, "Everywhere and Nowhere: Politics in Capital in the Twenty-First Century" in Heather Boushey, J. Bradford Delong, and Marshall Steinbaum, *After Piketty: The Agenda for Economics and Inequality* (Cambridge, MA: Harvard University Press, 2017), 533.

33. Gareth Jones, "The Geographies of Capital in the Twenty-First Century: Inequality, Political Economy, and Space," in Boushey et al., *After Piketty*, 280.

34. Jones, "The Geographies of Capital," 283.

35. Nimi Wariboko, *The Charismatic City and the Resurgence of Religion: A Pentecostal Social Ethics of Cosmopolitan Urban Life* (New York: Palgrave Macmillan, 2014), 137–153.

36. Thomas Piketty, *Capital in the Twenty-first Century*, trans. Arthur Goldhammer (Cambridge, MA: Harvard University Press, 2014); Joseph E. Stiglitz, *The Price of Inequality: How Today's Divided Society Endangers Our Future* (New York: W.W. Norton & Company, 2013).

37. Piketty, *Capital*, 34–35.

38. Piketty, *Capital*, 35.

39. Piketty, *Capital*, 168, 191–194, 308–312, 367–374, 477–593, 597, 618–619, 703–704, 746–748.

40. Jacobs, "Everywhere and Nowhere," 533–534.

41. Piketty, *Capital*, 746–747.

42. Mark L. Taylor, *The Executed God: The Way of the Cross in Lockdown America* (Minneapolis: Fortress, 2015); Michelle Alexander, *The New Jim Crow: Mass Incarceration in an Age of Color Blindness* (New York: The New Press, 2010).

43. United Nations, *Human Development Report* (New York: 2016), 60.

44. Slavoj Žižek, *Less than Nothing: Hegel and Shadow of Dialectical Materialism* (London: Verso, 2012), 166.

45. Paul V. Axton, *The Psychotheology of Sin and Salvation: An Analysis of the Meaning of the Death of Christ in the Light of the Psychoanalytical Reading of Paul* (London: Bloomsbury T&T Clark, 2015), 38–40.

46. The phrasing of these sentences relies on Slavoj Žižek, "The Abyss of Freedom," in F.W.J. Schelling, *Abyss of Freedom/Ages of the World* (2nd draft, 1813), trans. Judith Norman (Ann Arbor: University of Michigan Press, 1997), 10.

47. Žižek, *Parallax View*, 132, inspired this paragraph.

48. Žižek, *Parallax View*, 263.

49. Žižek, *Parallax View*, 268.

50. Žižek, *Parallax View*, 107.

51. Žižek, *Parallax View*, 109.

52. Nimi Wariboko, *Economics in Spirit and Truth: A Moral Philosophy of Finance* (New York: Palgrave Macmillan, 2014), 137.

53. There are "underlying law[s] which regulate what appears [as] a chaotic contingent interaction." Žižek, *Less than Nothing*, 460.

54. Friedrich A. Hayek, *Law, Legislation and Liberty: Volume 1: Rules and Order* (Chicago: University of Chicago Press, 1973).

55. Robert Pippin, *Henry James and Modern Moral Life* (Cambridge: Cambridge University Press, 2000), 10–11.

56. Eddie Glaude, Jr., *Democracy in Black: How Race Still Enslaves the American Soul* (New York: Broadway Books, 2016).

57. This way of putting across my thought was inspired by Leonardo Boff, *Liberating Grace*, trans. John Drury (Eugene, OR: Wipf and Stock, 1979), 165–166.

58. Lorenzo Chiesa, "Imaginary, Symbolic and Real Otherness: The Lacanian Subject and His Vicissitudes," thesis, University of Warwick, Department of Philosophy, 2004 (quoted in Žižek, *Parallax View*, 92). The phrases in quotation marks in the preceding sentence come from Chiesa's text.

59. Alain Badiou, "A Conversation with Alain Badiou," *Lacanian Ink* 23 (New York, 2004), 100–101; quoted in Žižek, *Parallax View*, 180–181.

60. Žižek, *Parallax View*, 181.

61. Žižek, *Parallax View*, 181.

62. Žižek, *Parallax View*, 181.

63. Lee Edelman, *No Future: Queer Theory and the Death Drive* (Durham, NC: Duke University Press, 2004), 4.

Chapter 4

1. Jacques Rancière, *Hatred of Democracy*, trans. Steve Corcoran (London: Verso, 2006), 41.

2. Jacques Rancière, *Disagreement: Politics and Philosophy*, trans. Julie Rose (Minneapolis: University of Minnesota Press, 1998), 6.
3. Rancière, *Disagreement*, 13.
4. Rancière, *Disagreement*, 9.
5. Rancière, *Disagreement*, 9.
6. Rancière, *Disagreement*, 18.
7. Rancière, *Disagreement*, 11.
8. Slavoj Žižek, *Less Than Nothing: Hegel and the Shadow of Dialectical Materialism* (London: Verso, 2012), 459. This is an adaptation of Žižek's sentence.
9. Žižek, *Less Than Nothing*, 459.
10. Achille Mbembe, "Life, Sovereignty, and Terror in the Fiction of Amos Tutuola," *Research in African Literatures* 34, no. 4 (2003): 4.
11. Jean-Pierre Vernant, *Mortals and Immortals: Collected Essays* (Princeton, NJ: Princeton University Press, 1991), 141.
12. Nimi Wariboko, *God and Money: A Theology of Money in a Globalizing World* (Lanham, MD: Lexington Books, 2008), 73–96.
13. Peter Hallward, *Badiou: A Subject to Truth* (Minneapolis: University of Minnesota Press, 2003), 257–258.
14. Ludwig Feuerbach, *The Essence of Christianity*, trans. Marian Evans (London: John Chapman, 1854), 13.
15. The thinking here is influenced by Kenneth Reinhard, "Paul and the Political Theology of the Neighbor," in Ward Blanton and Hent De Vries (eds.), *Paul and the Philosophers* (New York: Fordham University Press, 2013), 460. Reinhard was explaining how Paul in Romans 13 reduced Jesus Christ's dual commandment (love of God and love of neighbor) into one.

His radical intervention is to make a cut, a break—not, however, as is often claimed, a break between "the law" and "love," but between *the law to love God* (the Father) and *the law to love the neighbor*, embodied in Jesus, God's Son. The commandment to love God with "all your heart and with all your soul and with all your might" is the purest embodiment of the law's impossible demands and the infinite guilt for our failure to love absolutely that is its result. How, we might ask, can we find it in ourselves to love anyone else, let alone a neighbor, given this overwhelming absolute call to love God? The key "act" of Paul as apostle is neither to add anything to the law nor to take anything away from it, but to divide it from within. The commandment to love God is excised from its place beside the commandment to love the neighbor for the sake of freeing us all—Christians, Jews, and all other—from the guilt induced by the weight of the paternal law. This is not in any sense to diminish the role of God the Father or his laws, but to create a breathing space, a realm for living in the narrow place, not beyond but between the laws (460).

16. Slavoj Žižek, "The Necessity of a Dead Bird," in Ward Blanton and Hent De Vries (eds.), *Paul and the Philosophers* (New York: Fordham University Press, 2013), 184.

17. Peter Alexander Egom, *Global Joseph Project* (Ukala Okpunor, Nigeria: Adioné Publishing, 2009), xii.
18. Egom, *Global Joseph Project*, xiii.
19. Peter Alexander Egom, *Christian Society: Before and After Parousia* (Ukala Okpunor, Nigeria: Adioné Publishing, 2011); Peter Alexander Egom, *Compass for Economic Reform* (Ukala Okpunor, Nigeria: Adioné Publishing, 2006). He writes:

> A commodity payments standard does empower every member of an economy to equally participate in moving the economy forward, in a locally integrated manner, through effective demand from citizen-wage-and-vocation-fund bank accounts with local micro-finance and popular sovereignty basis for the inward-looking convertibility of any currency on the commodity payments standard. For, from the socio-political and economic dimensions, a currency has inward-looking or gold convertibility when the process of creating and distributing it within the currency market of an economy is equally owned by each and every member of the economy through the phenomena of the citizen wage and the vocation fund. (Egom, *Christian Society*, 201–202)

20. Roland Boer, "Paul and Materialist Grace," in Ward Blanton and Hent De Vries (eds.), *Paul and the Philosophers* (New York: Fordham University Press, 2013), 198.
21. Boer, "Paul and Materialist Grace," 207.
22. Alain Badiou, *Saint Paul: The Foundation of Universalism* (Stanford, CA: Stanford University Press, 2003).
23. Boer, "Paul and Materialist Grace," 191–193, 203, 207–209.
24. Kojin Karatani, *Transcritique: On Kant and Marx*, trans. Sabu Kohso (Cambridge, MA: MIT Press, 2003), 222.
25. Slavoj Žižek, *The Parallax View* (Cambridge, MA: MIT Press, 2009), 126–127.
26. Bruce Fink, *The Lacanian Subject: Between Language and Jouissance* (Princeton, NJ: Princeton University Press, 1995), 106.
27. Fink, *Lacanian Subject*, 107.
28. Fink, *Lacanian Subject*, 104.
29. Fink, *Lacanian Subject*, 106.
30. An economy is dynamic unity of depth and meaningfulness; this is a deployment of a Tillichian idea (Paul Tillich, *Systematic Theology, Volume 3: Life and the Spirit, History and the Kingdom of God* (Chicago: University of Chicago Press, 1965, 421–422). The depth of the economy is the ever-expanding sphere of economic production and the "immanence of creative potentiality," which together constitute the ground of satisfying human needs and wants. Meaning

stands here for the *principle of form* structuring the productive activities in the economy, the satisfaction of social wants. Let us try to explicate how *meaning* is implicated in the social practice of money. By *meaning* I am also referring to the individualistic, personal connection to this ground of production, which is to say a person's engagement in projects of worth. *Meaning* may express the urge of a woman to fulfill herself, to actualize her potentials. It is from here the animus of creativity feeds into the production process. This means a woman may approach her economic activities with purpose and may indeed interpret her action as fulfilling a purpose, but does not mean that the economy gives meaning on its own. Because individuals feel they can directly grasp the world of economic productive activities instead of the abstract world of stock exchange, forex, and gyrating interest rates, they think or harbor the illusion that there is a self and a world of production in interdependence. Meaning thus is the function (according to Tillich) of a person through which she actualizes herself and grasps and shapes this world. *Meaning* in this sense expresses the notion that every economic transaction is a "syndrome (i.e., a running-together) of facts and interpretation" (Tillich, *Systematic Theology, Volume 3*, 302). But this clinging to the sense of meaning in economy might be an illusion, as Mark C. Taylor argues. There is no possibility of closure in this system, as self-organizing, self-regulating, and coevolving interconnections increasingly create ever-expanding webs of countless relations. Hence, we are in a brave new world of no redemption where order is not imposed from outside by either a providential God or an institution. Taylor sums up his argument in these terms: "Since redemption presupposes closure as well as satisfaction, however it is figured, the ceaseless flux of life in network culture renders redemption impossible. Rather than the sign of certain death, the impossibility of redemption is the mark of endless life. To affirm this life is to embrace the infinitely complex networks that make us what we are and are not. . . . In the final analysis, the problem is not to find redemption from a world that often seems dark but to learn to live without redemption in a world where the interplay of light and darkness creates infinite shades of difference, which are inescapably disruptive, overwhelmingly beautiful, and infinitely complex (Mark C. Taylor, *Confidence Games: Money and Markets in a World without Redemption* (Chicago: University of Chicago Press, 2004, 330–331).

31. An empty or floating signifier is a name that does not actually refer to any one object (group of objects) and is itself empty of meaning and thus open to stand for an abundance of meanings. It is a signifier that is not tied to any number of signifieds. Thus, it means many things to many people, may mean whatever a person interprets it to be without reckoning with inherent contradictions in his or her understanding of it, and may stand in for any number of unfulfilled demands. An empty signifier, like "finance," points to a free-play of

overabundant signifieds around a signifier. Thus, it is difficult to anchor "finance" as a signifier to particular signifieds such as support of industry, the so-called substantial economy, and human flourishing.

32. Fink, *Lacanian Subject*, 121.

Chapter 5

1. Alenka Zupančič, *Ethics of the Real: Kant and Lacan* (London: Verso, 2011), 17.
2. Zupančič, *Ethics of the Real*, 15.
3. Zupančič, *Ethics of the Real*, 14.
4. Immanuel Kant, *The Metaphysics of Morals* (Cambridge: Cambridge University Press, 1996), 20.
5. Zupančič, *Ethics of the Real*, 17.
6. Zupančič, *Ethics of the Real*, 16–17.
7. Zupančič, *Ethics of the Real*, 19.
8. Zupančič, *Ethics of the Real*, 18.
9. Jacques Lacan, *The Seminar, Book XX, On Feminine Sexuality. The Limits of Love and Knowledge* (New York: W.W. Norton, 1998), 126.
10. Gilles Deleuze puts it in this way:

> The law is no longer regarded as dependent on the Good, but on the contrary, the Good itself is made to depend on the law. This means that the law no longer has its foundation in some higher principle from which it would derive its authority, but that it is self-grounded and valid solely by virtue of its own form . . . The moral law is the representation of a pure form and is independent of content or object, spheres of activity or circumstances. The moral law is THE LAW, the form of the law and as such it cannot be grounded in a higher principle. . . . Clearly THE LAW, as defined by its pure form, without substance or object or any determination whatsoever, is such that no one knows nor can know what it is. (Gilles Deleuze, *Masochism: Coldness and Cruelty* [New York: Zone Books, 1991], 82–84)

11. Immanuel Kant, *Critique of Practical Reason*, trans. by Mary Gregor, introduction by Andrews Reath (Cambridge: Cambridge University Press, 2015), 66.
12. Jodi Dean, "Still Dancing: Drive as a Category of Political Economy," *International Journal of Zizek Studies* 6, no. 1 (2012): 4.

13. Katerina Kolozova traces developments like this in the financial industry to the capitalist drive for profits "that is grounded in flawed metaphysical presupposition":

> In the last instance, the self-sufficient and self-enclosed universe of speculation (financial and beyond financial) feeds on the physical world, which it treats as mere material (not matter) for the (re-)production of abstract values. The role of the abstraction in the capitalist world is to (re)produce imperfect matter into numeric perfection (money) and to elevate it to a level where matter transcends itself by being transformed into "materialistic value" or "pure materialism. . . ." It is a pursuit of surplus value, rather than use value, which culminates in the surplus of "pure value." (Katerina Kolozova, *Toward a Radical Metaphysics of Socialism: Marx and Laruelle* [Brooklyn: Punctum Books, 2015], 54–55)

14. Kolozova, *Toward a Radical Metaphysics of Socialism*, 78.
15. Slavoj Žižek, *Tarrying with the Negative: Kant, Hegel, and the Critique of Ideology* (Durham, NC: Duke University Press, 1993), 78.
16. Zupančič, *Ethics of the Real*, 14.
17. Maurizio Lazzarato, *The Making of the Indebted Man: An Essay on the Neoliberal Condition*, trans. Joshua David Jordon (Los Angeles: Semiotext[e], 2012), 25.
18. Maurizio Lazzarato, *Governing by Debt*, trans. Joshua David Jordon (Los Angeles: Semiotext[e], 2015), 89. See also Slavoj Žižek, *Event: A Philosophical Journey Through a Concept* (London: Penguin Books, 2014), 162–163.
19. Roberto Esposito, "Foreword to the English Translation," in Electra Stimilli, *The Debt of the Living: Ascesis and Capitalism*, trans. Arianna Bove (Albany, NY: SUNY University Press, 2017), ix.
20. Gilles Deleuze and Félix Guattari, *Anti-Oedipus: Capitalism and Schizophrenia* (New York: Penguin, 2009), 197–198.
21. See Ilsup Ahn, *Just Debt: Theology, Ethics, and Neoliberalism* (Waco, TX: Baylor University Press, 2017) for a thorough analysis of debt and its socioethical impact on American society.
22. Kathryn Tanner, "Work, Debt, and Christian Witness," *Reflections: A Magazine of Theological and Ethical Inquiry*, Yale Divinity School, Spring, 2017: 28.
23. See Nimi Wariboko, "Freeing the Future," *Reflections: A Magazine of Theological and Ethical Inquiry*, Yale Divinity School, Spring, 2017: 56–57.
24. Nimi Wariboko, *Economics in Spirit and Truth: A Moral Philosophy of Finance* (New York: Palgrave Macmillan, 2014).
25. Maurizio Lazzarato, *Governance by Debt* (Semiotext[e], 2015).
26. Gilles Deleuze and Félix Guattari, *Anti-Oedipus: Capitalism and Schizophrenia* (Penguin, 2009), 197–198, original emphasis. See also Lazzarato, *Making of the Indebted Man*.

27. Dean, "Still Dancing," 6.
28. Dean, "Still Dancing," 6–7.
29. The work of Žižek influenced the formulation of the ideas here. See Slavoj Žižek, *The Most Sublime Hysteric: Hegel with Lacan*, trans. by Thomas Scott-Railton (Malden, MA: Polity Press, 2014), 81.
30. Žižek, *The Most Sublime Hysteric*, 111 inspired this paragraph.
31. Žižek, *The Most Sublime Hysteric*, 158.
32. See Žižek, *The Most Sublime Hysteric*, 159, for the source of inspiration for these ideas.
33. Žižek, *The Most Sublime Hysteric*, 171–174.
34. My expression of ideas here was inspired by Jacques Lacan, *Ecrits. The First Complete Edition in English*, trans. B. Fink, H. Fink, and R. Griggs (New York: W.W. Norton, 2006), 144; quoted in Žižek, *The Most Sublime Hysteric*, 174.
35. Bruce Fink, *The Lacanian Subject: Between Language and Jouissance* (Princeton, NJ: Princeton University Press, 1995), 46.
36. Jocelyn Pixley, *Emotions in Finance: Distrust and Uncertainty in Global Markets* (Cambridge: Cambridge University Press, 2004).
37. Pixley, *Emotions in Finance*, 3.
38. Pixley, *Emotions in Finance*, 29.
39. John Maynard Keynes, *The General Theory of Employment, Interest, and Money* (Orlando, FL: Harcourt Bruce Jovanovich Publishers, 1953), 161–162.
40. Todd McGowan, *Capitalism and Desire: The Psychic Cost of Free Markets* (New York: Columbia University Press, 2016).
41. Zupančič, *Ethics of the Real*, 19.
42. Slavoj Žižek, *Incontinence of the Void: Economico-Philosophical Spandrels* (Cambridge, MA: MIT Press, 2017), 47.
43. G.W.F. Hegel, *Phenomenology of Spirit*, trans by A.V. Miller (Oxford: Oxford University Press, 1977), 210.
44. Žižek, *Incontinence of the Void*, 50.
45. Žižek, *Incontinence of the Void*, 50.
46. Žižek, *Incontinence of the Void*, 28–32.
47. Jean-Luc Nancy, *The Inoperative Community*, trans. Peter Connor, Lisa Garbus, Michael Holland, and Simona Sawhney (Minneapolis: University of Minnesota Press, 1991), 25.

Chapter 6

1. Todd McGowan, *Capitalism and Desire: The Psychic Cost of Free Markets* (New York: Columbia University Press, 2016).
2. If we interpret the primordial and subsequent denials of consumption in terms of sacrifice, we might see the pursuit of empty forms as an attempt to create value where none exists. In this vein, one could interpret the birth of

finance from the undifferentiated primordial economy owing to the denial of present consumption in the distant past of our ancestors as sacrifice. Starting with the undifferentiated economy, sacrifice enabled the prehistoric prosumers "to create a value where none otherwise exist[ed]." See McGowan, *Capitalism and Desire*, 111.

3. Slavoj Žižek, *Incontinence of the Void: Economic-Philosophical Spandrels* (Cambridge, MA: MIT Press, 2017), 152.

4. Slavoj Žižek, *The Year of Dreaming Dangerously* (London: Verso Books, 2012), 134.

5. Žižek, *The Year of Dreaming Dangerously*, 134.

6. See the Introduction of this book for detailed explanations of the terms "omnipotent" and "impotentiality."

7. Frank Ruda, *Abolishing Freedom: A Plea for a Contemporary Use of Fatalism* (Lincoln, NE: University of Nebraska, 2016).

8. Ruda, *Abolishing Freedom*, 10.

9. This sentence is a reworking of a sentence in different context in Tsenay Serequeberhan, *Existence and Heritage: Hermeneutic Explorations in African and Continental Philosophy* (Albany, NY: SUNY Press, 2015), 14.

10. Lee Edelman, *No Future: Queer Theory and the Death Drive* (Durham, NC: Duke University Press, 2004), 4.

11. Karatani, *Transcritique*, 217.

12. Karl Marx and Friedrich Engels, *The German Ideology* (New York: International Publishers, 1989), 56–57; quoted in Kojin Karatani, *Transcritique: On Kant and Marx*, trans. Sabu Kohso (Cambridge, MA: MIT Press, 2003), 217.

13. Kojin Karatani, *Transcritique: On Kant and Marx*, trans. Sabu Kohso (Cambridge, MA: MIT Press, 2003), 293.

14. Karatani, *Transcritique*, 291.

15. Karatani, *Transcritique*, 289–290.

16. Karatani, *Transcritique*, 294; see also pp. 296–297, 300–301.

17. Karatani, *Transcritique*, 295.

18. Karl Marx, *Capital: A Critique of Political Economy*, vol. 3, trans. Ben Fowkes (New York: Penguin Books, 1981), 352. Karl Marx, *Capital: A Critique of Political Economy*, vol. 1, trans. Ben Fowkes (New York: Penguin Books, 1981), 268–269.

19. Marx, *Capital*, 268.

20. Marx, *Capital*, vol. 1, 269 ("Here is Rhodus, jump here!").

21. Marx solved its antimony by demonstrating that while within a single exchange value system, surplus value cannot be created in the process of circulation, but as multiple systems interact, such a possibility becomes possible (Marx, *Capital*, vol. 3, 472; Karatani, *Transcritique*, 225). I am transposing the Marxian idea from exchange between different value systems to differences between ethical systems or visions.

22. What follows is inspired by Joan Copjec, *Read My Desire: Lacan Against the Historicists* (London: Verso, 2015), 3.
23. Copjec, *Read My Desire*, 3.
24. Karen L. Carr, *The Banalization of Nihilism: Twentieth-Century Responses to Meaninglessness* (Albany, NY: SUNY Press, 1992), 140.
25. Carr, *Banalization of Nihilism*, 7.
26. Slavoj Žižek, *The Parallax View* (Cambridge, MA: MIT Press, 2009), 263.
27. G.W.F. Hegel, *The Science of Logic*, trans. George di Giovanni (Cambridge: Cambridge University Press, 2010), 119; quoted in McGowan, *Capitalism and Desire*, 137.
28. McGowan, *Capitalism and Desire*, 137.
29. McGowan, *Capitalism and Desire*, 140.
30. Nimi Wariboko, *Economics in Spirit and Truth: A Moral Philosophy of Finance* (New York: Palgrave Macmillan, 2014), ix, xiv–xvii, 10, 13, 15, 18, 76, 105–111, 120–121, 159–171, 177–178.
31. McGowan, *Capitalism and Desire*, 148.
32. McGowan, *Capitalism and Desire*, 148.
33. Marx, *Capital*, vol. 3, 358.
34. Giorgio Agamben, *Potentialities*, trans. Daniel Heller-Roazen (Stanford, CA: Stanford University Press, 1999), 182.
35. McGowan, *Capitalism and Desire*, 167.
36. Giorgio Agamben, *The Time That Remains: A Commentary on the Letter to the Romans* (Stanford, CA: Stanford University Press, 2005).
37. L.L. Welborn, *Paul's Summons to Messianic Life: Political Theology and the Coming Awakening* (New York: Columbia University Press, 2015), 2–10, 58–60.
38. G.W.F. Hegel, *Phenomenology of Spirit*, trans by A.V. Miller (Oxford: Oxford University Press, 1977).
39. See Molly Farneth, "How to 'Love thy Neighbor': Lessons from Hegel on Conflict and Reconciliation." Lecture delivered at the Boston University Institute of Philosophy and Religion, December 6, 2017; see also Molly Farneth, *Hegel's Social Ethics: Religion, Conflict, and Rituals of Reconciliation* (Princeton, NJ: Princeton University Press, 2017).
40. Farneth, "How to 'Love thy Neighbor,'" 14.
41. Farneth, "How to 'Love thy Neighbor,'" 10.
42. Jacob Taubes, *The Political Theology of Paul*, ed. Aleida Assmann with Jan Assmann, in conjunction with Horst Folkers, Wolf-Daniel Hartwich, and Christopher Schulte, trans. Dana Hollander (Stanford, CA: Stanford University Press, 2004), 53.
43. L.L. Welborn, *Paul's Summons to Messianic Life: Political Theology and the Coming Awakening* (New York: Columbia University Press, 2015), 3.
44. Welborn, *Paul's Summons*, 58.

45. Sigmund Freud, *Civilization and Its Discontents*, trans. Joan Riviere (New York: Doubleday Anchor Books, 1951), 57–58.
46. Freud, *Civilization and Its Discontents*, 60–61.
47. Welborn, *Paul's Summons*, 10.
48. Welborn, *Paul's Summons*, 2.
49. Welborn, *Paul's Summons*, 60.
50. Welborn, *Paul's Summons*, 61.
51. Farneth, "How to 'Love thy Neighbor,'" 2.
52. Farneth, "How to 'Love thy Neighbor,'" 10.
53. For an excellent analysis of the two subjectivities, see Farneth, *Hegel's Social Ethics*, 25–27, 65–79.
54. Farneth, "How to 'Love thy Neighbor,'" 12–13.
55. McGowan, *Capitalism and Desire*, 156.

Chapter 7

1. Lionel Robbins, *An Essay on the Nature and Significance of Economic Science* (London: Macmillan & Co., 19932), 15.
2. Jean-Luc Nancy, *Being Singular Plural*, trans. Robert D. Richardson and Anne E. O' Byrne (Stanford, CA: Stanford University Press, 2000), 185.
3. This interplay between abundance and scarce means is the key to increasing and preserving abundance. This relationship is similar to the way grace is presumed to operate in Pentecostal circles. Grace is abundant, and democracy is employed in its distribution. No one needs to get it at the hands of leaders in institutionalized hierarchy. There is, however, a means of grace, techniques of the self on the self, which demands sacrifices and choices. Abundant, democratized grace is appropriated through the scarce means of personal disciplinary regime. In the mainline churches there is a similar phenomenon at foot. There is also democratization of grace in the sense that God's grace is available to all, but the means of grace (at least, some of the sacraments) are in the hands of the priests and deacons in some of them and believers must get it through them. I need to quickly add that what is analogized here is not grace and material distribution per se, but the means of acquisition, the ways of acquiring what is presumably in abundance.
4. Something has to give in their interaction and intersection, which opens a community to its potentialities rather than to its destiny or totality.
5. Nancy, *Being Singular Plural*, 2; emphasis in the original.
6. Bruce Birch, *Let Justice Roll Down: The Old Testament Ethics and Christian Life* (Louisville, KY: Westminster John Knox, 1991), 171–182.

7. Kathryn Tanner, *Economy of Grace* (Minneapolis: Fortress, 2005), 140–142.

8. Albino Barrera, *God and the Evil of Scarcity: Moral Foundations of Economic Agency* (South Bend, IN: University of Notre Dame Press, 2005).

9. Before we proceed to discuss abundance, let us take a moment to ask how scarcity as an economic concept got its dismal reputation among theologians. Reverend Thomas Malthus misunderstood scarcity when he cast it in the first edition of his book *Essay on the Principle of Population* (1798) as the evil that compels human beings to perfectibility, the formation of the mind, growth in goodness. This clergyman, who with Adam Smith and David Ricardo invented the modern discipline of economics presented scarcity as the ontological evil that ultimately works to create the good. Evil for him is not a privation of the good; it is constitutive of the created order. For Malthus, that God created a world of scarcity and original sin is nothing but the torpor and corruption of chaotic matter from which human beings were molded, and this matter keeps them naturally lazy. Scarcity is the driver that moves them to progress and virtues. The penalty, the final judgment, eternal punishment for anyone who refuses or fails to employ the prodding of scarcity to develop him- or herself, to actualize his or her potentials is to fall back into the original insensible cloy of clay.

William Paley, the author of *Natural Theology* (1802), and John Bird Sumner, author of the 1816 book *A Treatise on the Records of the Creation and on the Moral Attributes of the Creator*, basically expanded on the Malthusian thesis of scarcity as the agent of human improvement. They, however, upheld the functional role of scarcity in animating improvement in moral qualities and progress toward future state of happiness without accenting his theological errors, which challenged the goodness of God's created order and soteriological basis of Christology.

Malthus, Paley, and Sumner regarded scarcity to be a material privation as a metaphysical given which warrants at best some kind of theodicy. This understanding of scarcity is what irks many theologians today as it fails to situate it as a phenomenon of competing claims at the level of social existence. Scarcity is the particular result of human modes of operations, of how lives hang together. The phenomenon of scarcity speaks to the allocative tasks in a society's economic and political lives and as such how society deals with human finitude, finite goods, contingency, and the moral agency of choice.

Finitude demands choice. Choice presupposes or retroactively activates freedom. He who is not free, having zero degrees of freedom, cannot make a choice. (In a capitalist society, choice and freedom are frequently linked to who gets what money or economic power, and when and how they got it.) Choice and freedom imply there is more than one alternative; there is a plurality of options. (In a democratic society, citizens need options about how they need to live their lives.) What are the institutional arrangements, norms, and procedures to enable and sustain the multiplicity of and platforms for choice? What are the identities of the moral agents who are making the choices? Are the choices of some agents predetermined or predictable? These questions speak to being and being-together, which are always at stake, and our existence being at stake is the nature of the political.

10. Walter Brueggemann, "The Liturgy of Abundance, The Myth of Scarcity." *Christian Century* (March 24–31, 1999): lines 24–26.

11. Brueggemann, "Liturgy of Abundance," lines 30–31.

12. Here I am using *nomos* (sharing, mutual sharing, and exposition) as defined by Jean-Luc Nancy. See Nancy, *Being Singular Plural*, 185.

13. Brueggemann, "Liturgy of Abundance," lines 150–154.

14. See Nimi Wariboko, *The Charismatic City and Public Resurgence of Religion: A Pentecostal Social Ethics of Cosmopolitan Urban Life* (New York: Palgrave, 2014), 137–153.

15. Is there no difference between a world of material abundance and superfluity and the belief in a God with limitless sovereign power to satisfy all desires of living things (Ps. 145:16)? I think there is a difference; the God who has an overwhelming power to create has put us in a world to enjoy sustenance with care.

16. Tanner, *Economy of Grace*, 136. See also p. 139.

17. Barrera, *God and the Evil of Scarcity*, 89.

18. Tanner, *Economy of Grace*, 64–67.

19. Tanner, *Economy of Grace*, 74.

20. Barrera, God and the Evil of Scarcity, 104–105. Barrera's theology is still problematic. How about those who reject God's law altogether? His notion of conditionality makes a cumbersome demand on the running for a political community with diverse comprehensive moral views.

21. Brueggemann, "Liturgy of Abundance," lines 73–74.

22. Barrera, *God and the Evil of Scarcity*, 74.

23. Barrera, *God and the Evil of Scarcity*, 74–75, 89.

24. See Jean-Luc Nancy, *The Inoperative Community*, ed. Peter Connor, trans. Peter Connor, Lisa Garbus, Michael Holland, and Simona Sawhney (Minneapolis: University of Minnesota Press, 1991).

25. Jean-Luc Nancy, *Birth to Presence*, trans. Brian Holmes et al. (Stanford, CA: Stanford University Press, 1993), 155; emphasis in the original.

26. Nancy, *Inoperative Community*, 35.

27. Nancy, *Inoperative Community*, 89. I have crudely adopted Nancy's thinking on dialectics and exposition here.

28. Nancy, *Inoperative Community*, 89.

29. Nancy, *Inoperative Community*, 89.

30. Catherine Keller, *Cloud of the Impossible: Negative Theology and Planetary Entanglement* (New York: Columbia University Press, 2014), 21.

31. This is an allusion to Alfred Whitehead's "process is the immanence of the infinite in the finite" (*Modes of Thought*, 54, New York: Free Press, 1968); quoted in Keller, *Cloud of the Impossible*, 231. See also pp. 177–178 for the inspiration of the statement, "scarcity inhabits abundance" as in Deleuze's "difference inhabits repetition."

32. Nancy, *Inoperative Community*, xxxviii–xxxix, inspired these couple of sentences.

33. Nancy, *Inoperative Community*, 36, inspired this definition.

34. Nancy, *Inoperative Community*, 39.

35. Hannah Arendt, *On Revolution* (New York: Penguin Books, 2004), 175.

36. Nancy, *Being Singular Plural*, 83.

37. Nancy, *Being Singular Plural*, 140.

38. Nimi Wariboko, *The Pentecostal Principle: Ethical Methodology in New Spirit* (Grand Rapids: Eerdmans, 2012); Nimi Wariboko, *Economics in Spirit and Truth: A Moral Philosophy* (New York: Palgrave Macmillan, 2014), 128–131.

Epilogue

1. Alenka Zupančič, *What is Sex?* (Cambridge, MA: MIT Press, 2017), 36.

2. Slavoj Žižek, *Incontinence of the Void: Economic-Philosophical Spandrels* (Cambridge, MA: MIT Press, 2017), 283.

3. Zupančič, *What Is Sex?*, 72.

4. Zupančič, *What Is Sex?*, 96.

5. Zupančič, *What Is Sex?*, 94–97, inspired the thought expressed in these last two sentences.

6. I have here adapted Freud's description of the death drive to my own purposes. See Sigmund Freud, "Beyond the Pleasure Principle," in *The Standard Edition of the Complete Psychological Works of Sigmund Freud*, vol. 18 (London: Vintage Books, 2001), 39.

7. Thought here was inspired by Jean-Luc Nancy. See *The Inoperative Community*, ed. Peter Connor, trans. Peter Connor, Lisa Garbus, Michael Holland, and Simona Sawhney (Minneapolis: University of Minnesota Press, 1991), p. 30.

8. Slavoj Žižek, *The Year of Dreaming Dangerously* (London: Verso Books, 2012), 28.

9. Žižek, *Year of Dreaming Dangerously*, 27–28.

10. Samo Tomšič, *The Capitalist Unconscious: Marx and Lacan* (London: Verso, 2015), 22.

11. Francis Ching-Wah Yip, *Capitalism as Religion? A Study of Paul Tillich's Interpretation of Modernity* (Cambridge, MA: Harvard University Press, 2009), 39–40.

12. Paul Tillich, *Theology of Peace*, edited by Ronald Stone (Louisville, KY: Westminster/John Knox, 1990), 52.

13. Bonnie Honig, *Political Theory and the Displacement of Politics* (Ithaca, NY: Cornell University Press, 1993), 210.

14. Paul Eisenstein and Todd McGowan, *Rupture: On the Emergence of the Political* (Evanston, IL: Northwestern University Press, 2012), 3.

15. Eisenstein and McGowan, *Rupture*, 4.

16. Eisenstein and McGowan, *Rupture*, 28.

17. Hannah Arendt, *Between Past and Future: Eight Exercises in Political Thought* (New York: Penguin, 2006), 13.

Works Cited

Acemoglu, Daron, and James A. Robinson. *Why Nations Fail: The Origins of Power, Prosperity, and Poverty*. New York: Crown Business, 2012.
Agamben, Giorgio. *The Kingdom and the Glory: For a Genealogy of Economy and Government*. Translated by Lorenzo Chiesa. Stanford, CA: Stanford University Press, 2011.
———. *Means Without End: Notes on Politics*. Translated by Vincenzo Binetti and Cesare Casarino. Minneapolis: University of Minnesota Press, 2000.
———. *Nudities*. Translated by David Kishik and Stefan Pedatella. Stanford, CA: Stanford University Press, 2010.
———. *Potentialities: Collected Essays in Philosophy*. Edited and Translated by Daniel Heller-Roazen. Stanford, CA: Stanford University Press, 1999.
———. *The Time That Remains: A Commentary on the Letter to the Romans*. Stanford, CA: Stanford University Press, 2005.
Ahn, Ilsup Ahn. *Just Debt: Theology, Ethics, and Neoliberalism*. Waco, TX: Baylor University Press, 2017.
Alexander, Michelle. *The New Jim Crow: Mass Incarceration in an Age of Color Blindness*. New York: The New Press, 2010.
Alperovitz, Gar, and Lew Daly. *Unjust Deserts: How the Rich Are Taking Our Common Inheritance and Why We Should Take It Back*. New York: New Press, 2009.
Arendt, Hannah. *Between Past and Future: Eight Exercises in Political Thought*. New York: Penguin, 2006.
———. *On Revolution*. New York: Penguin Books, 2004.
Aristotle. *Nicomachean Ethics*. Translated by Martin Oswald. Indianapolis: Liberal Arts Press, 1962.
Axton, Paul. *The Psychotheology of Sin and Salvation: An Analysis of the Meaning of the Death of Christ in Light of the Psychoanalytical Reading of Paul*. London: Bloomsbury T&T Clark, 2015.

Azzam, Abed. *Nietzsche versus Paul*. New York: Columbia University Press, 2015.
Badiou, Alain. "A Conversation with Alain Badiou." Interview by Mario Goldenberg. *Lacanian Ink*, 23, 2004.
———. *Saint Paul: The Foundation of Universalism*. Stanford, CA: Stanford University Press, 2003.
———. *Theory of the Subject*. Translated by Bruno Bosteels. New York: Continuum, 2009.
Barclay, John M.G. *Paul and the Gift*. Grand Rapids, MI: William B. Eerdmans Publishing Company, 2015.
Barnard, Suzanne, and Bruce Fink, eds. *Reading Seminar XX: Lacan's Major Work on Love, Knowledge, and Feminine Sexuality*. Albany, NY: SUNY Press, 2002.
Barrera, Albino. *God and the Evil of Scarcity: Moral Foundations of Economic Agency*. South Bend, IN: University of Notre Dame Press, 2005.
Barthes, Roland. *Camera Lucida: Reflections on Photography*. Translated by Richard Howard. New York: Farrar, Straus and Giroux, 2010.
Birch, Bruce. *Let Justice Roll Down: The Old Testament Ethics and Christian Life*. Louisville, KY: Westminster John Knox, 1991.
Blanton IV, Thomas R., and Raymond Pickett (eds.) *Paul and Economics*. Minneapolis: Fortress Press, 2017.
Blanton IV, Thomas R. *A Spiritual Economy: Gift in the Letters of Paul of Tarsus*. New Haven, CT: Yale University, 2017.
Blanton, Ward. *A Materialism for the Masses: Saint Paul and the Philosophy of Undying Life*. New York: Columbia University Press, 2014.
Boer, Roland. "Paul and Materialist Grace." In *Paul and the Philosopher*, 186–209. Edited by Ward Blanton and Hent De Vries. New York: Fordham University Press, 2013.
Boff, Leonardo. *Liberating Grace*. Translated by John Drury. Eugene, OR: Wipf and Stock, 2005.
Bowie, Andrew. *Schelling and Modern European Philosophy*. New York: Routledge, 1993.
Brecht, Bertolt. "Hollywood Elegies." Live Journal. August 2005: https://substitute.livejournal.com/986052.html
Brueggemann, Walter. "The Liturgy of Abundance, The Myth of Scarcity." *Christian Century*, March 24–31, 1999.
Carr, Karen L. *The Banalization of Nihilism: Twentieth-Century Responses to Meaninglessness*. Albany, NY: SUNY Press, 1992.
Chisea, Lorenzo. "Imaginary, Symbolic and Real Otherness: The Lacanian Subject and His Vicissitudes." Thesis, University of Warwick, Department of Philosophy, 2004.
Clark, J.P. "Ibadan." In *A Collection of Poems, 1958–1988: J.P. Clark-Bekederemo*. Washington, DC: Howard University Press, 1991.
Copjec, Joan. *Read My Desire: Lacan against the Historicists*. London: Verso, 2015.

Dean, Jodi. "Still Dancing: Drive as a Category of Political Economy." *International Journal of Zizek Studies* 6, no. 1 (2012): 1–19.
Deleuze, Gilles. *Masochism: Coldness and Cruelty*. New York: Zone Books, 1991.
Deleuze, Giles, and Félix Guattari. *Anti-Oedipus: Capitalism and Schizophrenia*. New York: Penguin, 2009.
Depoortere, Frederiek. *Christ in Postmodern Philosophy: Gianni Vattimo, Rene Girard and Slavoj Žižek*. New York: T&T Clark, 2008.
Derrida, Jacques. *The Post Card: From Socrates to Freud and Beyond*. Translated by Alan Bass. Chicago: University of Chicago Press, 1987.
———. *Writing and Difference*. Translated by Alan Bass. Chicago: University of Chicago Press, 1978.
Edelman, Lee. *No Future: Queer Theory and the Death Drive*. Durham, NC: Duke University Press, 2004.
Egom, Alexander Peter. *Christian Society: Before and after Parousia*. Ukala Okpunor, Nigeria: Adioné Publishing, 2011.
———. *Compass for Economic Reform*. Ukala Okpunor, Nigeria: Adioné Publishing, 2006.
———. *Global Joseph Project*. Ukala Okpunor, Nigeria: Adioné Publishing, 2009.
Eisenstein, Paul, and Todd McGowan. *Rupture: On the Emergence of the Political*. Evanston, IL: Northwestern University Press, 2012.
Esposito, Roberto. "Foreword to the English Translation." In Electra Stimilli, *The Debt of the Living: Ascesis and Capitalism*, vii–ix. Translated by Arianna Bove. Albany, NY: SUNY University Press, 2017.
Farneth, Molly. *Hegel's Social Ethics: Religion, Conflict, and Rituals of Reconciliation*. Princeton, NJ: Princeton University Press, 2017.
———. "How to 'Love thy Neighbor': Lessons from Hegel on Conflict and Reconciliation." Lecture at the Boston University Institute of Philosophy and Religion, Boston, MA, December 6, 2017.
Feuerbach, Ludwig. *The Essence of Christianity*. Translated by Marian Evans. London: John Chapman, 1854.
Fink, Bruce. *The Lacanian Subject: Between Language and Jouissance*. Princeton, NJ: Princeton University Press, 1995.
Flynn, Sean Masaki. *Economics for Dummies*. Hoboken, NJ: Wiley Publishing, 2005.
Fortuna, Robert T., and Beverly R. Gaventa (eds.), *The Conversation Continues: Studies in Paul and John, in Honor of J. Louis Martyn*. Nashville, TN: Abington Press, 1990.
Foucault, Michel. *Society Must Be Defended: Lecture at the Collège de France, 1975–1976*. Translated by David Macey. New York: Picador, 2003.
Freud, Sigmund. "Beyond the Pleasure Principle." In *The Standard Edition of the Complete Psychological Works of Sigmund Freud*, vol. 18. London: Vintage Books, 2001.

Friedman, Milton. *A Theory of the Consumption Function*. Princeton, NJ: Princeton University Press, 1957.

Glaude, Jr. Eddie. *Democracy in Black: How Race Still Enslaves the American Soul*. New York: Broadway Books, 2016.

Hallward, Peter. *Badiou: A Subject to Truth*. Minneapolis: University of Minnesota Press, 2003.

Hayek, Friedrich A. *Law, Legislation and Liberty: Volume 1: Rules and Order*. Chicago: University of Chicago Press, 1973.

Hegel, G.W.F. *The Phenomenology of Spirit*. Translated by A.V. Miller. Oxford: Oxford University Press, 1977.

———. *The Science of Logic*. Translated by George di Giovanni. Cambridge: Cambridge University Press, 2010.

Henriksen, Jan-Olav. *Desire, Gift, and Recognition: Christology and Postmodern Philosophy*. Grand Rapids, MI: Eerdmans, 2009.

Honig, Bonnie. *Political Theory and the Displacement of Politics*. Ithaca, NY: Cornell University Press, 1993.

Jacobs, Elizabeth. "Everywhere and Nowhere: Politics in Capital in the Twenty-First Century." In *After Piketty: The Agenda for Economics and Inequality*, 512–540. Edited by Heather Boushey, J. Bradford Delong, and Marshall Steinbaum. Cambridge, MA: Harvard University Press, 2017.

Jones, Gareth A. "The Geographies of Capital in The Twenty-First Century: Inequality, Political Economy, and Space." In *After Piketty: The Agenda for Economics and Inequality*, 208–303. Edited by Heather Boushey, J. Bradford Delong, and Marshall Steinbaum. Cambridge, MA: Harvard University Press, 2017.

Kant, Immanuel. *Critique of Practical Reason*. Translated by Mary J Gregor, with an introduction by Andrews Reath. Cambridge: Cambridge University Press, 2015.

———. *The Metaphysics of Morals*. Cambridge: Cambridge University Press, 1996.

Karatani, Kojin. *Transcritique: On Kant and Marx*. Translated by Sabu Kohso. Cambridge, MA: MIT Press, 2003.

Keller, Catherine. *Cloud of the Impossible: Negative Theology and Planetary Entanglement*. New York: Columbia University Press, 2014.

Keyes, John M. *The General Theory of Employment, Interest, and Money*. Orlando, FL: Harcourt Bruce Jovanovich Publishers, 1953.

Kolozova, Katerina. *Toward a Radical Metaphysics of Socialism: Marx and Laruelle*. Brooklyn: Punctum Books, 2015.

Koosed Jennifer L. *(Per)mutations of Qohelet: Reading the Body in the Book*. New York: T&T Clark, 2006.

Lacan, Jacques. *Ecrits: The First Complete Edition in English*. Translated by Bruce Fink, Heloise Fink, and Russell Grigg. New York: W.W. Norton, 2006.

———. *The Ethics of Psychoanalysis*. Edited by Jacques Alain-Miller. Translated by Dennis Porter. New York: W.W. Norton & Company, 1997.

———, ed. *Le séminaire: Les formations of de l'inconscient, 1957–1958. Livre V*. Paris: Champ Freudien, 1998.

———. *The Seminar, Book XX, Encore, On Feminine Sexuality, The Limits of Love and Knowledge*. Edited by Jacques Alain-Miller. Translated by Bruce Fink. New York: W.W. Norton, 1998.

———. *The Seminar of Jacques Lacan, Book XVII: The Other Side of Psychoanalysis*. Translated by Russell Grigg. New York: Norton, 2007.

Lazzarato, Maurizio. *Governing by Debt*. Translated by Joshua David Jordon. Los Angeles: Semiotext(e), 2015.

———. *The Making of the Indebted Man: An Essay on the Neoliberal Condition*. Translated by Joshua David Jordon. Los Angeles: Semiotext(e), 2012.

Le Gaufey, Guy. *Une Archéologie De La Toute Puissance*. Paris: EPEL, 2014.

Lukács, Georg. *History and Class Consciousness: Studies in Marxist Dialectics*. Translated by Rodney Livingstone. Cambridge, MA: MIT Press, 1971.

Malthus, Thomas. *Essay on the Principle of Population*. London: J. Johnson, 1798.

Marx, Karl. *Capital: A Critique of Political Economy*. Translated by Ben Fowkes. London: Penguin Books, 1976.

———. *Capital: A Critique of Political Economy*, vol. 1. Translated by Ben Fowkes. New York: Penguin Books, 1981.

———. *Capital: A Critique of Political Economy*, vol. 3. Translated by Ben Fowkes. New York: Penguin Books, 1981.

Marx, Karl, and Friedrich Engels. *The German Ideology*. New York: International Publishers, 1989.

Mbembe, Achille. "Life, Sovereignty, and Terror in the Fiction of Amos Tutuola." *Research in African Literatures* 34, no. 4 (2003): 1–26.

McGowan, Todd. *Capitalism and Desire: The Psychic Cost of Free Markets*. New York: Columbia University Press, 2016.

Nancy, Jean-Luc. *The Inoperative Community*. Translated by Peter Connor, Lisa Garbus, Michael Holland, and Simona Sawhney. Minneapolis: University of Minnesota Press, 1991.

Nancy, Jean-Luc. *Being Singular Plural*. Translated by Robert D. Richardson and Anne E. O' Byrne. Stanford, CA: Stanford University Press, 2000.

———. *Birth to Presence*. Translated by Brian Holmes et al. Stanford, CA: Stanford University Press, 1993.

———. *The Inoperative Community*. Translated by Peter Connor, Lisa Garbus, Michael Holland, and Simona Sawhney. Minneapolis: University of Minnesota Press, 1991.

Nancy, Jean-Luc, and Aurelién Barrau. *What's These Worlds Coming To?* Translated by Travis Holloway and Flor Méchain. New York: Fordham University Press, 2015.

Oliver, Mel, and Thomas Shapiro. *Black Wealth/White Wealth: A New Perspective on Racial Inequality.* New York: Routledge, 1995.

Paley, William. *Natural Theology: Oxford World Classics.* Edited by Matthew D. Eddy and David Knight. Oxford: Oxford University Press, 2008.

Piketty, Thomas. *Capital in the Twenty-First Century.* Translated by Arthur Goldhammer. Cambridge, MA: Harvard University Press, 2014.

Pippin, Robert. *Henry James and Modern Moral Life.* Cambridge: Cambridge University Press, 2000.

Pixley, Jocelyn. *Emotions in Finance: Distrust and Uncertainty in Global Markets.* Cambridge: Cambridge University Press, 2004.

Principe, Concetta V. *Secular Messiahs and the Return of Paul's "Real": A Lacanian Approach.* New York: Palgrave Macmillan, 2015.

Rancière, Jacques. *Disagreement: Politics and Philosophy.* Translated by Julie Rose. Minneapolis: University of Minnesota Press, 1998.

———. *Dissensus: On Politics and Aesthetics.* Edited and translated by Steven Corcoran. London: Continuum, 2010.

———. *Hatred of Democracy.* Translated by Steve Corcoran. London: Verso, 2006.

Reinhard, Kenneth. "Paul and the Political Theology of the Neighbor." In *Paul and the Philosophers*, 449–465. Edited by Ward Blanton and Hent De Vries. New York: Fordham University Press, 2013.

———. "Toward a Political Theology of the Neighbor." In Slavoj Žižek, Eric Santner, and Kenneth Reinhard, *The Neighbor: Three Inquiries in Political Theology*, 11–75. Chicago: University of Chicago Press, 2006.

Robbins, Lionel. *An Essay on the Nature and Significance of Economic Science.* London: Macmillan & Co., 1993.

Ruda, Frank. *Abolishing Freedom: A Plea for a Contemporary Use of Fatalism.* Lincoln: University of Nebraska, 2016.

Schatzki, Theodore. *The Site of the Social: A Philosophical Account of the Constitution of the Social Life and Change.* University Park: Pennsylvania State University Press, 2002.

Schelling, F.W.J. *Abyss of Freedom/Ages of the World.* Translated by Judith Norman. Ann Arbor: University of Michigan Press, 1997.

Serequeberhan, Tsenay. *Existence and Heritage: Hermeneutic Explorations in African and Continental Philosophy.* Albany, NY: SUNY Press, 2015.

Stiglitz, Joseph E. *The Price of Inequality: How Today's Divided Society Endangers Our Future.* New York: W.W. Norton & Company, 2013.

Sumner, John B. *A Treatise on the Records of the Creation and on the Moral Attributes of the Creator:* Charleston, SC: BiblioLife, 2009.

Tanner, Kathryn. *Economy of Grace.* Minneapolis: Fortress, 2005.

———. "Work, Debt, and Christian Witness." *Reflections: A Magazine of Theological and Ethical Inquiry.* Yale Divinity School (Spring, 2017): 27–28.

Taubes, Jacob. *The Political Theology of Paul*. Edited by Aleida Assmann and Jan Assmann, with Horst Folkers, Wolf-Daniel Hartwich, and Christopher Schulte. Translated by Dana Hollander. Stanford, CA: Stanford University Press, 2004.
Taylor, Mark L. *The Executed God: The Way of the Cross in Lockdown America*. Minneapolis: Fortress, 2015.
Taylor, Mark C. *Confidence Games: Money and Markets in a World without Redemption*. Chicago: University of Chicago, 2004.
Tillich, Paul. *The Religious Situation*. Translated by H. Richard Niebuhr. New York: Henry Holt, 1932.
———. *Systematic Theology, Volume 3: Life and the Spirit, History and the Kingdom of God*. Chicago: The University of Chicago Press, 1965.
———. *Theology of Peace*. Edited by Ronald Stone. Louisville, KY: Westminster John Knox Press, 1990.
Toffler, Alvin. *The Third Wave*. New York: Bantam Books, 1981.
Tomšič, Samo. *The Capitalist Unconscious: Marx and Lacan*. London: Verso, 2015.
Townes, Emilie M. *Womanist Ethics and the Cultural Production of Evil*. New York: Palgrave Macmillan, 2006.
United Nations. *Human Development Report*. New York: 2016.
Vernant, Jean-Pierre. *Mortals and Immortals: Collected Essays*. Princeton, NJ: Princeton University Press, 1991.
Wariboko, Nimi. *The Charismatic City and the Resurgence of Religion: A Pentecostal Social Ethics of Cosmopolitan Urban Life*. New York: Palgrave Macmillan, 2014.
———. *Economics in Spirit and Truth: A Moral Philosophy of Finance*. New York: Palgrave Macmillan, 2014.
———. "Freeing the Future." *Reflections: A Magazine of Theological and Ethical Inquiry*. Yale Divinity School, Spring, 2017: 56–57.
———. *God and Money: A Theology of Money in a Globalizing World*. Lanham, MD: Lexington Books, 2008.
———. *The Pentecostal Principle: Ethical Methodology in New Spirit*. Grand Rapids, MI: Eerdmans, 2012.
———. *The Split God: Pentecostalism and Critical Theory*. Albany, NY: SUNY Press, 2018.
Weber, Max. *The Protestant Ethic and the Spirit of Capitalism*. Translated by Talcott Parsons. New York: Charles Scribner's Sons, 1958.
Welborn L.L. *Paul's Summons to Messianic Life: Political Theology and the Coming Awakening*. New York: Columbia University Press, 2015.
Whitehead, Alfred. *Modes of Thought*. New York: Macmillan, 1938.
Yip, Francis Ching-Wah. *Capitalism as Religion? A Study of Paul Tillich's Interpretation of Modernity*. Cambridge, MA: Harvard University Press, 2009.

Žižek, Slavoj. "The Abyss of Freedom." In F.W.J. Schelling, *Abyss of Freedom/Ages of the World (Second Draft, 1813)*, 3–104. Translated by Judith Norman. Ann Arbor: University of Michigan Press, 1997.
———. *On Belief*. Oxford: Routledge, 2001.
———. *Event: A Philosophical Journey through a Concept*. London: Penguin Books, 2014.
———. *The Fragile Absolute, Or Why is the Christian Legacy Worth Fighting For?* London: Verso, 2008.
———. *Incontinence of the Void: Economico-Philosophical Spandrels*. Cambridge, MA: MIT Press, 2017.
———. *The Indivisible Remainder*. London: Verso, 2007.
———. *Less Than Nothing: Hegel and the Shadow of Dialectical Materialism*. London: Verso, 2012.
———. *The Monstrosity of Christ*. Cambridge MA: MIT Press Verso, 2009.
———. *The Most Sublime Hysteric: Hegel with Lacan*. Translated by Thomas Scott-Railton. Malden, MA: Polity Press, 2014.
———. "The Necessity of a Dead Bird." In *Paul and the Philosophers*, 175–185. Edited by Ward Blanton and Hent De Vries. New York: Fordham University Press, 2013.
———. *The Parallax View*. Cambridge, MA: MIT Press, 2009.
———. "The Real of Sexual Difference." In *Reading Seminar XX: Lacan's Major Work on Love, Knowledge, and Feminine Sexuality*, 57–75. Edited by Suzanne Barnard and Bruce Fink. Albany, NY: SUNY Press, 2002.
———. *Tarrying with the Negative: Kant, Hegel, and the Critique of Ideology*. Durham, NC: Duke University Press, 1993.
———. *The Ticklish Subject: The Absent Centre of Political Ontology*. London: Verso, 1999.
———. *The Ticklish Subject: The Absent Core of Political Ontology*. New York: Verso, 2008.
———. *The Year of Dreaming Dangerously*. London: Verso Books, 2012.
Zupančič, Alenka. *Ethics of the Real: Kant and Lacan*. London: Verso, 2011.
———. *What is Sex?* Cambridge, MA: MIT Press, 2017.

Index

Abolishing Freedom (Ruda), 8, 141, 187
"absolute contradiction," the split and, 184–85
abundance, 164–174
   Barrera and, 170–72, 208n20
   Brueggemann on, 164–65, 166
   material sufficiency and, 174
   multiple theological interpretations, 164
   political questions on, 174
   questions on application of interpretations, 172–73
   Tanner and, 170
   theological interpretation 1, 164–65
   theological interpretation 2, 165–66, 208n12
   theological interpretation 3, 167–68, 208n15
   theological interpretation 4, 169–170
   theological interpretation 5, 170–72
   theological interpretation 6, 172
   theological interpretation 7, 172
accounting, significance of, 107–8
accumulatable excess output, demand for, 117
Acemoglu, Daron, *Why Nations Fail*, 80

African Americans
   life expectancy of, 85
   as "part of no-part," 87
   wage disparity and, 86
   See also color gap: poverty and racialization
Agamben, Giorgio
   critique of modern economy by, 22
   definition of potentiality by, 149
   on divisions in law according to Paul, 29
   freedom brought to economy, 103–4
   on impotentiality and freedom, 8–9, 72
   on Paul's "abbreviation of Moses' commandment," 18
   on principle of law (7:23, NIV), 54
Alperovitz, Gar, 36
animal economy, as origin of split, 34–36, 181
animal spirits. *See under* Keynes, John Maynard
archi-spirituality, 66
Arendt, Hannah
   on abolishment of future, 142
   on dependence on one another, 177
   on each new generation discovering world anew, 48, 186

Badiou, Alain
  on God and religion, 94
  mentioned, 29, 50
  revolutionary militant figure of, 59
  Saint Paul: The Foundation of Universalism, 111
Badiousian *event* (defined), 111
Barrera, Albino, on abundance in scripture, 170–72
Barthes, Roland, on portrait of Queen of England, 69–70
being and thought correlation, 78–79
big Other, 49
Black Lives Matter movement, 88–89
Blanton, Thomas R.
  Paul and Economics, 20–21, 188n27
  Spiritual Economy, A, 20–21
Boff, Leonardo, on grace, 36
Brecht, Bertolt, "Hollywood Elegies," 14
Brueggemann, Walter, on abundance in scripture, 164–65, 166

Capital (Marx), 59
capitalism
  desire to produce abundance, 39–40, 155
  functioning of, 3–4
  hope for alternatives, 111
  as incompatible with liberal or Christian ethics, 112–13
  logic of, 113
  McGowan on, 132
  meaning and truth and, 94–95
  and negativity, 3, 5, 20, 27
  Pauline subjectivity and future orientation of, 57–58
  resistance against, 6
  scarcity and abundance, 156
  theological criticisms of, 40
  and theoretical framework, 5–6
  without exploitation, 90

Capitalism and Desire (McGowan)
  on Keynes, 132
  on psychic investment in future promise, 59, 89
  on repetition of failure key to capitalism's hold, 139
  thesis of, 4–5
capitalist economy, dimensions of split
  consumer responses to, 71–72
  disparity in wealth distribution in U.S. and, 78–79, 80, 92
  economy and finance of one substance, 75, 92
  empty signifier of human flourishing and, 74, 194–95n13
  Heisenberg's uncertainty principle and, 78
  impotentiality and, 72–73, 194n10
  normity of economic models ignored, 77–78
  primordial split and, 74–75
  split defined, 71
  urgency to act and, 72
  Žižek, Slavoj on void in human essence, 74
  See also color gap: poverty and racialization; split economy, dimensions of
CDOs (collateralized debt obligations), 13–14, 122
CDS (credit default swaps), 123–24, 129
churches, American, student debtors and, 128–29
collateralized debt obligations (CDOs), 13–14, 122
color gap: poverty and racialization, 80–89
  Black Lives Matter movement and, 88–89
  black neighborhoods in decline, 82

distribution of responsiveness and, 86–88
geographic dynamic and, 82
HDI (human development index) and, 85–86
income inequality and, 83
politics of inclusiveness and exclusion and, 86
poverty trap and, 80–81
prison- industrial complex and, 85
racialization of the economy, 81
Rancièrian politics and, 86–88
school system failure and, 85
spatial inequality and, 82, 93
splitting of part of no-part in America, 86–89
stars and stripes metaphor and, 81–83
Stiglitz on, 80
See also African Americans
credit and debt, emergence of, 1
credit default swaps (CDS), 123–24, 129

Daly, Lew, 36
Dean, Jodi, on market reflexivity, 122
debtor-creditor relationship, 125–26
Deleuze, Giles, debt ascendancy warning and, 127
de Saussure Ferdinand, 28

Economics in Spirit and Truth (Wariboko), 148
economic statistics and human lives gap, 77–78
economic theology: new direction, 157–180
  overview, 48, 156, 157–161
  approach to new direction, 157
  basic concepts in economics, 157
  methodology of the five-pointed star, 178–180

Robbins's definition of economics, 157
scarcity/abundance interplay emphasis, 157–59, 206ch7n3
sharing and, 158–160, 206ch7n4
Tanner and economic theology, 160–61
theology related to economics and, 160–61
See also abundance; pluralism; scarcity
Economy and Grace (Tanner), 160–61
Edelman, Lee, on "futureless capitalism," 143
Egom, Peter Alexander, on commodity payment system, 110–11, 199n19
Eisenstein, Paul, on Lucan, 28
Engels, Friedrich, *Germany Ideology, The*, 143
epilogue
  "absolute contradiction" is name for split, 184–85
  capitalism as demonic, 32, 185–86
  finance as crack in economy, 181–82
  finance as nightmarish disturbance to economy, 183–84, 209n6
  finance is economy as overarching insight of book, 185
  financialization of economy from Marxist perspective, 184
  fundamental arguments of book summarized, 181–86
  good news is economy is site of perpetual politics, 186
  permanence of primordial gap, 183
  present exposed to future, 184
  Zupančič, on fundamental contradiction, 183
  See also non-all economy
equalitarian politics potential gap, 86–89

equality, logic of, 155–56
essence as empty space, 74
essence of split, 66

fantasy of harmony, 99–116
  overview, 48, 50, 99
  accounting and, 107–8
  economy divided against itself, 104–5
  economy of three parts, 103
  finance emergence as primal form of "excess," 101–3
  finance opens crack in economic activity, 106–7
  finance's role in modern economy, 105–6
  freedom brought to economy, 8–9
  history of harmony between economy and finance, 99–101
  miscount of parts of economy, 104
  Wall Street/Main Street struggle and, 104, 105–6
  See also political economy of split
Farneth, Molly, *Hegel's Social Ethics*, 154
finance, ethical form of, 117–135
  affliction to economy, 130
  birth of finance, 2
  "Casino capitalism" and, 120
  churches and student debtors, 128–29
  as crack in economy, 181–82
  credit default swaps and, 123–24, 202n13
  creditor-debtor relationship, 125–26
  demand for accumulatable excess output and, 117
  Kantian ethical subject as split, 120, 201n10
  Lacanian notion of the *objet petit a*, 117, 118, 119–120, 121
  Lazarato on debt, 125
  morality vs. legality and, 118–19
  risk and, 123, 124
  sublimity of market, 121–22, 124
  See also global financial system; split economy, birth of; student debt; truths and afflictions of modern economy; Wall Street
finance capital, 10, 11, 19–20, 23, 30–31
  See also splitting the future of capital
finance-Industry gap, 75–77
financial market and morality, 31–32
financial meltdown of 2008, 182
finitude. See *under* scarcity
Fink, Bruce, 78–79, 114
flourishing, human, defined, 1
Foucault, Michel, analytical approach of, 68
Freud, Sigmund
  on capitalism, 3, 13
  commentary on Leviticus 19:18, 151–52, 153
Friedman, Milton, *Theory of the Consumption Function, The*, 2
"fundamental contradiction," defined, 183
future, abolishment of, 139–156
  overview, 48, 50, 134
  Arendt and, 142
  goal to exit from capitalism of future, 140
  hope for future of capitalism sustained, 139–140, 203ch6n2
  impotentiality and, 141, 204n6
  internal drive of past and present, 46–47
  introduction, 139–142
  Micaiah's prophecy and, 141–42
  preparation for, 7, 8
  Ruda on, 141

Index

surplus-future enemy of present, 140
Žižek, on, 140
See also self-limiting and connections to Saint Paul and Hegel; splitting the future of capital

gender-related issues, 114–15
Germany Ideology, The (Marx and Engels), 143
global financial system
   acts as its own "matter," 129–130
   Kantian ethics and, 120–21, 124
   Saint Paul and, 12, 19, 21, 62–63
   wealth creation and, 118
   See also finance, ethical form of
God, death of, 94
Governing by Debt (Lazzarato), 125
grace
   Adam Smith and, 35–36
   Boff on, 36
   in Pauline theology, 28–29
Guattari, Felix, 127

harvest into consumption, 10–11, 187n14
haves vs. have-nots, 15
Hayek, Friedrich, 91
HDI (human development index), 85–86
Hegel, Georg Wilhelm Friedrich
   on bad and good versions of infinite, 147–48
   on division of reality, 27–28
   on love of neighbor, 149–150
   Phenomenology of Spirit, 57, 132–33
   philosophy of conflict and, 154
   on Protestant ethic, 69
Hegel's Social Ethics (Farneth), 154
Heisenberg's uncertainty principle, 78
History and Class Consciousness (Lukács), 6–7

"Hollywood Elegies"(Brecht) (poem), 14
Human Development Report (UN) (2016), 85–86
human flourishing, 112
   defined, 1–3
   void in, 74, 109, 112, 194–95n13
   See also fantasy of harmony

impotentiality
   abolishment of future and, 141, 204n6
   Agamben on potentiality and, 149
   American consumer and, 72–73, 194n10
   defined, 9
   reckoning with, 8
Inoperative Community (Nancy), 134

Jacobs, Elizabeth, on inequality of capital accumulation, 84
Jones, Gareth, on neglect of spatial political economy, 82, 93

Kafka, Franz, 18, 125
   The Trial, 127
Kant, Immanuel
   ethics of, 112, 120–21, 124, 201n10
   Metaphysics of Morals, The, 118–19
   on our existence, 27
   Sollen, 155
Karatani, Kojin
   on capitalism, 113, 144
   on crisis in capitalist economy, 70–71
Keynes, John Maynard
   animal spirits and, 132–34
   economy and finance harmony promoted by, 99
   primordial split and, 12
Kolozova, Katerina, 124

Lacan, Jacques
  Le Gaufey on, 10
  objet petit a, 22, 116, 117, 118, 119, 120
  psychoanalytic theory of, 3–4
  on Romans 7::7-25 NIV, 52–53
  on rupture in being, 28
  on thinking (Seminar XIV), 78, 79
Lacanian-Žižekian tradition, 22
law as sin, 53–55
Lazzarato, Maurizio, *Governing by Debt*, 125
Le Gaufey, Guy, 10
LETS (local exchange trading system), 110
Lonergan, Bernard, on normity of economic models, 78
love
  as grace writ large, 36–38
  Paul on, 37
Lukács, Georg, *History and Class Consciousness*, 6–7

Malcolm X, on Plymouth Rock, 84
Marx, Karl
  on attainment of surplus value, 204n21
  Capital, 59
  on capitalism, 3
  on capital itself as true barrier to capitalist production, 149
  on communism, 143
  dream of capitalism without capitalism, 147
  Germany Ideology, The, 143
  on harvest into consumption, 10–11, 42, 187n14
  labor power and, 43
  on profit-making in capitalism, 20
  value as conceived by, 38
  on Wall Street commodities, 12–13

McGowan, Todd
  on limitation of desires, 149
  on logic of equality, 155–56
  on Lucan, 28
  on process of capitalism, 40, 58, 143, 148
  theory of, 8
  on true freedom, 60
  See also *Capitalism and Desire*
meaning and truth, capitalism and, 94–95
Metaphysics of Morals, The (Kant), 118–19
methodology of the five-pointed star, 178–180
  abundance, scarcity, pluralism concepts and, 178
  approach to economic theology, 178
  economic concepts translated into philosophical-theological language, 179
  fifth point of star is advancement of economic theology, 179
  generation of space for capitalism alternative, 179–180
  pluralism and something new, 178–79
  Tillich-Wariboko tripartite framework, 178
Micaiah, prophecy of, 141–42
morality vs. legality, defined, 118–19
Moses, and Exodus 16:4–26, 2

naked CDCs, 14, 30
Nancy, Jean-Luc
  on the "community" of sectors, 41
  Inoperative Community, 134
  on sharing, 175
  theory of, 63–64, 134–35
Niebuhr, Reinhold, 127

non-all economy, 63, 64, 90, 133–34, 182–83

objet petit a. *See under* Lacan, Jacques
Oliver, Mel, on African-Americans and FHA, 82

patrimonial capitalism, 83–84
Paul and Economics (Blanton and Pickett, eds), 20–21, 188n27
Phenomenology of Spirit (Hegel), 57, 132–33, 150, 153, 154
Pickett, Raymond, *Paul and Economics*, 20–21
Piketty, Thomas, on income inequality, 83–85
Pixley, Jocelyn, 132
Plato, on being, 27
pluralism, 174–78
  Arendt on, 177
  defined, 177
  dovetails into concept of scarcity, 177
  link to abundance and scarcity, 175–76
  Nancy on sharing, 175–76
  sharing and, 175–76, 177–78
political economy of split, 108–15
  absence of harmony between finance and economy, 114
  arguments summarized, 108
  Badiousian *event* and, 111
  economy and finance are alienated by ethical substance, 115, 199n30
  economy and finance as identical, 109
  Egom's commodity payment system and, 110–11, 199n19
  ethical life of societies and, 112–13
  on ethic of capitalism, 112, 113
  finance and economy lack compatibility, 115
  finance as part of no-part, 110
  finance separated from meaning, and empty signifier, 115, 200n31
  financial greed blamed for financial crises, 108–9
  gender-related issues and, 114–15
  politics as answer, 109–10, 198n15
  questions on approach to economic ethics, 116
  questions on capitalist ethos, 113–14
  Schopenhauer's Dionysian will and, 112
  sore points of argument, 111–12
  symbolic castration and, 115
potentiality to actuality, 8–9
PPF (production possibilities frontier), 45–46, 191n38
present-past collective, 46–47
primordial economy split, exploration of, 30–31. *See also entries beginning with* split economy
production possibilities frontier (PPF), 45–46, 191n38
prosumers, defined, 44, 190n31
Protestant Ethic and the Spirit of Capitalism, The (Weber), 2, 68–69
Protestantism, 68–69

Queen of England, portrait of, Barthes on, 69–70

Rancière, Jacques, notion of democracy, 64–65, 86–87, 88, 109, 112
revolutionary militant figure, 59–60
Robbins, Lionel, economics defined by, 157
Robinson, James, *Why Nations Fail*, 80

Romans 7. *See under entries beginning with* Saint Paul
Ruda, Frank, *Abolishing Freedom*, 8, 141, 187

Saint Paul
  basic beliefs of, 49–50
  disruptiveness of the crack in being and Wall Street, 50–51
  on human subjectivity as crack in human being, 28–29
  imagined visit to Wall Street as ethnographer by, 93–94
  on Jesus's command to love, 150–51
  on love (I Corinthians 13: 1–13), 37, 38
  on morality (unlike Hegel), 57, 193n19
  relationship to financial system of, 19
  relevance of to this study, 33
  Romans 7:7–24, NIV, 16–17, 18
  Romans 7 and, 5–6, 12–13, 19
  self is divided against itself, 65
  Žižek's summary and, 17–18
  See also Saint Paul, split subjectivity and; split subjectivity
Saint Paul, split subjectivity and
  accent on future, 57–58
  capitalism and, 57–58, 60–61
  Lacan on, 52–53
  Lacan-Žižekian and, 56
  law as sin, 53–55
  law divides self, creating gap between self and desires, 54, 192n9
  militant figures and, 59–61
  Romans 7::7-25 NIV, 51–52
  splitting within law that can (re)produce itself, 55, 192n10
  subjectivity as crack, 55
  subjectivity emerges from split, 54, 192n8
  what Paul is saying in Romans 7, 53
  who will rescue me,(Paul's cry), 57
  Žižek on Paul's problem, 55–56
Saint Paul: The Foundation of Universalism (Badiou), 111
sarx/pneuma, 29
scarcity, 161–64
  concept of, 161–62, 175–77
  conflation of scarcity concept and competition, 163
  finitude and, 162–63, 164, 176–77
  theologians' dislike of word, 161
  what scarcity is, 163–64, 207n9
  Whiteheadian prose and, 176, 209n31
Schelling, F. W. J., 44–45
Schelling's Godhead, 44–45, 191n34
Schopenhauer's Dionysian will, 112
self-limiting and connections to Saint Paul and Hegel
  Freud's commentary on Leviticus 19:18, 151–52
  Hegel on love of neighbor, 149–150, 153, 154–55
  Hegel' philosophy of conflict and, 154
  Pauline theology on love and, 150–51, 153
  politics of reciprocal recognition and, 155
  Welborn on mandate to love one's neighbor, 151–52, 153
Shapiro, Thomas, on African-Americans and FHA, 82
sickness unto excess, 27–48
  overview, 23, 27–30
  birth of split economy, 30–41
  looking forward, 47–48
  split economy and split time, 44–47

split economy to split commodity,
      42–44
Smith, Adam, 35–36
social justice, 89–92
   affirmation of split, 91–92
   capitalism without exploitation
      and, 90
   contingency as necessity, 91–92
   laws and economic activities
      emerge, 91, 197n53
   McGowan on, 89
   so-called "real economy" and, 91
   as way of covering gap, 89
   See also non-all economy
Sollen (Kant), 155
Spiritual Economy, A (Blanton), 20–21,
      188n27
split economy, birth of, 1, 30–41
   ambiguity of split, 31
   born from excess, 33–38
   cautious optimism of author and, 32
   financial market and morality,
      31–32
   fragmentation of economy and, 41
   healing of economy problematic,
      38–39
   origin traced to *animal economy*,
      34–36, 181
   Paul's theology and, 33
   primitive economy and, 30–31, 47
   primordial split and, 12, 31, 47
   tragic quality of split, 32–33
   withdrawal as constriction
      shedding light on future, 47
   See also finance, ethical form of;
      grace; love; Saint Paul; Wall
      Street
split economy, character of
   defined in four senses, 13–14,
      188n17
   fragmentary sectors of, 41
   nature of, 14–15, 20

self-identity as unachievable, 41
   Wall Street and, 16
split economy, dimensions of, 67–97
   overview, 47–48, 66
   economic statistics-human lives
      gap and, 77–78, 92–93
   equalitarian politics potential gap
      and, 86–89
   finance-industry gap and, 75–77
   uprootedness and, 92–93
   work-reward gap and, 78–80
   See also capitalist economy,
      dimensions of split; color gap:
      poverty and racialization; social
      justice
Split Economy, The (Wariboko)
   focus of book on Lacanian-Žižekian
      tradition, 21–23
   lessons to be learned from, 24
   new approach to theory of finance
      capital, 23
   primordial economy and, 30
split economy and split time, 44–47
   fractured time and, 44
   PPF and, 45–46, 191n38
   present-past collective and, 46–47
   primordial freedom and, 45
   Schelling's Godhead and, 44–45,
      191n34
split economy to split commodity
   harvest process, 42
   and human *prosumers*, 44, 199n31
   labor power and, 43, 44
   Marx and, 42
   primordial split between economy
      and finance, 42
   saved consumption and time-
      power, 43–44
split subjectivity (Saint Paul's), 49–66
   overview, 23, 47, 49–51
   future orientation of capitalism
      and, 57–58

split subjectivity (Saint Paul's) (*continued*)
   militant figures and, 59–61
   Paul and split subjectivity, 51–56
   split economy and, 61–66
   See also entries beginning with Saint Paul
splitting the future of capital, 142–155
   Agamben on potentiality and love, 149
   alternative future comes from capitalism itself, 143
   capitalist future as split within itself, 143
   dream of capitalism without capitalism, 147
   Economics in Spirit and Truth (Wariboko), 148
   Engels and, 143
   exploitation endemic to capitalism, 147
   Hegel on bad and good versions of infinite, 147–48
   internal split rips capitalism, 143
   Karatani on two parts in capitalism, 144
   Marx, and, 143, 145, 149, 204n21
   movement must consist of consumer/workers, 144
   political response to, 142, 155
   possible objection to idea of limit within capitalist time, 147
   sphere of capitalism and, 145
   splits in late capitalism and, 146–47
   true infinite as possible destiny of finance capital, 148–49
   two kinds of future in movement, 144
   unpredictability of human behavior as limit to capitalism, 148, 155
   what "abolish the future" means, 145–46

   See also finance capital; McGowan, Todd
Stiglitz, Joseph
   on divided society in America, 80
   government and economic growth, 36–37
   on income inequality, 83
student debt
   amount of current debt, 126
   churches and, 128–29
   imbalance of power and, 127
   poster children of exploitation and, 127
   See also finance, ethical form of
subjectivity split, economy and
   debit/credit as signifiers, 61
   economy as living thing, 61
   "essence" of the split, 66
   exploitation of working class and, 63, 147
   gap between signifier and signified, 61–62
   language (accounting system) as problem, 62
   non-all economy and, 63, 64, 90, 133–34, 182–83
   political theory by Rancière and, 65, 194n32
   questions on gap examined in this book, 62–63, 194n32
   Rancière and, 64
   Romans 7 and gap in human subjectivity, 62, 64, 65–66
   solutions, 63–64
   solutions not offered, 63–64
surplus future (surplus promise), defined, 7–8

Tanner, Kathryn
   on abundance in scripture, 170
   economic theology and, 160–61

Economy and Grace, 160–61
  on indebtedness, 126
Theory of the Consumption Function, The (Friedman), 2
Ticklish Subject, The (Žižek), 56
Tillich, Paul, 32, 178, 185
Tillich-Wariboko tripartite framework, 178
time, fractured, defined, 44
time-power, defined, 43
Townes, Emilie, 81
Trial, The (Kafka), 127
truths and afflictions of modern economy, 129–134
  overview, 129–130
  capitalist future as split within itself, 134
  economy's creation of financial sector, 131
  finance as affliction to economy, 130
  future as unknowable, 131–32
  Keynes conception of "animal spirits" and, 132–33
  on the penis that is the animal spirits, 134
  trust as financial product, 132
  See also global financial system; Hegel; Wall Street

United States
  levels of splitting and, 14–16
  as split society, 10–13
  See also Wall Street
uprootedness, 92–93

Vernant, Jean-Pierre, 106

Wall Street, 129
  as demonic, 32, 185–86
  disruptiveness of the crack in being and, 50–51
  evil as being for itself, 129, 130
  "future-oriented emotions" and, 132
  Kantian logic and, 120–21, 122
  mechanization and, 134
  objet petit a and, 118
  origin of name, 126
  risk is reflexive, 124
  Saint Paul confronts, 93–94
  "sin" of, 35
  vulnerability lacking in, 38, 40
  See also finance, ethical form of; United States
Weber, Max
  analytical approach of, 68–69
  Protestant Ethic and the Spirit of Capitalism, The (Weber), 2, 68–69
Welborn, L. L., on mandate to love one's neighbor, 151–53
"Who will rescue me?," 49, 52, 57, 109
Why Nations Fail (Acemoglu and Robinson), 80
work-reward gap, 78–80

Žižek, Slavoj
  on abolishing future, 140
  on essence as empty space, 74
  on exploitation in capitalism, 147
  on meaning and truth in capitalism, 94
  Pauline notion of subjectivity summary, 17–18
  on Saint Paul's problem, 55–56
  Ticklish Subject, The, 56
Zupančič, Alenka
  on fundamental contradiction, 183
  on legality and morality, 118–19

www.ingramcontent.com/pod-product-compliance
Lightning Source LLC
Chambersburg PA
CBHW021140230426
43667CB00005B/194